The Visitor's Guide
to
AUSTRIA

D1125619

2 1 AVR '96	**DATE DUE**	
0 3 MAI '97		
1 3 MAR '98		
4 AVR '98		

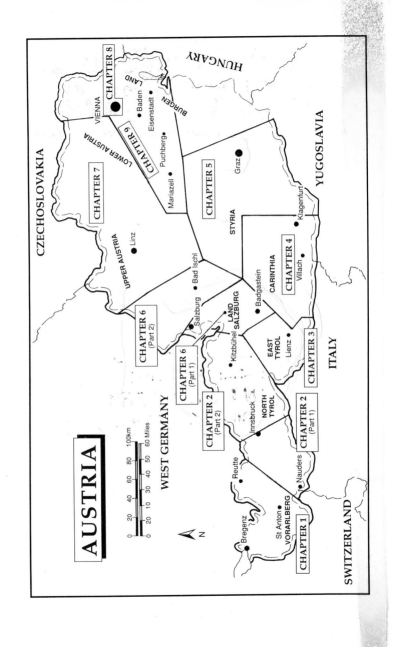

AUSTRIA

CZECHOSLOVAKIA

HUNGARY

YUGOSLAVIA

ITALY

SWITZERLAND

WEST GERMANY

0   20   40   60   80   100km
0   10   20   30   40   50   60 Miles

N

CHAPTER 8

CHAPTER 7

CHAPTER 9

CHAPTER 5

CHAPTER 6 (Part 2)

CHAPTER 6 (Part 1)

CHAPTER 2 (Part 2)

CHAPTER 2 (Part 1)

CHAPTER 4

CHAPTER 3

CHAPTER 1

VIENNA

LOWER AUSTRIA

UPPER AUSTRIA

BURGEN LAND

STYRIA

CARINTHIA

LAND SALZBURG

EAST TYROL

NORTH TYROL

VORARLBERG

- Baden
- Eisenstadt
- Puchberg
- Mariazell
- Graz
- Linz
- Klagenfurt
- Bad Ischl
- Salzburg
- Badgastein
- Villach
- Kitzbühel
- Lienz
- Innsbruck
- Reutte
- Nauders
- Bregenz
- St Anton

THE VISITOR'S GUIDE TO AUSTRIA

Ken Allan

MPC

HUNTER
PUBLISHING INC

914.3604
ALL

dce
88

British Library Cataloguing in
Publication Data:
Allan, Ken
   The visitor's guide to Austria. —
   (MPC Visitor's Guide).
   1. Austria — visitor's guides
   I. Title
   914.36'0453

Published by:
Moorland Publishing Co Ltd,
Moor Farm Road,
Ashbourne,
Derbyshire DE6 1HD
England

ISBN 0 86190 226 2 (paperback)
ISBN 0 86190 225 4 (hardback)

Published in the USA by:
Hunter Publishing Inc.,
300 Raritan Centre Parkway,
CN94, Edison, NJ 08818

ISBN 1 55650 073 4

Colour and black & white
origination by:
Eurographics Ltd, Nottingham

Printed in the UK by:
Butler and Tanner Ltd, Frome

Cover photograph:
Kufstein (MPC Picture Collection).

Photographs on pages:14, 19, 23,
25, 34, 35, 39, 42, 43, 50-51, 71,
74-5, 78, 79, 82, 83, 86, 87, 102,
103, 114, 115, 126, 139, 141, 142,
178, 179, 182, 186-7, 190
are from the MPC Picture Collection; all the remaining photographs
were supplied by the author.

ACKNOWLEDGEMENTS
The author is pleased to acknowl-
edge the assistance he has
received from all of the staff of the
Austrian National Tourist Office in
London, especially Dr L. Oberrie-
der and Herr J. Stockinger, and of
the regional and local tourist
offices in Austria, especially Herr
E. Mayr, of Lienz; Herr J. Silober,
of Innsbruck; Herr H. German, of
Graz; Frau F. Kobenter and Herr J.
Steiner, of Klagenfurt; and Frau
Moosbrugger, of Egg. He is
grateful also to Mr Donald Smith,
of Llandeilo, Dyfed, for his help
and encouragement, and to his
wife Vera for her continuing
patience.

CONTENTS

Key to Symbols Used in Text Margin

 Recommended walk

 Parkland

 Archaeological site

 Nature reserve/Animal interest

 Birdlife

 Garden

 Beautiful view/Scenery, Natural phenomenon

 Church/Ecclesiastical site

 Building of interest

 Castle/Fortification

 Museum/Art gallery

 Other place of interest

 Sports facilities

Wintersports

Note on the Maps

The maps drawn for each chapter, while comprehensive, are not designed to be used as route maps, but locate the main towns, villages and places of interest. For touring, the Ö. A. M. T. C. (Touring Club Austria) maps (1:200,000, 1cm=2km, approx 1in=3.1 miles) which are distributed in the U. K. by the Automobile Association and are available in all good book shops in the U. K. and in Austria are recommended.

INTRODUCTION

Austria is enchanting. Visitors are welcomed by a friendly people to a countryside rich with wild-flower meadows and charming villages, and to beautiful romantic cities. It is a country of contrasts. To the west, along the border with Bavaria, country folk work their patchwork farms, tend their belled cattle, and enjoy boisterous evenings in alpine inns. Three hundred miles to the east, on the shores of Lake Neusiedl, low white houses are topped by storks' nests, while gipsy caravans and spicy foods are reminders of nearby Slav and Magyar cultures. To the south, in Carinthia, a passionate love of poetry, music and the arts hints at their Celtic blood. This simple country life contrasts with the sophistication of the cities and Vienna. The Austrians are an industrious, contented, and hospitable people who cherish their traditions, and for the visitor that means security, clean, comfortable accommodation and courteous, helpful service.

Austria is a scenic wonderland. From the wooded hills of the Bregenzerwald to the reeded plains of Burgenland, through the leafy lanes of the Vienna Woods, along the beautiful Danube and Inn Valleys, to the majestic, awesome, snow-capped peaks of the High Alps, the traveller enjoys an unending panorama of natural beauty. Singing hills, milky-white rivers, sailing boats bobbing on blue lakes, green forests, and everywhere geranium-clad farmhouses.

In winter, skiing is the major sport and the resorts provide warm hospitality to complement the sparkling *pistes*, while in summer Austria is known for mountaineering and climbing, but for the less agile there are easier, clearly marked walks. Water sports, tennis, golf, bowling, hang-gliding, angling, white-water canoeing are all readily available at reasonable cost and there are are many lakeside resorts where sun-lovers can chase that much prized bronze look.

Austria is a cultural paradise. The European tradition in classical music reaches its peak in Vienna but its influence is everywhere. Mozart in Salzburg, Haydn in Eisenstadt, Beethoven in Baden, Bruckner in Linz. Their music is played in concert halls, churches, and salons throughout the land. For lighter tastes there are evenings of Strauss waltzes; Lehar fans may visit his villa at Bad Ischl; and the original White Horse Inn is at St Wolfgang. Music festivals occur all year long: Salzburg at Easter and in August; Vienna in June; Bregenz and Villach in

August; Graz in October. When the State Opera House was re-opened after World War II Vienna, capital of the world of opera, was born again.

The abbeys and churches, palaces and castles, and museums are the cultural treasure houses of the nation. Austria is a baroque country. The first sight of a richly decorated church interior is breathtaking. Particularly rewarding examples can be found at Melk, St Florian, and Stams abbeys, in St Peter's church at Salzburg, in the Hofkirche at Innsbruck, and the Karlskirche in Vienna. The national shrine at Mariazell is a wonderful sight. In the smallest, simplest churches, such as St Adolari on the Pillersee in Tyrol, and in unexpected places — at Frauenkirchen in the Seewinkel, perhaps — the visitor may find ancient art masterpieces which have miraculously survived the centuries. The superb libraries at the great abbeys of Admont, Melk, and Kremsmünster testify to their contribution over the centuries to the minds as well as to the hearts of the people.

It is a land of palaces and castles. The Hofburg, Schönbrunn, and the Belvedere in Vienna, the Hohensalzburg fortress, Hochosterwitz, Riegersburg, Eggenburg, Forchtenstein are outstanding examples. Splendid buildings, magnificent apartments, the finest furniture, marble sculptures, ceramic stoves, tapestries, china, gold- and silver-ware, and all of the charivari needed to support the lifestyles of imperial personages are set in grand gardens and parklands designed to give panoramic views and sylvan walkways. The everyday things of bygone ages are the jewels of today. There are many museums of international renown. The Joanneum in Graz, the Ferdinandeum in Innsbruck, and Vienna's wealth of museums of all kinds.

To understand modern Austria it is necessary to appreciate its history. The story of the Austrian people hinges upon the strategic location of their country at the crossroads of Europe. As the ancient Celts journeyed on their tradeways to the east, they emerged from the last foothills of the High Alps and saw, beckoning them forward, the plains of Hungary stretching away to the distant Carpathians. Only the Danube lay between them and the riches of Asia. They chose to ford the river on a southerly bend and there erected a pagan temple. It became the site of the Roman outpost of *Vindobona* which survived centuries of onslaught by the Turks, the scourge of the plague, and two World Wars, to become Vienna today.

Austrian history is dominated by great families and outstanding personalities. In 1273, after 270 years of reign by the Babenbergs, the imperial crown passed to Rudolph I, so founding the house of Habsburgs which was to rule for a remarkable 645 years. During that period the fortunes of the empire flourished by marriage, diplomacy, and war. At one time or another the empire embraced the Netherlands, parts of eastern France and northern Italy, the kingdom of Naples, the Balkans, Hungary, Rumania, Czechoslovakia, Poland and Galicia. Its power and influence were unbounded. Kaiser Franz Josef inherited the throne in 1848, and while much remains of the majesty and splendour of his reign, the empire was characterised as much by inefficiency and bureaucracy as its lifestyle. But although this is a source of nostalgia for some Austrians even today, modern Austria is forward-looking and embraces the benefits of the hi-tech society.

Preparing for the Journey

Everyone travelling to Austria must carry a valid individual passport, or be included in a family passport. Visas are not required for British, American or Canadian subjects. Every driver must carry a full national (for Europeans) or international (for others) driving licence, the registration book for the vehicle, and, if the driver is not the legal owner, a letter of authorisation from the owner (if the vehicle is hired then a hire car registration certificate is necessary); and, for British vehicles more then 3 years old, a valid Ministry of Transport test certificate. All of these documents must remain valid during the visit. Trailers and caravans also require a 'Carnet' if they are to be taken into Italy. Vehicle insurance is compulsory. Normal UK insurance policies will provide the 'legal minimum' in European countries but a Green Card must be obtained from the UK insurer for full insurance cover.

Personal and vehicle insurance policies are widely available. Austria has a reciprocal arrangement with the UK so that visitors may obtain some free medical treatment. To qualify for this privilege the visitor must be able to produce a certificate of entitlement (Form E111), obtainable from local Social Security offices. However, the amount of free treatment is limited and further cover — up to about £10,000 per person — is desirable. Visitors from the USA and Canada should arrange in advance medical insurance up to about US$25,000 per person. The motorist must also consider vehicle breakdown and recovery insurance, usually as an extension of the basic insurance package. It is prudent to ensure that cover includes alternative vehicle and/or transport home in the event of total breakdown.

There is currently no limit on the amount of money that may be taken abroad by British travellers. Some cash will be needed to meet the costs of the journey, and initial costs on arrival. However, it is safer to carry traveller's cheques rather than cash. Eurocheques can be used to settle hotel and other bills, or to obtain cash, when presented with a Eurocheque Card. They are widely acceptable throughout Europe as are UK and USA credit cards.

Automobile hire is readily available at airports and in the larger cities and towns. An international driving licence is required. Advance booking can be made through travel agents or airlines.

The major towns and cities of Austria are served by the **Austrian Federal Railways' network** which extends into the European railway system. Coach travel is also a cheap and convenient means of travel. Local tourist offices and railway and coach stations provide timetables and will advise on connections. Regular travellers should enquire about runabout tickets which afford considerable savings.

For leisurely and cost-effective touring **bicycles** are available for hire at about seventy railway stations throughout Austria. They may be hired by the day or longer. Passports are required as proof of identity.

The Journey to Austria

BY AIR

Austrian Airways operate daily flights from New York (with Trans World Airlines) and from Toronto (with Air Canada) via Frankfurt to Vienna. Internal flights (with Austrian Air Services) connect the capital to Graz, Klagenfurt, Linz, Salzburg, and (with Tyrolean Airways) to Innsbruck. Austrian Airways, in cooperation with local airways, also operate scheduled services from Vienna to thirty European cities, fifteen Mediterranean cities and the Middle Eastern cities, and to Moscow. Other international airlines operate internal services from major airports in North America either via New York, or directly to European cities with connections to Vienna. For example, Pan American fly three flights each week from New York to Vienna with a stop at Hamburg, as well as services from Seattle, San Francisco, Los Angeles, Dallas, Miami, Baltimore, and Detroit with connecting flights from Hamburg.

CROSSING THE ENGLISH CHANNEL

There can be no 'best' way of getting to Austria. The most appropriate route depends upon the starting point and the destination, and upon personal preferences. From Scotland, the north of England, north Wales, Northern Ireland and perhaps the Midlands, travellers may choose Hull and Harwich/Felixstowe. North Sea Ferries operate a service from Hull overnight to Rotterdam (Europoort) which tends to commit the traveller to following the motorways across Holland and Belgium to Cologne and up the Rhine Valley. This also applies to services from Harwich to the Hook of Holland, and from Sheerness to Vlissingen, in Holland. North Sea Ferries from Hull, and P. & O. from Felixstowe, also operate ferries to Zeebrugge.

Travellers from the West Country may cross from Plymouth, Weymouth, Southampton, Portsmouth, or Newhaven, then travel across northern France, rather than drive along the south coast of England to the Dover area. These routes cannot take advantage of fast roads however, and are likely to delay arrival in Austria. The motorway system

USEFUL INFORMATION

•The native language of Austria is German but many — though not all — Austrians speak English.

•Electricity supply is 220 volts with a standard two-pin, round plug. It is best to carry a universal adapter.

•Bank opening hours: Monday, Tuesday, Wednesday, and Friday 8.30am-12.30pm and 1.30-3pm; Thursday 8am-12.30pm and 1.30-5.30pm.

•Shop opening hours: Generally, Monday to Friday 8am-6pm; Saturday, 8am-12noon; but with local variations according to season.

•Drinking water is safe.

•It is customary to leave a tip in restaurants, and for taxi drivers, of about 10 per cent of the bill.

•To telephone abroad from Austria from a payphone first lift the receiver; then insert coins (the slots take 1, 5, 10, 20 schilling coins) to the value of 9 schillings. When the dialling tone is audible dial 00 44 (for the UK) or 01 (for USA and Canada) then the home number, including the area code (but omit the initial 0 for the UK). Where there are only three coin slots press the red button when the dialled number answers. An audible tone warns that the time is about to expire. In hotels press the button on the handset then dial the number as before. Hotel telephone charges are high.

Public Holidays

1 January	New Year's Day
6 January	Epiphany
	Good Friday
	Easter Monday
1 May	Labour Day
	Ascension
	Corpus Christi
15 August	Assumption
26 October	National Day
1 November	All Saints' Day
25-6 December	Christmas

now brings the Dover ports within reach of the west of England, south and west Wales, and the Midlands.

The 'short' routes across the Channel start at Folkestone, Ramsgate, and Dover. Disembarkation may be at Boulogne, Calais, Dunkirk, Ostend, or Zeebrugge, after crossing times of between 35 minutes and up to $4^1/_4$ hours.

Driving in Austria

Motorists should become familiar with the international road signs. Seat belts must be worn by the driver and front-seat passenger, and by rear-seat passengers if rear seat belts are fitted. Children under the age of 12 are not allowed to travel in the front seats. Traffic police may issue on-the-spot fines.

Driving on side lights is not allowed. Parking (or side) lights are required at night where there are no street lamps or where they go out at midnight (red band around the lamp-post).

Use of the horn is prohibited in towns at all times. Trams have priority when coming from left or right, and vehicles must stop behind trams which have stopped to load or unload passengers.

Vehicles coming from the right have priority at uncontrolled cross-roads. On motorways passing is on the left; passing on the right-hand side of a vehicle is prohibited.

Drunken driving is a serious offence. **Do not drink and drive!** Rudeness to other travellers is also an offence punishable by an on-the-spot fine.

Speed Limits

Motor-cars:
  Built-up areas 50 kmh (31mph)
  Open roads 100 kmh (62mph)
  Motorways 130 kmh (81mph)
With Trailer under 750 kg (1,650 lb):
  Open roads 100 kmh (62mph)
  Motorways 100 kmh (62mph)
With trailer over 750 kg (1,650 lb):
  Open roads 80 kmh (49mph)
  Motorways 100 kmh (62mph)

1   THE VORARLBERG

Vorarlberg is the westernmost province of Austria and the smallest, with a population of about 300,000 scattered over 1,000sq miles. Its northern boundary is formed by the mountains of the Allgäu on the border with West Germany, the Ratikon range, together with the river Rhine is the border with Switzerland, except where Liechtenstein intrudes onto the right bank; the Arlberg and the peaks of the Silvretta guard the eastern passes to the Tyrol, and it has 20 miles of shoreline on Lake Constance. Its people originate from Celtic, Alemmanic, and Romansh stock mixed with Bavarian and Valaisian immigrants. In the hills and valleys of the Bregenzerwald they are dairy farmers; in the Rhine valley and the Walgau they manufacture textiles, embroidery, and chocolates; in the Montafon they grow fruit and generate hydroelectricity; throughout the province they extend their hospitality to their many visitors .

Bregenz, the capital, is strategically placed on Lake Constance, 5 miles from West Germany and 8 miles from Switzerland. For many visitors it is the gateway to Austria. The Illyrians and Celts settled there long before the Romans constructed the port of *Brigantium*. After the collapse of the Roman Empire, Vorarlberg suffered many centuries of disruption from successive wars, and from hostility between powerful landowning families. When Napoleon came over the Alps in 1797 his army suffered a notable defeat at Feldkirch. In 1945 the French came again as an army of occupation.

Today Vorarlberg derives a quarter of its income from tourism. Its facilities are excellent, its scenery spectacular, and its welcome warm.

BREGENZ
Approaching Bregenz from West Germany along Route 18 or Route 12, the signposts lead to the A14 motorway which bypasses the town. Note that it is necessary to leave the motorway at the Lochau junction in order to enter Bregenz from the north, along the lakeshore. Otherwise the motorway passes through the 4-mile-long Pfänder Tunnel and the town is entered from the south.

Bregenz (population 25,000) enjoys a scenic location at the foot of the Pfänder (1,064m, 3,490ft) and the Gebhardsberg (567m, 1,860ft) where the river Rhine enters Lake Constance (Bodensee). In addition

*Gebhardsberg,
near Bregenz*

to the natural and man-made wonders of the surrounding area and the churches and museums, the town has excellent modern water- and land-based sporting facilities as well as a casino. From the last week in July to the last week in August the Bregenz Festival offers a programme of international artistes, groups, and orchestras in performances of opera and ballet, recitals, and concerts on the floating stage of the **Festspielhaus**. The tiered, open-air auditorium seats 4,300 people and runs down to the water's edge. The festival ends with a fireworks display reflected in the waters of the lake.

In the old town around the cornmarket, and in the walled, upper town, there are many elegant period houses from the seventeenth and eighteenth centuries. The **Lake Chapel** (Seekapelle) of St George, on the corner of Rathausstrasse and A-Schneiderstrasse, was on the edge of the lake when it was first built in 1408. The present building, which was erected in 1698, has a beautiful Renaissance altar (1610), and relics of soldiers who died in the Appenzell war of 1408. Around the corner from the Rathaus (town hall, 1685) are the **Cornmarket Theatre** (converted in 1955 from the cornmarket of 1838), the **Johann**

Nepomuk chapel (1757), and the **Vorarlberg provincial museum** which has collections of prehistoric and Roman finds, and paintings by Angelika Kaufmann.

There is a regular boat service to Lindau, Friedrichshafen, Constance, and eight other townships. Between the harbour and the playhouse there are delightful gardens and promenades alongside the lake. At the north end of Kornmarktstrasse, Schillerstrasse leads to Belruptstrasse and the Pfänderbahn cable car. From the top of the Pfänder there are superb views across the lake, the town, and up the Rhine valley to Liechtenstein and the High Alps, and there is an alpine zoo.

The parish church of **St Gallus**, consecrated in 1318, is in Kirchstrasse. The baroque altar depicts Sts Gallus, Peter, Paul, and Ulrich, and, with the organ loft and choirstalls, dates from 1738 when the church was restyled by Franz Anton Beer and Peter Thumb. In the side chapel are St Magnus, a Benedictine monk from St Gallen and the Apostle of the Allgäu, and St Nicholas, the patron saint of the Lake Constance boatmen. Note the gilded statue of St Gallus and the little black bear.

In the upper town, **St Martin's Tower** (Martinsturm) dates from the fourteenth century but the present building was erected in 1602. On the upper floor there is a small **local history museum** with a collection of items connected with navigation on Lake Constance. Beneath it is **St Martin's chapel** which contains frescoes from the late fourteenth century. The picturesque **old town hall** is half-timbered and was built in 1662.

Around Bregenz

On the Gebhardsberg, a mile to the south-east of the town centre, Burg Hohenbregenz, ruined in 1647, provides spectacular views. The pilgrimage church of St Gebhard (1723-42), perched on the edge of a sheer cliff, was originally part of the castle where Gebhard was born. He became Bishop of Constance in 949 and founded the Benedictine abbey of Petershausen, near Constance, where he was buried in 995.

At **Mehrerau-Wettingen**, about a mile to the west along the lakeshore, the Cistercian abbey was founded in 1097 by the Benedictines from Petershausen. The abbey church is a Romanesque basilica built over an earlier crypt, the burial place of the abbots. In 1743 F.A. Beer built a baroque church which was restyled in 1856, and rebuilt in 1960. It contains notable panels painted by Adelbert Brouts, and two late Gothic statues of the Madonna.

At **Fussach**, about 5 miles to the west of Bregenz, across the Rhine bridge on the border with Switzerland, is the Rheinholz nature reserve which is popular with bird-watchers.

From Bregenz there are three routes eastward to the Tyrol. The northern route passes through the Bregenzerwald and over the Hochtannberg Pass to Reutte (1a); the central route via Bludenz and the Arlberg (1b); and the southern route through the Montafon and over the Silvretta Pass to Landeck (1c).

Route 1a   Bregenz to Imst in Tyrol via the Bregenzerwald (Northern Route) (see maps pages 17 and 22)

Leave Bregenz on Route 190 and after 6 miles turn left onto Route 200 signposted Beznau/Bregenzerwald. The road twists and turns upward for about 2 miles affording splendid views across Bregenz and Lake Constance. At **Alberschwende** (population 2,500) the parish church is neo-Romanesque and there is a memorial chapel to Pastor Merbot who died a martyr's death in 1121. Turn right here towards Egg. The Bregenzerwald got its name from the woodland which extended from the border with West Germany to the Rhine valley. Today most of the forest has been replaced by green pasture. The mountains are slashed by the torrent of the Bregenzerach which rises on the slopes of the Mohnenfluh (2,542m, 8,338ft), above Schröcken in the south-east, then flows through a series of wide basins, past meadows full of bell-clanking cattle, before tumbling through a narrow gorge above Bregenz and into Lake Constance. The people of the upper end of the valley are descendants of settlers who came here from the Valais in Switzerland, in the thirteenth and fourteenth centuries, and they may sometimes be seen in their traditional costume. The Bregenzerwald is a region of gentle scenic beauty and is rightly popular as an all-year-round holiday area.

The regional tourist office is very enterprising in ensuring that visitors find the kind of holiday they want. A full programme of events, for adults and for children, includes a 2-day walking tour on the mountains; a 7-mile cycling excursion away from traffic; an evening trip to see the sunset in the mountains; a tour of the mountain huts with cheese tasting; a photographic safari; a BMX bicycle rally; a botanical field trip; a tour of the bridges of the Bregenzerwald; a farm tour for children; underground caves; and a 'culture bus' which takes visitors on an escorted tour of churches, museums, etc. In the region there are seven outdoor swimming pools, and one indoor pool at Lingenau; an alpine climbing school at Schoppernau; a gliding club at Egg; and riding schools at Sibratsgfäll, Reuthe, and Riefensberg. There are 300 miles of marked footpaths. The Bregenzerach provides plenty of white water for canoeing, and clear water for fishing. In winter the landscape is transformed and facilities for skiing and other winter sports are excellent.

THE BREGENZERWALD BUNDESSTRASSE

The pretty town of **Egg** (population 2,800) is the capital of the Bregen-

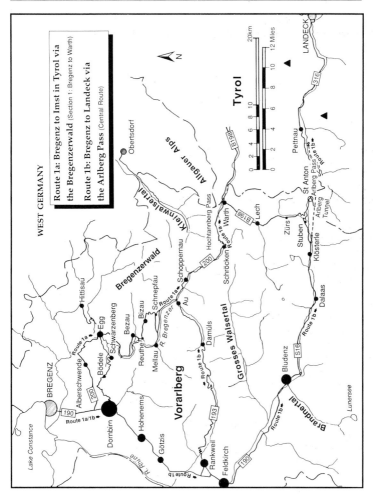

zerwald. Here there is a local history museum and a statue commemo-rating the Swedish invasion during the Thirty Years' War, and the parish church of St Nikolaus dates from 1307. Egg is an excellent centre for walking, and for touring the nearby villages of **Schwarzenberg** (popu-lation 1,500, home of the famous artist Angelika Kaufmann, 1741-1807), **Hittisau** (fourteenth-century church and a museum of old farm implements), **Lingenau** (parish church built in 1150), and for an excur-sion up the Balderschwangertal into West Germany.

Route 200 — the Bregenzerwald Bundesstrasse — rises up the Bregenzerach valley. **Andelsbuch** is a health resort, and a good starting point for walking on the Bezegg, and to the waterfalls of the Brühlbach. Beyond Andelsbuch the road then enters a magnificent gorge with tree-covered lower slopes and high cliffs. At 22 miles follow the signpost into the unspoilt village of **Bezau** (population 1,600). The parish church of St Jodok is early Gothic, seventeenth century, and has a high altar dating from 1684. The local history museum is located in a 300-year-old house and has an interesting collection of eighteenth-century costumes. At the eastern end of the village, at Oberhalden, there is a cable car up to the Baumgartenhöhe (1,631m, 5,350ft).

At **Reuthe** the Gothic parish church of Sts Jakob and Magdalena was built in 1289, and has frescoes from the fifteenth century and a sacristy from 1500.

At 30 miles, Route 200 passes through Mellau, another pretty village nestling in the hills. The peaks of the Hochtannberg now appear ahead, as well as the high crags of the Kanisfluh (2,044m, 6,704ft). The sleepy hamlet of **Hirschau** is tucked into the side of a steep, wooded hill, as are **Bizau**, with its onion-domed church, and **Schnepfau**. **Au** (population 1,500), lies to the right of the road across the river. It was the home of the Masterschool of the Bregenzerwald, founded in 1657, which, during the seventeenth and eighteenth centuries, trained many of the baroque architects who made such a great contribution to the cultural heritage of Austria and West Germany. The most famous families were the Beers, Thumbs, and Moosbruggers who between them produced thirty-one architects. Their works can be seen in Ottobeuren (Bavaria), St Gallen, Rottenburg, Landshut, and 300 other churches. The parish church has a consecration stamp dated 1372.

Schoppernau (population 900), is a delightful rustic village, a community of farmhouses where the Franz Michael Felder museum commemorates his life and work. From the elevated, simple baroque parish church (1682) there is a lovely view across the rooftops of the flower-decked, wooden houses to the surrounding peaks, all of them over 2,000m (6,560ft) high. The air is filled with the sound of goat bells and bird song, the smell of drying timber, and the sight of butterflies, geraniums, dahlias, and of cheesecloths hung out to dry in the sunshine.

Continuing up the valley the road rises through a narrow gorge to reach, at 45 miles, the little village of **Schröcken** (population 350). This is the end of the valley of the Bregenzerach and to travel further the road must rise over the Hochtannberg Pass (1,679m, 5,507ft).

THE HOCHTANNBERG HOCHALPENSTRASSE

The Hochtannberg Hochalpenstrasse is steep, twisting, and narrow. It is not an easy road. It is used by large vehicles, especially coaches, and

Sibratsgfäll in the Bregenzerwald

oncoming traffic can sometimes force ascending vehicles to stop and restart on the hairpin bends. Work to improve the road is in hand and will doubtless soon result in a first-class highway. While work is in progress the unavoidable disruption to the carriageway, and the heavy transport required, may cause added difficulties. The problem should not be exaggerated but it would be wise to enquire about road conditions before starting the journey.

After nine hairpin bends (gradients up to 14 per cent, 1 in 7), the road reaches Nesslegg then continues through four more hairpin bends to the final, very narrow section to the top of the pass at **Hochkrumbach**. Here there is wild moorland with a small lake half a mile to the south of the road, and a footpath which leads northward into the Kleinwalsertal which, although part of Austria, can only be reached by road from Oberstdorf in West Germany.

From the pass the road descends easily through a short tunnel and, at 51 miles, the red steeple of the little seventeenth-century parish church welcomes the traveller to **Warth**. The village enjoys a superb setting on the hillside, across the green valley from the majestic Biberkopf (2,599m, 8,525ft) on the border with West Germany.

As a diversion from the main route, go ahead at Warth on Route 198 down a narrow, tree-lined gorge, some 5 miles to the winter resort of **Lech** (population 1,200) which, together with Zürs, Stuben, and St Anton, is one of the best winter sports centres in Austria. The road goes on a further 5 miles to the Arlberg Pass, but return to Warth to follow the Lechtal to Reutte.

THE LECHTAL

From Warth, Route 198 descends into the valley of the river Lech by means of two hairpin bends, crosses into the Tyrol, then runs alongside the river. The narrow valley is flanked by the Allgäuer Alps, at about 2,500m (8,200ft) to the north-west, and the Lechtaler Alps, rising to around 2,900m (9,512ft). The road winds gently downward through the villages of Steeg, Holzgau, and Bach, each with its little white church. At **Elbigenalp** (population 600), which is known for its woodcarvers, the Falger museum is devoted to the works of Anton Falger (1791-1876), artist and sculptor. The parish church of St Nicholas dates from 1399. The interior is baroque and rococo and the painted ceiling is by Johann Jakob Zeiller. In St Martin's chapel there are late fifteenth-century Gothic frescoes and a painting of *The Dance of Death* by Anton Falger.

At Elmen and Stanzach the valley widens and the broad river bed is a measure of the torrents which rush down from the mountains after storms. The scenery is reminiscent of the Rocky Mountains with towering hills of bald rock, scree slopes clad with green conifers, and blue-green water in the glacier-fed river. A sign reads 'Aufwiedersehen Lechtal' and the road runs past the turn to Weissenbach and the Oberjoch Pass into West Germany, and past an airstrip, before entering Reutte at 88 miles.

The village of Warth and the Biberkopf

Reutte (population 5,000) is an industrial town with several eighteenth-century buildings. At No 1 Untersteig the decorated house with bay windows was built in 1780 and was the home of the Zeiller family. The paintings of Paul Zeiller and his sons Franz Anton and Johann Jakob may be seen in the churches of the area, and in the local history museum at Unterer Markt 24. In the Hauptstrasse the Rathaus (town hall) has an external, balustraded staircase and is prettily decorated, as is the administrative building next door with its curved gable. On the corner is the Golden Crown Hotel which has a coach fresco painted in 1777. Across the road is the church of St Anna, originally 1490, rebuilt after a fire in 1846. At the southern end of the Hauptstrasse is the Gasthof Schwarzer Adler which has a very attractive façade and stands alongside Route 314, signposted Fernpaß.

Route 314 rises quickly, passing the ruins of Schloß Ehrenberg, then descends through Heiterwang. It bypasses **Bichlbach** (population 750) but it may be worth turning into the village to see the frescoes by Johann Jakob and Franz Anton Zeiller in the fifteenth-century church of St Lorenz. With the nearby village of **Berwang**, this is a popular winter sports centre with good facilities. Back on the main road the majestic Zugspitze (2,962m, 9,715ft), on the border with West Germany, soon comes into view. Again it may be worth pausing at **Lermoos** (population 950) to see the baroque church of St Katherine (1753), the ceiling paintings by Giuseppe Gru of Verona (1784), and the gilded pulpit. The health resort and winter sports centre of **Ehrwald** (population 2,200),

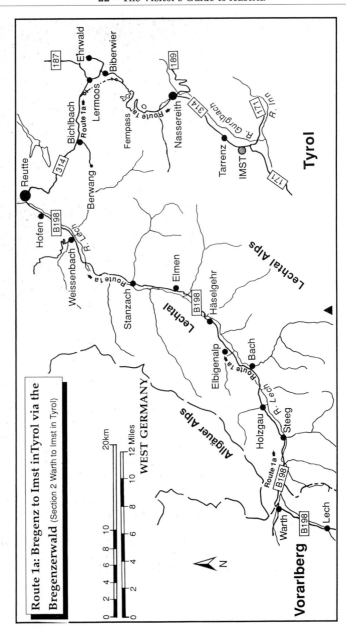

Route 1a: Bregenz to Imst in Tyrol via the Bregenzerwald (Section 2 Warth to Imst in Tyrol)

Zürs, one of Austria's main winter sports centres

at the foot of the Zugspitze, is 2 miles beyond Lermoos on Route 187 to Garmisch-Partenkirchen.

A superb view of the mountains across the Blindsee can be enjoyed from the Zugspitzeblick restaurant, and at 108 miles the road reaches the Fernpaß (1,209m, 3,966ft). A rapid descent follows through a hairpin bend to the bridge over the Fernsteinsee. In the middle of the lake is the ruin of Siegmundsburg, a fifteenth-century hunting lodge. Looking west from the bridge, half hidden in the trees and clinging to the side of a deep gorge, is Schloß Fernstein. In the thirteenth century the castle was a toll station and guard post for the Fernpaß. It has notable stucco decoration and frescoes in the great hall, and a late Gothic chapel (1478).

The road then drops into the Gurglbachtal where at **Nassereith** and at **Tarrenz** there are old houses and fifteenth-century churches. At 120 miles from Bregenz the road reaches **Imst** in the Inn valley.

Route 1b   Bregenz to Landeck via the Arlberg Pass (Central Route) (see map page 17)

The central route from Bregenz to the Tyrol may follow either the A14 motorway, or Route 190. The former avoids the hindrances of towns, and passing through the Arlberg Road Tunnel can enable the motorist to drive the 90 miles from Bregenz to Imst in about an hour, and to reach Innsbruck, 36 miles further on, in less than 2 hours.

For a more leisurely route which takes in the attractions of the Walgau and the Klostertal, depart from Bregenz on Route 190 to **Dornbirn** (population 40,000), centre of the textile industry. In the market square the Red House (Rote Haus), which dates from 1639, has a richly decorated interior. The parish church of St Martin dates from 1840. At No 35 Marktstrasse is the Vorarlberg natural history museum (Vorarlberger Naturschau) which has exhibits of plant and animal life of the region and a large collection of minerals.

Slightly off the route, about 3 miles south-east of Dornbirn along the right bank of the Dornbirner Ache, there is a spectacular gorge — the Rappenlochschlucht — and a footpath leads up to the Alplochschlucht where there is a waterfall 120m (390ft) high. A mile-and-a-half to the south there is a cable car to the top of the Karren (975m, 3,198ft) with superb views. East of the town, some 5 miles along the mountain road towards Egg, is **Bödele**, in a lovely setting surrounded by alpine pastures and pine forests and with views over Lake Constance.

South of Dornbirn the road keeps close to sheer cliffs on the left while ahead the humped back of the Kummenberg breaks the level valley floor and obscures the view of the distant snowclad peaks of Switzerland.

Hohenems (population 13,000), just over a mile from the border with Switzerland, derives its name from the Ems family of the now ruined Alt-Ems castle. Wolf Dietrich of Ems married Clara de Medici, sister of Pope Pius IV, who had three sons, one of whom was Marcus Sitticus. In 1560 the head of the family was raised to the status of Imperial Count, and a year later Marcus Sitticus became the Cardinal Bishop of Constance. He began the construction of Schloß Hohenems, a Renaissance palace with a courtyard and fountains, where a Schubert Festival (Schubertiade) is held each June. Marcus Sitticus gave the incomplete palace to his brother Hannibal who, after the death of his 28-year-old wife Hortense, built a memorial church. The present parish church of St Carlo Borromeo (half-brother of Hortense) was built in 1796. It has a remarkable carved wooden high altar in Renaissance style from 1580, and houses the tomb of the last count, Kaspar von Ems, who died in 1635. In the palace library, in the eighteenth century, two Nibelungen songs were found amongst the family manuscripts.

The Damülser Mittagspitze, from Damüls

The village of **Götzis** (population 850) is squeezed between the Kummenberg and the foothills of the Hohe Kugel (1,645m, 5,396ft). The parish church dates from 1340 and has a baroque altar and a sacristy from 1597. The new church was built in 1865 in neo-Romanesque style and has notable stained glass windows. Beyond Götzis the valley opens into a large basin with the Rätikon Mountains dominating the view ahead.

The road bypasses **Rankweil** (population 10,000), at the bottom of the Laternsertal. A detour can be made along Route 193 which winds its way up to 1,769m (5,802ft) then down again (gradients up to 14 per cent, 1 in 7) via Damüls to Au. The parish church of St Peter dates from the thirteenth century, and has a branched wooden cross dated 1400 depicting the martyrdom of the Abbess of Valduna. The pilgrimage church of Maria Heimsuchung stands on a hill, and was converted in 1377 from one of the Count of Montfort's castles — it is still enclosed by the old parapet. The Chapel of Grace (Gnadenkapelle) is by Michael Beer of Au and contains a wrought-iron screen and altar paintings from 1450, and a carved Madonna from 1470. The nearby silver cross is dated 1233 and came from Augsburg.

Retracing the road back to Route 190, **Feldkirch** (population 23,000), 23 miles from Bregenz, stands on the river Ill, barely a mile from the border with Liechtenstein. The one-time capital of the province still preserves some of the town walls and gated towers which protected the old quarter where there are many period houses, alleyways, and arcaded squares to delight the eye — especially in and around the Marktplatz and Neustadtstrasse. Feldkirch has a tradition of artistic achievement and of scholarship which dates back to the Middle Ages. The late Gothic cathedral church of St Nikolaus was first consecrated in 1287, the double nave being completed in 1478. On the left side altar three paintings, including a notable *Lamentation*, are by Wolf Huber, a native of Feldkirch, who was a member of the Danube school of artists. The pulpit (1521) was converted from a tabernacle and is considered the best example of Gothic wrought-iron work in Austria. Near the high altar there is a tomb of one of the Counts of Montfort dating from 1320.

On the corner of the Domplatz and Neustadtstrasse is the Rathaus (1493) which has interesting seventeenth- and eighteenth-century decoration in the council chamber. At the end of the Herrengasse is the Cat's Tower (Katzenturm) (1491) named after a cannon decorated with lion heads. In the Schloßergasse is the Liechtenstein palace which is the town library and venue for cultural events. In Johannitergasse is the headquarters of the Knights of St John, and the church of St John, built in 1218 by Count Hugo von Montfort who is buried there. The Schattenburg, the best preserved castle in the province, was built in the twelfth and thirteenth centuries on a hilltop now tunnelled by Route 190, and houses the local history museum.

Feldkirch has several other churches to visit — the Kapuzinerkirche (1605), the church of Sts Peter and Paul (sixteenth century), Kreuzkapelle-im-Kehr (1380), Margarethenkapelle (fifteenth century), Magdalenenkirche (fourteenth century), Martinskapelle (1222), Dominikanerinnenkloster (seventeenth century), and St Cornell's church at Tosters. Schloß Amberg (1502), at Levis, is now a hotel, and at Tosters there is a ruined castle built in 1260. Feldkirch is a convenient centre for visiting Vaduz and the rest of Liechtenstein; for exploring the Großes Walsertal; and for climbing in the Rätikon Mountains which include the Schesaplana (2,965m, 9,725ft).

Leave Feldkirch on Route 190 up the Illtal to **Bludenz** (population 13,000), home of Suchard chocolate. There has been a settlement on this site since the Bronze Age but fires in the fifteenth and seventeenth centuries destroyed most of the town except the church and the castle. The latter, Schloß Gayenhofen, is now an administrative centre. Like the neighbouring parish church of St Laurentius (1514) it overlooks the town and may be reached via a steep pathway. The church contains five baroque marble altars (1720), and two Gothic pictures from 1510. In the Upper Gate (Obere Tor) there is a local history museum with ecclesiastical exhibits from the fifteenth century. Bludenz is a working town near the junction of five valleys. On the north side there is a cable car to the Muttersberg (1,384m, 1,504ft) and a splendid view of the Großes Walsertal to the north, Klostertal to the east, Montafon to the south-east, Brandnertal to the south-west, and the Walgau to the north-west. The

many hairpin bends of the road up the Brandnertal lead to the picturesque Lunersee (1,976m, 6,481ft) at the foot of the Schesaplana.

Beyond Bludenz Route 190 becomes Route S16, the Arlberg
expressway, which is mostly dual carriageway. Along the Klostertal
there are several villages which are starting points for walks. From
Dalaas (836m, 2,742ft) there is a pathway northward to the Formarin-
see (1,915m, 6,281ft) and on up the Roten Wand (2,704m, 8,869ft); on
the south side a footpath snakes up to Innerkristberg (1,150m, 3,772ft)
and over into the Silbertal. From **Klösterle** (1,073m, 3,519ft) a path
rises northward to the Spullersee (1,827m, 5,993ft) and on to the
Spuller Schafberg (2,680m, 8,790ft); and, on the south side of the
valley, several paths lead over to the Silbertal.

Just beyond Klösterle, Route S16 enters the Arlberg Tunnel which
is $8^1/_2$ miles long. Alternatively, bear left up the road to **Stuben** to enjoy
the wild mountain scenery. The Flexenstrasse, on the left, goes over the
Flexenpass to Zürs and Lech. From the Arlberg Pass (1,793m, 5,881ft),
which is the border between Vorarlberg and Tyrol, the road descends
steeply (gradient 13 per cent, 1 in 7.7) down the mountainside, with a
lovely view of the peaks of the Verwall group ahead, into the valley of
the Rosanna to reach **St Anton-am-Arlberg** (population 2,000) at 60
miles from Bregenz.

St Anton is an international centre for winter sports and home of the
Arlberg Ski School, founded by Hannes Schneider (1890-1955). The
cable cars, chairlifts, and ski-lifts are so numerous that they are referred
to as a 'circus', and they enable skiers to reach peaks ranging from
1,845m (6,052ft) to 2,809m (9,214ft) high. St Anton is also a pleasant
summer holiday resort and a good centre for walking and climbing in the
Verwall group and the Lechtaler Alps.

Below St Anton is the pretty village of **Pettnau**. Here rejoin Route
S16 and run down past the junction with Route 188 to **Landeck**, 78
miles from Bregenz, in the Inn valley.

Route 1c   Bregenz to Landeck via the Montafon and Silvretta Pass (Southern Route)

(see map page 29)

The southern route from Bregenz to the Tyrol is the most spectacular.
It follows the central route to the junction, beyond Bludenz, where Route
190 becomes Route S16. There take Route 188 signposted Silvretta
Hochalpenstrasse/Schruns. The road passes through **St Anton-im-
Montafon** with its parish church on the left, separated from the road by
a small orchard. In the Montafon when the snows of winter have melted
then the warm valley is white again with spring blossom. At harvest time

the red-and-yellow apples burst with sap.

Note at St Anton, the road to the left which goes up to **Bartholomäberg** where there is a remarkable parish church built in 1732. On the baroque high altar the tabernacle dates from 1635, and on a panelled side altar there is a notable wooden relief of the *Last Supper* from 1525. The Romanesque processional cross is decorated with enamel and precious stones and was made in Limoges, in France, in 1150. The church occupies a beautiful, elevated setting from which there are splendid views.

The road continues past Vandans (population 2,000), where there is a ruined castle, and Tschagguns (population 2,000), to **Schruns** (population 3,500), 44 miles from Bregenz, pretty principal town of the Montafon, and end of the railway line from Bludenz. The parish church is neo-Romanesque and has attractive stained glass windows, and ceiling paintings by Hans Bertle. The local history museum is housed in a seventeenth-century house. Schruns is a good centre for walking and touring in the Silbertal and in the Rätikon and Verwall Mountains, and has a two-stage cable car up to 1,850m, 6,068ft.

From Schruns Route 188 rises steadily up the narrowing valley to **St Gallenkirch** (population 2,000), with a late Gothic parish church from 1478. A side road leads up the Gargellental, to the south-west, to **Gargellen** in a superb alpine setting almost surrounded by high peaks. The main road continues through Gortipohl, where there is a waterfall, to **Gaschurn** (population 3,000), with a seventeenth-century church, a good base for excursions. **Partenen** is located at the top of the Montafon valley, at the foot of the Verwall and Silvretta Mountains, 55 miles from Bregenz.

THE SILVRETTA HOCHALPENSTRASSE

After the toll booth the Silvretta Hochalpenstrasse rises swiftly (gradients up to 10 per cent, 1 in 10) through eighteen hairpin bends stacked on top of each other with several stopping points with admirable views, until the road reaches the 50m-high (164ft) dam of the Vermunt-Stausee (1,743m, 5,717ft). The road continues to rise steeply southward, overlooking the lake, before climbing through another six hairpin bends up to the Bielerhöhe at 2,032m (6,665ft) 64 miles from Bregenz. The beautiful lake is created by a 80m-high (262ft), 432m-wide (1,382ft) dam. There are boat cruises, a small church and shrine, and accommodation and refreshments at the Bielerhöhe Hotel.

The scenery around the Bielerhöhe is spectacular. To the east and south are the broken peaks of the Silvretta group, with the Vermunt Glacier glistening against the backdrop of the Silvrettahorn (3,244m, 10,640ft) and Piz Buin (3,312m, 10,863ft) on the border with Switzerland; to the west the Hochmaderer (2,823m, 9,259ft) and its foothills are even more rugged; to the north is the Schattenkopf (2,654m, 8,705ft).

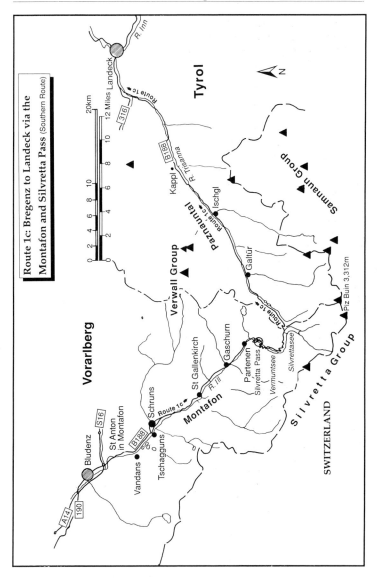

Route 1c: Bregenz to Landeck via the Montafon and Silvretta Pass (Southern Route)

This is good walking country for fit, well equipped people of all ages. The road then descends into the Paznauntal, crosses into the Tyrol,

The Bielerhöhe on the Silvretta Pass

and runs alongside the river Trisanna. The landscape is like that of Scotland, with grassy moorland broken by occasional pine woods on the long sides of the cup-shaped valley, and the little river gurgling over smooth stones. Passing two small lakes on the right, the road crosses a wooden bridge where, through the clear water, trout may be seen rising in the pools. At **Galtür** (population 700) there is a baroque parish church from the fourteenth century. A track southward goes up the Jamtal to the Jamtalhütte at 2,165m (7,101ft) below the Jamtalferner Glacier.

Below Galtür the valley widens. At **Ischgl** (population 1,000), an international winter sports centre, there is the longest funicular railway in Austria 3,600m (11,808ft) up to the 2,320m-high (7,610ft) station on the Idalpe. The parish church of St Nikolaus is baroque (1757), built on the site of a late Gothic, fifteenth-century church.

Below Ischgl the valley is bounded on the north side by the Verwall group — Fatlárspitze (2,986m, 9,794ft), and Madaunspitze (2,961m, 9,712ft), and on the south side by the Samnaungroup — Bürkelkopf (3,032m, 9,945ft), Grübelekopf (2,894m, 9,492ft), Kreuzjoch (2,853m, 9,385ft), and Hexenkopf (3,035m, 9,955ft). At Versahl there is a wooden, late Renaissance chapel from the seventeenth century. The road then passes beneath the Trisanna bridge which is 86m (282ft) high and 230m (754ft) long and was built in 1882 to carry the Arlberg railway to St Anton am Arlberg. Route 188 then joins Route S16 to reach Landeck, 94 miles from Bregenz.

2 NORTH TYROL

For many holidaymakers the province of Tyrol represents Austria. When they conjure in their mind's eye a vision of an old wooden house with a balustraded balcony laden with bright red geraniums, sited on a steep, sunny pasture at the foot of a snow-capped mountain, with a farmer in his leather trousers (*lederhosen*), his wife in a blouse and long skirt (*dirndl*), and his cattle weighed down with heavy bells, they recall a picture that is more likely to be found in the Tyrol than in any other province. Tourism may be said to have started here more than a century ago and receives greater recognition than perhaps anywhere else in the world. Catering for the visitor is a major source of income for all Tyroleans and is therefore of primary concern to them. That is reflected in the availability of tourist information, ease of accessibility to the many worthwhile places to visit, and the high quality of service from hotels, shops etc. Because holiday facilities are so well developed, the Tyrol is very popular with visitors, especially those who are English-speaking because almost every Tyrolean speaks some English. Consequently it can become crowded in high season, but its reputation as a holiday venue is well deserved.

The province of Tyrol is divided into a large northern area and a south-eastern section known as East Tyrol. Before 1919 there was also a southern section — South Tyrol — which elected at that time to join Italy. This chapter describes North Tyrol which comprises an area of 4,100sq miles inhabited by 550,000 people and bounded to the west by the Arlberg and the province of Vorarlberg, to the north by the Limestone Alps, to the east by Land Salzburg, and to the south by the High Alps. Between the two alpine ranges is the glacial valley of the river Inn which runs diagonally across the province from the Finstermünz ravine for 120 miles to the Kufstein gap. The major side valleys are all to the south — the Ötztal, the Sellraintal, the Wipptal with the Stubaital, and the Zillertal. The rugged peaks of the white-faced limestone Alps give way to upland terraces at Seefeld, Leutasch, and Mieming, and to the west lie the lovely Gurgltal, and the more austere Paznauntal and Lechtal. It is an area of great natural beauty, with high mountains and deep valleys covered with forests and meadows, dressed with colourful flowers, and inhabited by deer, birds of prey, marmots, and mountain goats, which combine to provide wonderful landscapes.

An unusual feature of the Inn valley is the Föhn — a hot wind which blows up from the south over the high mountains, to pour along the Ötztal and into the deep trench cut by the Inn. The dry wind clears the air and burns the grasses causing a risk of fire, and melts the snows so that rivers run in spate and avalanches thunder down the mountainsides. The populace lives in fear and trepidation, school examinations are suspended and it has been said (by the defendants) that the Föhn has been the cause of criminal actions!

Innsbruck, the capital, is close to the geographic centre of the province. It is a city with many historic features as well as cultural and sporting activities. It is a good base for exploring the Tyrol, having excellent road and rail connections, and excursions may be made to Salzburg and Vienna or into West Germany and Italy. Along the Inn valley there is a succession of old towns with period houses and buildings. The lakes of the Tyrol are warm and beautiful and offer good facilities for water sports.

The Tyrol has a rich cultural heritage. The Hofkirche in Innsbruck together with the abbey at Stams are the highlights of church architecture in the province. The baroque style is well represented also by the Hofburg palace, St Jakob cathedral and Wilten basilica in Innsbruck, and the parish churches of Brixen-im-Thale, Ebbs, Götzens, Hopfgarten, Neustift, and Volders. The Ferdinandeum museum in Innsbruck has an outstanding collection of finds from throughout the Tyrol but much of interest can be found in numerous smaller museums, many housed in old castles. The history of the province is inevitably one of many wars since it is strategically placed on both north-south and east-west routes. The best loved patriot is Andreas Hofer who led a peasants' revolt against Napoleon's armies in 1809. There are Passion Plays every 6 years at Thiersee and at Erl, the 'Antlass-Ritt' Corpus Christi procession in the Brixen valley, the 'Gauderfest' beer festival in the Zillertal, the European Forum at Alpbach, and the masked carnivals at Imst, Nassereith, Telfs, Lans and Axams which are held in February.

For sporting visitors the Tyrol offers a full range of facilities. In winter it has some of the best downhill skiing in the world as well as cross country skiing, and skating and curling rinks. In summer there is walking and climbing, sailing, boating, swimming, white-water canoeing, riding, cycling, gliding and hang-gliding, tennis, rifle-shooting, golf, bowling, fishing, and summer skiing. There are casinos at Seefeld and Kitzbühel. On the Achensee there are steamer excursions, and in the Zillertal there is a steam railway. There are also many 'hobby' holidays on offer. They include wood carving, wax making, cookery, watercolour painting, photography, handicrafts, language courses, and music. The programme varies considerably from year to year, so visitors should seek up-to-date information from the Austrian National Tourist Office or from their local tourist office in Austria.

Three roads from Vorarlberg have already been described in Chapter 2. This chapter describes the main route which follows the river Inn, then roads which go off to the north and south, and finally journeys into Land Salzburg via the Gerlos Pass, and via St Johann, in both cases terminating at Zell-am-See. The Grossglockner Hochalpenstrasse, Lienz and East Tyrol are described in Chapter 3.

PART 1 THE UPPER INN VALLEY AND INNSBRUCK

Route 2a Nauders to Innsbruck (see map page 37)

The river Inn enters Austria from the Engadine region of Switzerland through the Finstermünz ravine. As the river flows northward, then eastward, then northward again for 120 miles, the deep, broad valley is the backbone of the province. For 2,000 years it has been a highway for east-west transport and a respite for traffic travelling across the passes to north and south. In prehistoric times the Celts settled in its warm meadows and many Bronze Age and Roman finds have been made. Its fertile, alluvial soil has supported dairy, arable, and fruit farming as well as market gardening to feed the industrial towns which lie along the river banks, and its mineral wealth has provided the raw materials for silver, copper, and chemical works.

Travellers from the Engadine may enter Austria either by following the river along Route 27/184, or by crossing Martin's bridge over the Inn then climbing up the steep (gradients up to 15 per cent, 1 in 7) road to **Nauders** (population 1,300) enjoying the splendid views. West of the Norberthöhe (the highest point of this road) about 20 minutes' walk away, is the Schöpfwarte (1,438m, 4,717ft), which affords splendid views of the Engadine. Just beyond there are views of the river Inn far below, and the pathway marked No 2 then swings around the Sellesköpfe to return to the start. This is an easy walk which should take about 2 hours. Nauders is a good centre for touring and walking. The eleventh-century parish church of St Valentin was rebuilt in the sixteenth century, and later restyled. It has a neo-Romanesque altar and nineteenth-century frescoes by Johann and Stefan Kärle. Two carved side altars date from 1480 and 1510. South of the village, Schloß Naudersberg dates from 1300 and is very picturesque. At the foot of the castle the little church of St Leonhard is Romanesque and was built in 1391. It has frescoes from the twelfth century in the apse and paintings from 1500 in the nave. A cable car goes up to Bergkastelboden at 2,184m (7,164ft). Italy is only $2\frac{1}{2}$ miles to the south and Route 315 comes up from the border and carries on northward via several hairpin

The Inn valley looking west

bends and the Finstermünz Pass. Just after Hochfinstermünz there is a car park with views across the gorge to the Samnauntal in Switzerland. At Kajetanbrücke Route 315 joins Route 184 and a mile later enters Pfunds.

Pfunds (population 2,000) is a double town with Pfunds-Stuben sited between the road and the left bank of the Inn, and Pfunds-Dorf on the opposite bank. In the former the church of Our Lady is Gothic, with frescoes in the nave and a sixteenth-century winged altar. In Pfunds-Dorf the parish church is also Gothic and has a richly decorated interior.

Below Pfunds, the old road runs parallel to the S15 and passes through the village of Tösens to reach **Ried** (population 900). The church of St Leonhard (1516) is late Gothic with notable paintings and altar sculptures. Schloß Siegmundsried, a thirteenth-century fortified keep, was enlarged in 1470 by Count Siegmund. It has a two-storey late Gothic hall, and sixteenth-century paintings of coats of arms in the entrance hall. West of Ried a tortuous road rises 6 miles via the hamlet of **Fiss** (where there is a cable car up to the Fisser Joch (2,436m, 7,990ft) to the mountain village of **Serfaus** (population 900). Here there are three remarkable churches. The parish church of Maria Himmelfahrt (1500) has notable paintings, carved figures and chancel. The church of Our Lady in the Woods (1332) has Gothic frescoes, a painting of the Holy Mother and Child from 1300, and a striking plague chapel (1635). Half a mile south is St George's chapel which has frescoes from 1482, a panelled altar from 1500, a high altar from 1680, and a copy of a shrine

Stams abbey

of 1270, the original being in the Ferdinandeum museum in Innsbruck. Serfaus has two cableways up to the Komperdell (1,980m, 6,494ft).

After Ried the road soon reaches **Prutz** (population 1,300) where the parish church (1521) is late Gothic, and the Antonius chapel dates from 1676. The chapel of rest has a sixteenth-century *pietà*. The Kaunertal runs east of Prutz to the Gepatsch reservoir where a pleasant and easy walk around the lake takes about 3 hours. From Prutz Route 315 then follows the right bank of the Inn to the Pontlatzer bridge where a memorial commemorates victory over Bavarian and French forces in 1703, and over the French army in 1809. Since 1511 the people of Tyrol have had the right to bear arms, and have been required at all times to be prepared to defend their homeland. In 1703 Innsbruck surrendered after a surprise attack and it was left to the peasants of the Inn valley to repel the insurgents. In 1809 a French force marching on Finstermünz found their way blocked by armed citizens. Many of the villages today have a rifle brigade and the people maintain their shooting skills. A mile further on a side road rises to **Fließ** (population 2,400) where the parish church (1493), has external frescoes of St Christopher, and the new parish church (1804) has two towers in the classic style.

Landeck (population 7,500) 27 miles from Nauders, is a small industrial town at a strategic location for traffic to and from the west and south. It is overlooked by Burg Landeck which was built about 1200 and has a notable great hall and a chapel with sixteenth-century frescoes. It now houses the local history museum. The parish church dates from

1280, and was rebuilt in the style of a Gothic basilica in 1493. The relief over the west door depicts the Madonna and Child with two angels (1506), and on the south wall is the figure of St Oswald of Schrofenstein (1530). The little Pestheiligenkirchlein (1656), on the high ground of the 'Burschl', contains a beautiful Gothic choir, and a high altar by Adam Payr (1651). North of the town, the privately owned Schloß Schrofenstein (1196) stands on a picturesque site some 300m (984ft) above the river. Landeck is a convenient centre for touring the upper Inn valley.

After Landeck the road runs down the valley through the villages of Zams — where a cable car rises to the Venet (2,208m, 7,242ft) — and Schönwies, and past the ruined Burg Kronburg, to **Imst** (population 6,500) 39 miles from Nauders. It is located at the junction of the Gurglbach and the Inn rivers, on the route northward to West Germany, and has long been an important staging post for travellers — it was mentioned in 763. It stands on an uneven hillside site so that it divides naturally into upper and lower towns, the town centre being in the latter. There are picturesque houses from the seventeenth and eighteenth centuries including the Old Post Hotel and the Rathaus (town hall) which houses a local history museum with finds from early times as well as carnival masks and nativity cribs. The fourteenth-century Johanneskirche has notable frescoes. The parish church, in the upper town, dates from 1305, though it has been altered many times. The west façade has a stepped gable and a rose window over the door. On the west and south walls there are external frescoes from the fifteenth to eighteenth centuries, now sadly weathered and in need of restoration. The interior is simply decorated in Gothic style except for a striking modern altar of copper and white stone. The oil paintings and stained glass windows are magnificent. In the arcaded churchyard the chapel of St Michael is a late Gothic, two-storey rotunda and has frescoes from 1490. Also worth seeing is the Kalvarienberg where the seventeenth-century chapels of the Stations of the Cross lead up to the Laurentiuskirche and the Heilig-Grab-Kapelle, and on to the plague chapel (1694), which is built of stone and wood and is unique in the Tyrol.

Imst shares with Nassereith and Telfs the honour of organising the February carnival to drive out the devils of winter and prepare a welcome for spring. Costumed figures wear grotesque masks, most of which are displayed during the rest of the year in the museum of folk art in Innsbruck. Some of the carnival figures originate from the seventeenth-century trade in canaries which were exported to London, Madrid, and many other distant cities. In 1822 a fire destroyed many buildings in the town and the breeding stock was lost.

Next the road crosses the Inn to pass the Ötztal Railway Station on the left, opposite Route 186, signposted Ötztal/Sölden/Oetz. Continuing along Route 171, here lined with fruit trees, the green onion-dome belongs to the parish church of **Haiming** which is late Gothic from the

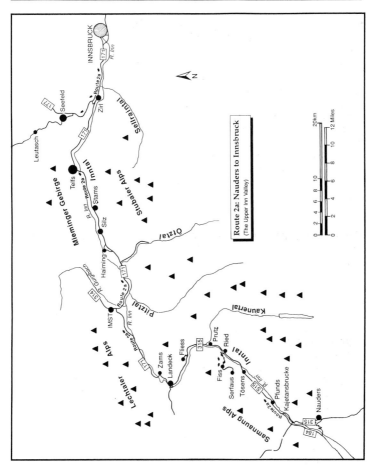

Route 2a: Nauders to Innsbruck
(The Upper Inn Valley)

fourteenth century. It has notable net vaulting and stained glass windows from 1521. Beyond the village to the north, is the peak of Simmering (2,096m, 6,875ft). Shortly the twelfth-century Schloß Petersberg comes into sight on the right-hand side. It has a chapel with interesting windows and now houses a youth hostel. The next village is **Silz** which has a neo-Romanesque parish church (1847) with a sharp steeple, as has the baroque church of Maria Schnee, the parish church of Mötz, which can be seen high on a hill to the left.

After Silz the lovely buildings of **Stams** abbey come into view on the southern side of the valley, below the wooded slopes of the Stubaier

View across the city of Innsbruck to the Karwendel Mountains

Alps. Across the valley the skyline is determined by the ragged white ridge of the Mieminger Mountains. The Cistercian abbey seems to be at peace and in harmony with its natural surroundings. When the voices of the choir in the abbey church have died away then the silence is broken only by the sound of birds on the abbey roof.

The abbey was founded in 1273 by Elizabeth of Bavaria and her husband Meinhard II, Count of Tyrol. The buildings were developed from 1440 to 1660, and again from the late seventeenth century to 1740. The two-storey, dormitory building encloses a rectangular courtyard. Among the most notable features of the accommodation is the princes' hall which has paintings denoting scenes from the life of St Bernard by Franz Michael Hueber and George Zoller. The magnificent sweeping banister on the staircase is the work of Bernhard Bachnetzer, of Silz.

The abbey church of the Virgin Mary is resplendent baroque, the work of George Anton Gumpel who rebuilt the church in the eighteenth century to replace a Romanesque church from 1284. The high altar (1613), by B. Steinle, is a massive piece reaching up to the top of the 15m-high (50ft) vaulting, and bearing eighty-four carved wooden figures depicting the Tree of Life. Adam and Eve, at the base, represent the beginning of human life on earth, and at the top Christ on the Cross represents the spiritual life. A truly remarkable work. The stucco decoration is by F.X. Feichtmayr, and J. Vischer; the statues and carvings are by Andreas Damasch, Andreas Kölle, and J. Reindl; and the wrought-iron grilles are by Bernhard Bachnetzer and Michael Neurauter. These

Herzog Friedrich Strasse with the Golden Roof in the background, Innsbruck

artists worked under the direction of Johann George Wolker who also painted the beautiful frescoes. The tomb of the Dukes of Tyrol dates from 1681 and is adorned by twelve gilded statues. This was the work of Andreas Damasch, as was the large Crucifixion group. The magnificent choirstalls are by Christopher Gumpp, and George Zoller.

The village of Stams is overshadowed by the abbey but it has a quiet beauty of its own. The parish church of St John the Baptist was built in 1316. The structure is partly Gothic but the interior is wholly baroque, and it has eighteenth-century ceiling paintings by F.A. Zeiller, and altar sculptures by J. Reindl.

Continuing on Route 171, the fourteenth-century church of St Valentin at **Riez** was redecorated in baroque style in 1765. The lovely high altar (1774) is by Hans Reindl. The road then crosses to the north side of the valley to **Telfs** (population 6,500) at the foot of the Hochmunde (2,662m, 8,731ft), once the home of the baroque painter Anton Zoller (1695-1768). There are old houses in the town, a local history museum, and the parish church of Sts Peter and Paul is neo-Romanesque. The Gothic chapel of St Veit was built in 1384.

The road then runs alongside the A12 motorway through **Oberpettnau** where the parish church has ceiling decoration from 1774 by Josef Anton Zoller, and past fruit orchards and old farmhouses to **Zirl** (population 4,000). The parish church dates from 1850 and has a Gothic altar and frescoes by Franz Plattner (1867). The ruins of thirteenth-century Schloß Fragenstein look down on the town, and nearby is Martinsbühel, former hunting lodge of Maximilian I. It stands on the site of the Roman fortification of *Teriolis* (or *Cyroleum*) which guarded the road north to the Scharnitz Pass. The road reaches Innsbruck 76 miles from Nauders.

INNSBRUCK

Innsbruck (population 116,000) has been the capital of the province of Tyrol since 1406 when Duke Friedrich the Penniless moved his residence from Meran. Today it is the fourth largest city in Austria. It is particularly well sited for road connections, with the Scharnitz Pass to the north, the Brenner Pass to the south, the Arlberg Pass to the west, and the Inn valley to the east. Because of its strategic position it has always been an important military stronghold and trading post. It is a major rail terminus, and there are scheduled flights by Tyrolean Airways from Frankfurt, Zurich, and Vienna to the city's airport. The public bus and tramway systems extend across and beyond the city and, with private bus companies, operate excursions to Vienna, Salzburg, Venice, Oberammergau, and many other places.

Innsbruck occupies a most spectacular location, on a double bend of the river Inn, at the foot of the Patscherkofel (2,246m, 7,367ft), with the massive Karwendel Mountains to the north, rising to the rugged peak of the Brandjochspitze (2,560m, 8,397ft), dominating the heart of the city.

The principal thoroughfare is Maria Theresien Strasse which runs
northward from the **triumphal archway** — a monument which commemorates, on the south side, the marriage of Leopold, Grand Duke of
Tuscany, to Princess Maria Ludovica, Infanta of Spain, in 1765, and is,
on the north side, a memorial to Emperor Franz I, Leopold's father and
husband of the Empress Maria Theresa, who died during the wedding
celebrations. On the east side of the street is the **Landhaus**, built by
G.A. Gumpp in 1728, next to the **Fugger-Taxis palace gallery** which
dates from 1679. They are superb examples of the secular baroque
style. At No 38 the seventeenth-century **Trapp palace** has a baroque
doorway and a lovely balcony with basketwork railings. **St Anna's
column** (Annasäule) was designed by Christoforo Benedetti and
erected in 1706 to commemorate victory, on 26 July, 1703, over the
Bavarians during the War of the Spanish Succession. The view, looking
north, of the Annasäule with the busy street and the white peaks of the
Nordkette in the background, is one of the best known scenes in Austria.

In Herzog Friedrich Strasse there are elegant arcaded shops and
restaurants and tall, colourful old houses, and in the narrow Riesen-
gasse, and in Seilergasse, which run off it, the houses lean out toward
each other as they have done for many centuries. The **city tower**
(Stadtturm) was built in the fourteenth century and from March to
October visitors may climb to its top for a splendid view across the city.

Where the street widens, the **Golden Roof** (Goldenes Dachl) is a
famous landmark. The roof is covered with 2,657 gold plated tiles and
for many years it was amusingly attributed to Duke Friedrich the
Penniless (or, literally, Friedrich of the Empty Pocket) who was said to
have erected it to disprove his nickname. Alas, it is now accepted that
it was built by Maximilian I, in 1500, as a royal box from which he and
his guests could watch events in the square below. The first storey has
a painted façade, is supported by two red marble pillars, and bears a
stone relief of the coats-of-arms of the Emperor. On the front balustrade
of the second storey loggia two reliefs show members of the court
watching performances from the loggia itself, while reliefs on either side
display the antics of the performers. Above the pillars supporting the
roof there are grotesque animals. The building at the rear now houses
the registry office and the **Olympiamuseum** which has exhibits of the
Innsbruck Winter Olympic Games of 1964 and 1976.

On the corner of the square is the **Helblinghaus**, the most beautiful
example of a late baroque house in Austria. The original medieval
house was redecorated with stucco in 1740.

Herzog Friedrich Strasse goes around this corner to the **Golden
Eagle** (Goldener Adler), the oldest *Gasthof* in the city, where Goethe,
Paganini, and many other notables once stayed. On the right is the
Ottoburg, built in 1495 and now an inn. Before it is a bronze statue in
memory of those who fought for the freedom of Tyrol in 1809. Across

The Hofburg palace and Leopold's Fountain, Innsbruck

from the junction with Herzog Otto Strasse is the **Old Bridge** over the river Inn which gave the city its name, and there is a view of fine old houses on the far bank, and of the river, valley, and mountains downstream.

On the other side of the Golden Roof is the Pfarrgasse which leads to the Domplatz and the **cathedral of St Jakob**. The present baroque edifice was built in 1720 after an earlier building was demolished following an earthquake. The façade, with two towers, is rather plain except for the statue of St Jakob on horseback. The beautiful ceiling frescoes were painted by Cosmas Damian Asam, of Munich, in 1722-3. There are no side chapels but the seven magnificent altars were designed by Christoforo and Theodore Benedetti from 1726 to 1732. On the high altar the 'miracle picture' in the silver frame is by Lucas Cranach (1530). The bronze tomb, in the left-hand transept, is that of Maximilian II, German Master of the Teutonic Order, and dates from 1620.

The Hofgasse is a quaint little street of high buildings and small shops and cafés and leads to the **Hofburg palace** and Hofkirche. The palace was built by Empress Maria Theresa in 1755-77. Conducted tours include the magnificent two storey-high Reisensaal with white and gold rococo decoration and beautiful ceiling frescoes by Franz Anton Maulpertsch (1776). In the south wing is the rococo imperial chapel. The palace has an especially attractive façade onto the Rennweg.

The Tyrolean State Museum Ferdinandeum, Innsbruck

The **Hofkirche** was built to plans by Andrea Crivelli of Trento in 1563, and the interior was redecorated in baroque style by George Anton Gumpp in 1731. It is a very grand and unusual hall church. The imperial tomb (Kaisergrab) occupies the centre of the nave and is very striking. The white marble cenotaph of Maximilian I was completed in 1584 by Alexander Colin and is surrounded by twenty-four alabaster reliefs by Colin and the brothers Bernhard and Arnold Abel of Cologne. Particularly remarkable are the twenty-eight larger-than-life, black, bronze statues of Austrian royalty flanking the tomb, which were cast between 1509 and 1550 in Munich, Nuremberg, and Innsbruck. Nos 10 (Bianca Maria Sforza, Maximilian's second wife), 13 (Karl the Bold, King of Burgundy), and 26 (Leopold IV of Babenberg) were designed by Albrecht Dürer. No 8 is Arthur, King of England. The high altar, by Nikolaus Pacassi, dates from 1755. On the left of the altar is the Renaissance Prince's Gallery (1567) by Hans Waldner, which looks down on two lead statues, of St Francis and St Theresa, by Balthasar Moll, and the sixteenth-century organ. On the east side is the white marble statue to the patriot Andreas Hofer who was buried here in 1810. Also notable are the twenty-three small bronze statues of members of the house of Habsburg on the balustrade of the west gallery, and the twenty busts of Roman emperors. The Silver Chapel (Silberne Kapelle) was built from 1564 to 1595 by Archduke Ferdinand II of Tyrol. It contains the marble tomb of the Archduke (1596), and that of his wife Philippine Welser (1580), both by Alexander Colin. The altar has a silvered Madonna and reliefs in silver by Anton Ort.

Alongside the Hofkirche is the **museum of Tyrolean folk art** (Tiroler Volkskunstmuseum) which has collections of national costumes, furniture, artefacts, glass, pottery, and nativity cribs, and is the most important folk museum in Austria. Further along Universitäts Strasse is the **Jesuit church**, a pure example of the early baroque style. It was built in the seventeenth century and rebuilt after World War II. The altar dates from 1680. In the crypt is the tomb of Archduke Leopold V (1632) and his wife Claudia von Medici.

In the Rennweg is the Renaissance **Leopold's Fountain** with an equestrian statue of Leopold V. Further along is the **theatre** and the pleasant **royal gardens** (Hofgarten) where band concerts are held on summer evenings. Across the road is the congress house and conference centre. In Museum Strasse is the **Tyrolean State Museum Ferdinandeum** which has prehistoric, Celtic and Roman collections; a gallery of paintings by German and Dutch masters — including one by Rembrandt; Gothic and baroque collections; a gallery of modern art; and a relief model of Tyrol to a scale of 1:20,000. In Zeughausgasse, in the armoury erected by Maximilian I in 1502, is the **Tyrolean regional museum** (Tiroler Landeskundliche Museum). It has collections of natural history, maps, paintings, wood carvings, musical instruments, and minerals.

At the northern end of the Rennweg, is the **Rundgemälde** which houses a panoramic painting of more than 1,000sq m (3,280sq ft) depicting the Battle of Berg Isel on 14 August 1809. It was painted in 1895 under the direction of M. Zeno Diemer.

Near the Rundgemälde is the Hungerbergbahn which crosses the Inn to the Hungerberg (288m, 945ft) and the cableway station. By car this may be reached from the Old Bridge via Höttinger Gasse and the Höttinger Höhenstrasse. The cable car rises to Station Seegrube at 1,905m (6,248ft), and a second cable car goes up to Station Hafelekar at 2,260m (7,413ft) affording superb views.

Alpenzoo Innsbruck is in Weiherburggasse, on a terrace above the Inn. It has a collection of 350 animals representing over 100 species, including wolf, chamois, deer, marmot, bison, lynx and ibex; many birds, including griffon, vulture, golden eagle, and owl; reptiles in an open-air terrarium; and indigenous fish in a series of aquaria. The Alpenzoo is 30 minutes' walk from the town centre (take the footbridge from Rennweg across the river, cross the Hoher Weg to the zig-zag path up onto the Hungerberg plateau, then left), or may be reached in summer by bus route Z from the Taxis palace, or by car from Innstrasse via St Nikolaus Gasse. A tour of the enclosures takes about an hour.

Innsbruck is a city of music with an all-year programme of classical concerts and recitals — as many as ten per week in July and August during the Summer Festival. Folk music can be heard in the Goldener

Adler Hotel and other venues, and band concerts in the Hofgarten and in the city's squares. Oratorio is regularly sung in the churches. In the crypt of the Jesuit church a mass is sung in English every Saturday evening at 6pm. It is also a city of the arts with twenty-six galleries, and the Landestheater has two auditoriums which offer nightly perform-ances of drama or ballet. There are also four smaller theatres in the city.

The Innsbruck tourist office is very active in organising events for visitors throughout the year. The programme offers hiking and moun-taineering tours with qualified guides, and guided cycling tours, with free buses to start/finish points, from June to September (bicycles may be hired). Skiing is available throughout the year at the head of the Stubai valley. A gondola cableway starts from Mutterbergalm (1,750m, 5,740ft) and goes up to Bergstation Eisgrat (2,900m, 9,512ft), where there is a restaurant with a panoramic view, and a protected 45-minute walk across the Eisjoch Glacier. Tow lifts then take skiers up to the top of the Eisjoch, and on to the Gaißkar Glacier. The tourist office also manages Club Innsbruck (and Club Igls) which offers discounts on admission fees, golf and tennis fees, etc.

Around Innsbruck
On the south side is the district of **Wilten**, the oldest part of the city, whose name is derived from the Roman settlement of *Veldidena* which stood on this site. According to legend, the giant Raymon, having killed his old rival Thyrsus, was filled with remorse and started to build a monastery. But the work was hindered by a dragon which knocked down the limestone blocks with its great tail, and so Raymon chased it until he cornered it in a cave and killed it. The work then proceeded and Wilten abbey was founded. The abbey church of St Lorenz is twelfth century, restyled in baroque form by Christopher Gumpp in 1655, and again by George Anton Gumpp in 1716. The interior stucco is by Bernard Pasquale (1702); the high altar is by Paul Huber (1665); and the ceiling paintings are by Kasper Waldmann (1707).

The nearby parish church (Wilten basilica) attracts many visitors (Bus J; tramline No 1). It was completed in 1755 by Franz de Paula Penz on the site of a twelfth-century church. The elaborate west façade and portal are a portent of the glorious rococo interior. The high altar carries a 'miraculous image' from the earlier Gothic edifice, and is surmounted by a superb open canopy supported by four columns, and attributed to Franz Karl Fischer, of Füssen. The ceiling frescoes (1754) are by Matthäus Günter, and the stucco decorations are by Franz Xavier Feichtmayr. The votive table (1418) was donated by Friedrich the Penniless. Nearby, in Klostergasse, is the Tiroler Kaiserschützen-museum which has colourful displays of the history of the Tyrol Light Infantry Regiments since 1864.

At **Berg Isel** the patriotism of Andreas Hofer is commemorated by

The baroque dome of Wilten basilica, Innsbruck

a large bronze statue. On 10 April 1809 fires on the mountain tops around Innsbruck called to arms some 15,000 Tyroleans. Carrying only scythes and shotguns, and led by Hofer, they defeated the French and Bavarian troops who occupied Innsbruck. The regular Austrian army took over and within a month the invaders were back in the city. Again Hofer and his compatriots drove them out, and again the army lost the city. From his mountain hideout Hofer sent his instructions signed 'Andreas Hofer, from where I am'. Replies were addressed to 'Andreas Hofer, wherever he may be'. With his lieutenant, Speckbacher, Hofer and his peasant army returned to Berg Isel, and, at dawn on 14 August 1809, the Capuchin priest Haspinger celebrated mass before they charged into the city. By nightfall they were victorious and Hofer was in command. Then came tragedy. In October, Emperor Johann signed the Treaty of Vienna which gave the Tyrol to Bavaria. Hofer became an outlaw, was hunted down, captured, and taken to Mantua where, in 1810, he was executed. His last words, to the corporal in charge of the firing squad, were 'shoot straight'. Today he is Tyrol's greatest hero. A

room at the Ferdinandeum museum is devoted to his relics and his tomb is in the Hofkirche.

Also at Berg Isel are the Tyrol cenotaph, Tomb of the Unknown Soldier, the Chapel of Honour and regimental museum of the Tyrolean Imperial Rifles (Kaiserjäger). At Berg Isel too is the Olympic ski-jump and a panoramic view of the city and the mountains beyond. Immediately below is the suburb of Wilten.

Seefeld

South-east of the city is **Schloß Ambras** which contains collections of swords, spears, guns and armour, domestic artefacts, and paintings. The tenth-century castle was rebuilt from 1564 to 1589 in Renaissance style by Archduke Ferdinand II of Tyrol. By the end of the sixteenth century his great personal collection occupied five rooms but most of these items were transferred to Vienna in 1806. Nevertheless, the modern collection is worth seeing. The Spanish room, designed by Giovanni Lucchese and built in 1573, is especially notable, being the largest Renaissance hall north of the High Alps.

Amongst the exhibits is Philippine Welser's bathtub. In 1557 the Archduke Ferdinand II secretly married Philippine, the beautiful daughter of a merchant from Augsburg. The marriage took place without the permission of his father, Emperor Ferdinand I, and was therefore invalid under imperial law. The Emperor forgave them, so validating the marriage, but insisted that it be kept secret. For twenty years it remained so and their children were treated as foundlings. Ferdinand and Philippine became the best loved couple in the Tyrol, and their tombs are in the Silver Chapel of the Hofkirche.

Guided tours of the castle last about 1³/₄ hours. The gardens and parkland of Schloß Ambras provide delightful walks and picnic areas.

Igls is 3 miles south of the centre of Innsbruck on a wooded hillside which rises southward to the Patscherkofel (2,246m, 7,367ft) and overlooks the city and the valley as far as the Karwendel massif. It is easily reached from Innsbruck by busline J or by tramline No 1 to Berg Isel then the Igls tram (No 6) which crawls up the hillside dodging the pine trees. In Igls the fifteenth-century parish church has a ceiling painted by Josef Schmutzer in 1777, and in the chapel of rest there are frescoes from 1486.

Igls is an ideal centre for walking on and around the Patscherkofel. The cable car rises to the Berghotel at 1,944m (6,376ft) and then a ski-lift goes to the top of the mountain. There are some seventy-five marked footpaths. For example, from the Patscherkofel hut follow AV350 down the hill toward the south-west. After a swift but easy descent the path reaches the Patscher Alm then continues downwards to Ochsenschlag where Almensweg 1600 goes left. Note that the latter is an alpine pasture route at 1,600m (5,248ft) and runs around the Patscherkofel. AV350 joins walk No 31 for a short way to the right, then after a left bend, it drops to Heiligwasser, where there is a *Gasthof*. The seventeenth-century chapel contains an altar with a fifteenth-century carving of the Madonna which once attracted many pilgrims. AV350 continues down through the trees, bending left across open hillside, then turns off to the right to cross the Speckbacherweg at Schwellerkap where there is a small shrine. From here the ground slopes gently across pastureland and the pathway runs down to the cable car station. It is a moderately easy walk and can be covered comfortably in about 1$^1/_2$ hours.

The Speckbacherweg starts from the church of St Peter in Ellbögen beyond the village of Patsch — 4$^1/_2$ miles south of Igls — and passes Sistrans and Rinn to end at Tulfes — 7 miles east of Igls. It keeps close to the 1,050m (3,444ft) contour and is very easy to walk along. This pathway can be reached from Igls via AV350 to the Schwellerkap, there turning right toward Patsch, or left toward Tulfes.

To walk from Igls into Innsbruck follow Eichlerstrasse past the school and the graveyard down to the hamlet of Vill. Turn right towards Grillhof, following pathway No 10. Take the left fork before the forest then descend gently between the pines to the Poltenhütte. The path then goes left along the Patschbergweg to reach Berg Isel. This is an easy downhill walk and should take about 1$^1/_2$ hours into the city.

Igls also has two golf courses, twelve tennis courts, an indoor tennis hall, health cure centre, beauty farm, indoor shooting range, as well as swimming and boating in the Lansersee.

South-west, and within 10 miles of Innsbruck, there are several small resorts in pleasant walking country, conveniently placed for touring and for excursions into the city. **Völs**, on the south bank of the river Inn, has a notable pilgrimage church of St Blasienberg (1733) with a bronze crucifix from 1522. **Götzens** has a pretty baroque parish church with notable stucco by Franz Singer and ceiling paintings by Matthäus Günter, both from 1775. **Axams** parish church has a chapel of St Michael with Romanesque windows, and an octagonal Linden chapel dating from 1634. About 5 miles south of Axams is **Axamer Lizum** (1,578m, 5,176ft), where some of the events of the 1964 Winter Olympics were held. This is a good area for walking and a cable car rises to the Hoadl (2,340m, 7,675ft) affording superb views of the Kalkögel range to the south. Just off Route 182, south of Innsbruck, are the villages of **Natters** and **Mutters**. Natters has a Gothic parish church dating from 1451, and a bathing lake — the Natterer See. The nearby Schloß Waidburg is a sixteenth-century hunting castle. Mutters has retained its simple, rustic air despite its popularity as a ski resort. The parish church of St Nikolaus dates from 1510 and contains eighteenth-century paintings by Anton Zoller of Telfs, and his son Josef Anton Zoller. A cableway goes up in two stages to the Nockhof (1,255m, 4,116ft) and to the Muttereralm (1,608m, 5,274ft).

Seefeld

Leave Innsbruck along Route 171 westward past the airport and, at Zirl, turn right onto Route 177 signposted Seefeld. The road rises steeply (gradients up to 16 per cent, 1 in 6) through a right-hand hairpin bend — with a restaurant and escape road for descending vehicles — then flattens out through Leithen, where there is an interesting plague column (*Pestsäule*) from 1604. At the *Rasthaus* on the left, there is a car park with exceptional views of the patchwork of fields below and across the Inn valley to the magnificent mountains to the south. Above, and reached by a side road, is Reith-bei-Seefeld with its pink parish church (1893). After 14 miles turn left toward Seefeld Sud. As the road runs into Seefeld there are lovely views of the Wetterstein peaks ahead. At the Wildsee, a swimming and boating lake, there is minigolf, and ample car parks. The centre of the village is pedestrianised (*Fußgangerzone*).

Seefeld (population 2,500) is an international resort and sports centre which can conveniently be reached by railway or by bus from either Innsbruck or Garmisch-Partenkirchen, in West Germany. The heart of the village is a small wooded garden — where horse-drawn carriages await their passengers — bounded by flower-decked hotels and restaurants, the prettily decorated Tiroler Schmuckkastl, in Innsbrucker Strasse, being notable.

On the west side of the square is the red-steepled **parish church of St Oswald.** According to legend, in 1384 a knight named Oswald Milser, on receiving the Sacred Host at communion, sank up to his knees in the ground and blood ran from the Host. The church is dedicated to this miracle and the Sacred Host was on exhibition until 1919. The first church was mentioned in 1320 but the present edifice

The Leutasch valley, near Seefeld

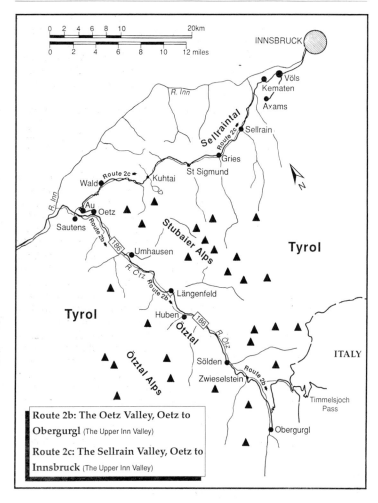

Route 2b: The Oetz Valley, Oetz to Obergurgl (The Upper Inn Valley)

Route 2c: The Sellrain Valley, Oetz to Innsbruck (The Upper Inn Valley)

was started in 1432, by Friedrich the Penniless, and completed in 1474 by Archduke Sigmund the Rich. It has a late Gothic doorway, and richly decorated ribs on the vaulting. The frescoes in the choir depict the life of St Oswald, and a picture by Jörg Kölderer dating from 1502, describes the miracle of the Sacred Host. In the right-hand side altar there are figures from 1515; the font is sixteenth century with a wooden cover from 1608; and the pulpit, by Peter Dosser, dates from 1525. The red and white steps of a wide marble staircase lead up to the Holy Blood chapel which was added in 1574, by G. Luchese, for Archduke Ferdinand II. The altar contains the Sacred Host. A painting of *The Last Supper*, by Giovanni Baptista Fontana, dates from 1580, and the ceiling frescoes are by Josef Anton Puellacher from 1772. The adjacent Hotel Klosterbräu was once an Augustinian monastery founded by Maximilian I in 1516 and retains the old courtyard, doorways, and baroque frescoes.

On the west side of the village, past the Olympia sport and congress centre, and standing in an open meadow, is the baroque **Lake Chapel** (Seekapelle). It was built in 1628 by Archduke Leopold V to house a miraculous early sixteenth-century crucifix which is now on the rococo high altar.

Seefeld has extensive sports facilities which are the venue for national and international events. It also has a championship golf course, outdoor and indoor swimming pools, a riding club, tennis, bowling, and many marked pathways. It is a famous ski-resort and hosted the Winter Olympic Games in 1964 and 1976. At the top of Andreas Hofer Strasse is the station for the funicular railway which goes up to the Roßhütte at 1,754m (5,753ft), where there is a restaurant. From there cable cars go up to the Seefelder Joch (2,063m, 6,767ft), and to the Hermelekopf (2,045m, 6,708ft). During the summer there is a programme of day and evening entertainments, and there is a casino.

About 4 miles north-west of Seefeld is **Leutasch** (population 400) at the foot of the Wetterstein Mountains. It is a good base for walking and climbing, and has a trout farm with fishing (☎ 05214 6455). The parish church in Oberleutasch was built in 1821 and has altar and ceiling paintings by Leopold Puellacher. The parish church in Unterleutasch dates from 1831. The valley of the river Leutasch (the Gaistal) to the west, between the Mieminger group to the south and the majestic Zugspitze (2,962m, 9,715ft), is one of the most beautiful valleys in the Tyrol. Beyond the Igelsee, at 1,543m (5,061ft), at the head of the valley, is the town of **Ehrwald**, some 12 miles from Leutasch.

Beyond Seefeld the road runs through the narrow gap at Scharnitz across the border to Mittenwald.

Route 2b   The Oetz Valley: Oetz to Obergurgl

To reach the Ötztal from Innsbruck travel 30 miles westwards along Route 171 as far as the Ötztal Railway Station (note — there is no railway up the Ötztal), and turn left onto Route 186, signposted Ötztal/Sölden/Oetz.

The road runs alongside the Ötztaler Ache, in this lower reach a

The village of Sölden in the Ötztal

rushing river frothing over its rocky bed. **Oetz** (or Ötz) (population 2,000) 33 miles from Innsbruck, is built into the steep side of the valley which rises to the Acher Kogel (3,010m, 9,873ft). In the centre of the village is the old, highly decorated Gasthof Stern with sixteenth-century outside frescoes and a wealth of geranium-laden balconies. The parish church of St George and St Nikolaus stands on a clifftop. In fact it is two churches. The Unterkirche is below the choir of the Oberkirche. The former, also known as St Michael's chapel, dates from the fourteenth century and has Gothic ribs and notable vaulting. The remarkable altar is by Ignaz Waibl and dates from 1683. The upper church was built in 1660 and redecorated in baroque style in 1745. It has Gothic doorways from 1667 and 1744, and the pulpit is also Gothic, as is the small altar (1500). The baroque statues of Sts Kassian and Nikolaus are by Hans Reindl, of Stams, and there is a baroque crucifix in the sacristy.

Oetz is an excellent base for touring and walking. A small road to the west goes up to the Piburger See (915m, 3,001ft), where there is swimming and boating. This lovely lake was given to Stams abbey in 1282 and became a source of food for the monks when meat was forbidden. The lake remained the property of the abbey until the nineteenth century when it was sold. In 1929 it became a nature reserve and its use as a leisure amenity is strictly controlled. It is one of the warmest lakes in Tyrol and there are pleasant walks along its banks. In Piburg St Blasius chapel has a rococo altar and a late Gothic figure of St Sebastian. Just above Oetz the river passes through a narrow ravine — the Achenfälle — which produces a wild spate of water after rain.

About 1$\frac{1}{2}$ miles after Oetz, at **Habichen**, there is a house with a façade which was painted in 1632. The road then rises through four hairpin bends to **Umhausen** (population 2,000), the oldest village in the Ötztal, where the parish church of St Vitus is fifteenth-century Gothic. The octagonal Johannes chapel was an eighteenth-century addition, and has notable ceiling frescoes by Josef Keill (1771). About 50 minutes' walk to the south-east of the village, on the road to Niederthei, is the 150m (492ft) Stuibenfällen Waterfall — the highest in the Tyrol.

Längenfeld (population 3,000) is 44 miles from Innsbruck. Its springs have long made it a popular health resort, and it was a favourite haunt of the artist Albin Egger-Lienz (1868-1926). The village square is dominated by the 74m-high (243ft) steeple of St Katharine's church. It dates from the fourteenth century and has a notable late Gothic and baroque entrance which dates from 1690, and a fifteenth-century font. In the church of the Holy Trinity (1661) the rococo side altar has beautiful carving by Hans Reindl (1770). The Schneiderkirchl is an octagonal chapel from 1710. On the west side of the valley, and easily reached on foot, there is a plague chapel set amongst woodland. Up the Sultztal, to the east, a steep road (gradients up to 16 per cent, 1 in 6) follows the river Fischbach to **Gries-im-Sultztal** where the seventeenth-century parish church has ceiling paintings by Josef Anton Puellacher (1792).

The road rises past heavily wooded slopes, small patches of meadowland, and scattered farmhouses to **Sölden** (population 2,500), 53 miles from Innsbruck. This is a busy resort with many hotels, restaurants, and shops along the main street which slices through the narrow valley. The parish church (1521) has beautiful ceiling paintings by Josef Anton Puellacher (1779). A chairlift and chain railway connect the village to **Hochsölden**, high above the valley floor, where there are hotels with wonderful views. The Ötztaler Gletscherbahn is the highest cable car in Austria. It goes up to the Gaislachalm, at 2,180m (7,150ft), then on to the Bergstation on the Gaislachkopf at 3,040m (9,971ft), from which there are spectacular panoramas. A mile beyond Sölden is the start of the Ötztaler Gletscherstrasse, a toll road which rises through steep hairpin bends (gradients up to 13 per cent, 1 in 8) to the Rattenbach glacier.

Above Sölden there are four hairpin bends before **Zwieselstein** (population 400), a pretty village in a small basin cut by the fast flowing river, and enclosed by near-vertical mountainsides. Here the Venter and Gurgl rivers join to form the river Oetz. The church dates from 1749.

The final ascent up the Gurgltal goes through another four hairpin bends (gradients up to 15 per cent, 1 in 7) with superb views to the rear. Leaving the timber line behind, the road then rises steadily with the Nöderkogel (3,166m, 10,384ft) towering on the right across the little valley, and the snows and glaciers of the Diemkogel (3,380m, 11,086ft) and the Romolkogel (3,551m, 11,647ft) ahead. At the bend which is the start of the Timmelsjoch Hochalpenstrasse, over the 2,497m (8,190ft) pass into Italy, turn right to reach **Obergurgl** (population 600), 62 miles from Innsbruck, and **Hochgurgl** at the end of the valley.

Obergurgl is the highest parish in Europe and a winter sports centre. In front of the parish church there stands a bronze statue of an old mountain guide pointing his outstretched hand toward the high peaks. A chairlift goes up to the Gaisberg (2,095m, 6,871ft) and then on to the Hohe Mutt (2,663m, 8,735ft) with a panorama of twenty-one glaciers in the Ötztaler Alps. It was from the Gurgl Glacier, at 1,300m (4,264ft) on 27 May, 1931, that Professor Piccard flew his balloon into the stratosphere to reach a record-breaking altitude of 16,000m (52,480ft).

Route 2c   The Sellrain Valley: Oetz to Innsbruck (see map page 52)

On the return journey from Obergurgl, turn right just before Oetz onto a road which goes to the east (gradients up to 14 per cent, 1 in 7) up the Nedertal via Au and Wald, past the Längental reservoir, to the little village of **Kühtai** (population 400). This is a holiday centre with two chairlifts, and good walking and climbing. To the south are the little Plenderle mountain lakes, and the lovely Finstertal See, surrounded by mountains up to 3,019m (9,902ft) high, where there is a limnological research centre. The Berghotel was built in 1445 as a hunting lodge for the Princes of Tyrol, and, in 1628, was used by Archduke Leopold V. The Prince's Room has been kept in Renaissance style with the original wood panelling.

The road passes over the Kühtai saddle (2,017m, 6,616ft) before descending through the wild scenery of the Obertal to **St Sigmund-im-Sellrain** (population 400). The parish church dates from 1490 and has late Gothic frescoes and baroque ceiling paintings (1779 and 1790) by Josef Schmutzer and Josef Leopold Strickner. The high altar dates from 1800, and the reliquary on the side altar dates from 1487. The road then runs down the Sellraintal (gradients up to 16 per cent, 1 in 6) through Gries to reach **Sellrain** (population 1,250) 22 miles from Oetz. Sellrain is a summer resort with walking and climbing in the Fotschertal, to the south. The parish church (1701) has baroque external frescoes (1743) by Leopold Praxmarer, altar paintings (1825) by Leopold Puellacher, and ceiling paintings (1877) by Johann Kärle. North of the village is the church of St Quirin (1496) which has remarkable Gothic frescoes, fifteenth-century pictures, and a wooden figure of St Quirin from 1390.

Below Sellrain is **Kematen** where the parish church of St Victor has notable late Gothic wall paintings from the fifteenth century. The altars are baroque, and the ceiling paintings over the organ loft are by Franz Anton Zeiller. Two miles west of Kematen is **Oberperfuss** (population 1,750). The parish church of St Margaret was restored in 1735. It has frescoes from the nineteenth century, and a statue of Peter Anich (1723-66), the Tyrolean cartographer who was born here and whose work is preserved in the Anich museum in the school house. From Kematen it is 7 miles to Innsbruck via the motorway or Route 171.

Route 2d   The Wipptal and the Brenner Pass

The Wipptal, the valley of the river Sill, lies directly south of Innsbruck, between the Stubaier Alps to the west and the Tuxer Alps to the east. At its head the Zillertaler Alps are broken by a pass at the watershed between the Sill and the southward flowing Eisack, on the slopes of the Brenner (1,374m, 4,507ft) Mountain. It is the lowest pass through the High Alps and is least affected by adverse weather conditions. Except in the severest of winters, the Brenner Pass remains open all year round. Historically it has been an important commercial and military

The village of Gries-am-Brenner in the Wipptal

route. Today it is a heavily trafficked means of transit between Austria and Italy, traversed by rail, by Route 182, and by the E6 Brennerstrasse motorway over the spectacular Europa Toll Bridge. Together with the Stubaital and seven smaller side valleys it is a deep, steep-sided, and strikingly beautiful valley.

As an alternative to Route 182 along the valley bottom, start the journey up the Wipptal from **Igls**. At Gasthof Stern take the Patsch/Matrei road past the Igls Kongresshaus. Turn right at the 'T' junction, pass the highly decorative old hunting lodge, Grünwalderhof, now a hotel, then bear left into **Patsch** (population 800). The parish church (1479) has a ceiling painted by Anton Zoller (1767).

Beyond Patsch the road — the Ellbögenerstrasse — runs high above the valley, and although narrow and sometimes twisting, it is easily travelled with a little consideration for oncoming vehicles. It rewards the careful traveller with wonderful views across the Europa Bridge and up the Stubaital.

At the church of St Peter, topped by a green onion dome, the alpine air rings with the sound of cow-bells. Then the road descends rapidly (gradient 18 per cent, 1 in 5.5) through Mühltal and into Ellbögen at the foot of the Viggartal. The road winds between pretty farmhouses before levelling off at Gasthof Neuvert.

With the deep gorge of the Wipptal on the right, the road then winds down again to the hamlet of **Erlach**, where the church has a tiny steeple, then undulates past painted farmhouses with spectacular views to the west. At **Pfons**, Gasthof Pension Fuchs has colourful balconies of flowers. As the road descends again, a rocky outcrop on the right is surmounted by the ruined Schloß Trautson, damaged by bombing in 1945. At Mühlbach turn right across a 'planked' bridge then left to **Matrei-am-Brenner** (population 1,200), 10 miles from Igls. There was a settlement here in the Bronze Age (finds in the Ferdinandeum museum in Innsbruck), and here the Romans built the town of *Matreium*. There are several period houses from the fifteenth to the eighteenth century in the old part of the town. The parish church dates from 1311. In 1754 Josef Adam Mölk redecorated it in baroque style, and he himself designed the high altar and painted the ceiling. In the graveyard the Johannes chapel was built in 1521 on the site of a chapel which dated from 1284.

With the Brenner motorway high above on the right, the road joins Route 182 and runs swiftly up to **Steinach** (population 3,000). This is the principal town of the Wipptal, at the bottom of the Gschnitztal which runs to the south-west. In the town centre there are pleasant old houses. The twin-towered parish church of St Erasmus is neo-Romanesque and dates from 1867, and the high altar is by Johann Perger.

The road then rises gently to Stafflach where a road on the left goes up the Schmirntal via **St Jodok-am-Brenner** (population 300). A cluster of houses encircle the red-steepled parish church whose simple outside appearance belies the beautiful baroque interior. It is delight-

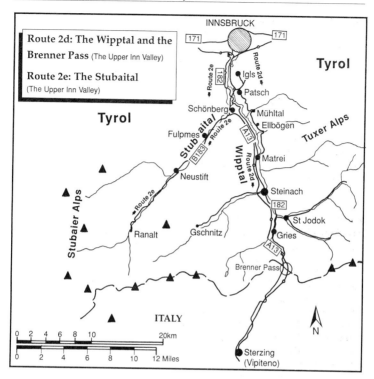

Route 2d: The Wipptal and the Brenner Pass (The Upper Inn Valley)

Route 2e: The Stubaital (The Upper Inn Valley)

fully set beside the little river Schmirnbach where a narrow bridge leads to old peasant houses on the far bank. The road goes on for another 6 miles up the valley. Note that the old road on the right bank of the river goes up a hill with a gradient of 28 per cent (1 in 3.6). St Jodok is also at the bottom of the Valsertal which runs around the southern flank of the Gammer Spitze (2,537m, 8,321ft).

Beyond Stafflach is **Gries-am-Brenner** (population 1,500) which has a sixteenth-century parish church with paintings by Josef Arnold (1827). The chapel of St Jakob is fourteenth-century and has a Gothic panelled altar from 1490. Alongside the road out of the village there is a shrine which dates from 1530.

Above Gries the valley narrows as the road rises rapidly through **Luegg** with the peak of the Kraxentragger (2,999m, 9,837ft) ahead closing the top of the valley. Then it turns right to cross the motorway and, 20 miles from Igls, reaches the Brenner Pass (1,370m, 4,494ft) and the frontier with Italy. A visit to Sterzing (Vipiteno), about 10 miles beyond the border, is popular with package-tourists who are tempted by promises of cheap leather goods. Buyer beware!

To return to Innsbruck-Igls a journey down the Brennerstrasse motorway toll-road affords superb views from its forty-two fly-overs and bridges. At the Europa Bridge there is a restaurant, a modern chapel, and a viewing terrace. To return to Igls take the narrow, uphill, right-hand exit immediately after the Europa Bridge which, as it rises to the Patsch fork, gives splendid rearward views. For Innsbruck exit from the next access point onto Route 182 for a spectacular view across the city.

Route 2e   The Stubaital

From the Brennerstrasse the third exit leads to the village of **Schönberg** (population 700) at the foot of the Stubaital. The parish church was built in 1748 by Franz de Paula Penz and has notable paintings in the transept by Giuseppe Gru, of Verona, from 1752. Josef Mages, of Imst, executed the paintings in the choir which date from 1752, as do those in the nave, in the organ loft, and on the façade which are by Franz Anton Leitensdorfer of Reutte. Andreas Hofer's headquarters were at the Gasthaus Domanig which has a pretty painted façade from 1713.

From Schönberg Route 183 goes up the Stubaital. At **Mieders**, there are eighteenth-century houses and a parish church by Franz de Paula Penz who also built the parish church of St Pankras at Telfes (population 1,000). **Fulpmes** (population 3,000), once the centre of an iron and steel industry with over fifty factories, is now a resort with chairlifts up to the Kreuzjoch (2,139m, 7,016ft), and the Sennjoch (2,240m, 7,347ft), and is a good base for walking and climbing in the Kalkkögel peaks (up to 2,808m, 9,210ft) to the north-west. The parish church of St Vitus is another example of the work of Franz de Paula Penz. The façade frescoes are by Johann George Bergmüller, as are the ceiling paintings. The high altar is by George Graßmayr, and the organ loft by Clemens Holzmeister who was born in Fulpmes in 1886.

After Fulpmes the road passes through the health resort of Medraz and, after 8 miles, reaches the winter resort of **Neustift** (population 3,000) in its beautiful setting amongst the high mountains. The parish church of St George (1774), again by Franz de Paula Penz, is considered to be one of the best examples of the baroque style. The painting in the nave is by Josef Anton Zoller (1772), and the altar paintings are by Johann Josef Henrici, of Schlesien and date from 1780. The chapel of remembrance was built in 1922 by Clemens Holzmeister.

Beyond Neustift the road rises up the narrow Unterbergtal to **Ranalt**. From there a track (gradients up to 15 per cent, 1 in 7) goes up to the Mutterbergalm where lifts go up to the ski area of the Eisgrat (2,900m,

9,512ft) (see Innsbruck). Another track from Neustift goes up the Oberbergtal to the Stöcklenalm and the Oberisshutte (1,742m, 5,714ft) at the foot of the Hoher Viller Spitze (3,104m, 10,181ft).

PART 2   THE LOWER INN VALLEY

Route 2f   Strass to Zell-Am-See via the Gerlos Pass

The third of the southern valleys is the Zillertal, which is described here as part of the route from the Inn valley over the Gerlos Pass into the Pinzgau (in Land Salzburg), making a detour up the Kaprunertal and terminating at Zell-am-See.

THE ZILLERTAL
The Zillertal is bounded by the Tuxer Alps, the Kitzbüheler Alps, and the Zillertaler Alps, which rise to more than 3,000m (9,840ft). The river Ziller starts on the border with Italy, joins the Stillupbach and Zemmbach rivers at Mayrhofen, then runs northward to meet the river Inn near the village of Strass. Half-way up the valley Route 169 goes ahead while Route 165, the Gerlosstrasse, turns east to follow the Gerlosbach up to the pass (1,507m, 4,943ft) and then down the Pinzgau valley via Mittersill. The Zillertal is a beautiful valley, understandably popular for summer and winter holidays. Perhaps it was the sunny hills and meadows that inspired the valley's musicians who, in London in 1837, performed for Queen Victoria.

From **Strass** — which has a parish church dating from 1520 — Route 169 is signposted Zillertal/Gerlos Pass. The road bypasses Schlitters (population 1,000) where the late Gothic parish church dates from 1504 and has ceiling paintings by Christopher Anton Mayr from 1750. Then it runs alongside the railway to **Fügen** (population 2,500), a resort with a cable car to the top of the Spieljoch (1,865m, 6,117ft), and a good centre for walking and cycling. The parish church dates from the fifteenth century. Amongst its many notable features are frescoes in the choir from 1330; the late Gothic (1500) reliefs of the apostles on the high altar; Maria with Child (1460) on the left side-altar; and the organ which came from the convent at Hall-in-Tirol where, in 1772, it was played by Wolfgang Amadeus Mozart. St Michael's chapel dates from 1497 and has a mural of the *Adoration of the King* from 1500. Schloß Fügen was built in the fifteenth century.

The road then passes Uderns, Ried and Kaltenbach — where there is a cable car up to Forstgartenhöhe (1,740m, 5,707ft) on the Zillertaler Höhenstrasse — to **Stumm** (population 1,250). There the fifteenth-century parish church has ceiling paintings by Christopher Anton Mayr (1756), baroque carvings on the side altar by Franz Xavier Nissl, and, in the choir, a crucifix by Franz Seraph Nissl (1842). At Rohr a cable car goes up to Gründlalm (1,150m, 3,772ft). About 13 miles from Strass turn right to enter Zell-am-Ziller.

Zell-am-Ziller (population 1,900) is a delightful resort at the foot of the Gerlosstrasse. The domed parish church of St Veit stands on the site of a seventh-century monk's retreat and was first mentioned in 1304. The present edifice was redecorated in rococo style by Andreas Hueber in 1784. It has a central cupola with magnificent paintings by F. A. Zeiller (1779), who also produced the paintings on the high altar and six side altars. The wrought-iron crosses in the churchyard are also remarkable.

Zell was once famous for its garnets and aquamarines, and for the mining of gold, silver, asbestos, cobalt, copper, iron, lead and magnesia, but the deposits were small and the industry died out. Today farming, timber and tourism are the main sources of income. Zell also has the oldest brewery in the Tyrol, dating from about 1500, and a special strong beer is brewed for the 'Gauderfest' beer festival which is held each year on the first Sunday in May.

There are many enjoyable walks around Zell on marked footpaths. On the east side of the valley, for example, the Gründlalm cableway may be used to overcome the initial slope. From the Wiesenalm, at 1,309m (4,294ft), an easy footpath (No 10), which takes about $1\frac{1}{2}$ hours, may be taken up to the Rosenalm (1,780m, 5,838ft). Then several opportunities occur. Path No 10 rises steeply to the Törljoch (2,189m, 7,180ft) and then up the ridge path to the Kreuzjoch (2,559m, 8,394ft), which may be reached in about 4 hours from the Rosenalm. Alternatively, bear right off No 10 to follow No 11 which skirts around the Karspitze along the old mountain road to the Kreuzwiesenhütte and then to the Außerertensalm. A good path then snakes up the mountainside to the Karhütte (2,072m, 6,796ft), from which point the gradient increases on the narrower, westward path up to the Karspitze (2,263m, 7,423ft). From there a ridge path leads northward and downward to the Törljoch to rejoin No 10 for a gentle walk through alpine pastures down to the Rosenalm which can be reached in 4 hours. Both of these walks are of moderate difficulty. They afford splendid panoramas as well as the chance of seeing chamois, red deer, marmots, eagles, hawks, and delicate and colourful alpine flowers.

Passing the turn for the Gerlos Pass, Route 169 goes up to **Mayrhofen** (population 3,500), 18 miles from Strass. The town caters for every need of its many visitors. It has a modern entertainment and congress centre in the Europahaus, and is the terminus of the picturesque Zillertal steam railway which opened in 1902 and provides a regular service between Jenbach and stations along the valley.

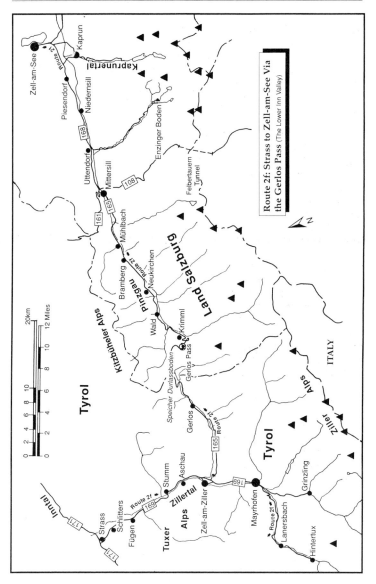

Route 2f: Strass to Zell-am-See Via the Gerlos Pass (The Lower Inn Valley)

Mayrhofen is an excellent centre for walking in the four adjacent high-level valleys. The Ahornbahn cable car goes up to the Filzenalm

Flowers and wrought-iron crosses in the churchyard at Zell-am-Ziller

(1,962m, 6,435ft) and a marked path then leads south-eastwards to the Aschaffenburger Weg which rises, high above the Stilluptal, to the Kasseler Hütte (2,177m, 7,141ft). This is not a difficult walk but a long one, allow 6 hours. Alternatively, a car or bus may be taken up to the Stillup reservoir, then one may either walk up the valley, or take a mini-bus up to the Grüne-Wand Hütte. The Kasseler Hütte can then be reached in about 2 hours of steep walking. Return via the mini-bus.

Another example of the many good walks in the area begins at Breitlahner (1,256m, 4,120ft), 11 miles from Mayrhofen along the Zemmgrund valley. The path follows the Zemmbach river to the south-east, rises via the Schwemmalm to the Grawand Hütte (1,636m, 5,366ft), then goes on via the Alpenrose Hütte (1,873m, 6,143ft) to the Berliner Hütte (2,042m, 6,698ft) which can be reached in about $3^1/_2$ hours. From there a path leads north-east to the beautiful Schwarzensee (2,472m, 8,108ft) whence it descends through the Gunggltal to Rauth, 3 miles below Breitlahner. Allow $3^1/_2$ hours for the return.

The Penkenbahn cable car operates from Mayrhofen to the Gschoßwand Hütte (1,762m, 5,780ft), and chairlifts go on to the Penken Alm (2,000m, 6,560ft); the Finkenburger Almbahn chairlift starts from the quiet little village of Finkenberg, about 3 miles above Mayrhofen, and goes up to the Penkenjoch Hütte (2,095m, 6,872ft). From these high points there are many opportunities for walks into the Tuxertal, which is well served by post-bus for the return journey, or down to the Horberg Stüberl (1,650m, 5,412ft), in the Horbergtal, and

Gasthof Schönmoosalm on a corner of the Gerlos Pass road

then via the Horbergbahn cableway to Schwendau, just below Mayrhofen. At the head of the Tuxertal, at Hintertux (1,493m, 4,897ft), there is a cable car up to the Sommerbergalpe (2,080m, 6,822ft) and on to the Tuxer Ferner (2,609m, 8,558ft).

THE GERLOS PASS AND THE PINZGAU

To reach the Gerlos Pass from Mayrhofen return along Route 169 and turn onto Route 165. The road climbs through four steep hairpin bends to reach the hamlet of **Hainzenberg**. The pilgrimage church of Maria Rast (1739) has a magnificent rococo altar by Stefan Föger (1748). From here there is a cablecar up to the Gerlosstein (1,620m, 5,314ft). The road then rises through the lovely meadows of the Gerlostal before flattening out past a lake below the Gasthof Pension Knoller at Gmünd, a place of peace and rural beauty. At 36¹/₂ miles from Strass (via Mayrhofen) the road reaches **Gerlos** (population 700), a pleasant village with a spectacular baroque parish church (1730) with paintings by Josef Michael Schmutzer. At the Durlaßboden dam there are facilities for watersports. Here the road swings through a right-hand hairpin bend to climb the north bank of the reservoir, and cross the border into Land Salzburg, affording spectacular views of the Wilderglostal and to the Wildkarspitze (3,073m, 10,079ft).

At about 43 miles a road to the left goes up to Almdorf Königsleiten, a ski resort some 3 miles south of the source of the river Salzach. The steep (gradients up to 20 per cent, 1 in 5), narrow side road which winds down alongside the Salzach to Wald is not recommended. A mile further on Route 165 is the toll booth for the Gerlos Hochalpenstrasse, and at Gerlosplatte there is a picnic area with superb views of the rugged mountains ahead, including the Hütteltalkopf (2,962m, 9,715ft). The road then drops rapidly past the Schönmoosalm, overhanging the long drop into the valley. After six hairpin bends it turns right through a helix to pass under itself. A rare piece of highway engineering! Another hairpin bend past the lower toll booth, and a large car park affords access to the 400m-high (1,312ft) Krimml Waterfalls. They are the highest waterfalls in Europe, and are located in a beautiful, romantic setting in a dark and narrow valley. After a walk of about an hour through the damp trees the middle and upper falls can be viewed from the Gasthof Schönanger. At the top of the falls is the Tauern Haus from which there are better views of the upper falls. **Krimml** (population 800), is the terminus for the railway line from Mittersill, and has a Gothic parish church.

The road then descends the deep valley bounded to the north by the Kitzbüheler Alps, and to the south by the 3,000m (9,840ft) peaks of the Hohe Tauern. After the twelfth-century Burgfried ruins at **Wald-im-Pinzgau**, the road bypasses **Neukirchen** which has an interesting parish church with fourteenth-century frescoes. Two miles further down the valley the ruin of Weyerburg was once a residence of the Bishop of Chiemsee. At **Bramberg-am-Wildkogel** there is a local history museum with a collection of minerals and stained glass, and the Gothic parish church is known for its Brambacher *pietà*. Passing Mühlbach the road crosses the railway and the river to Hollersbach-im-Pinzgau. Mittersill is reached 68 miles from the beginning of the route.

Mittersill (population 5,000) is at the crossroads of the road from the Gerlos Pass to Zell-am-See, and so to Salzburg and Vienna, and of the road from Kitzbühel via the Felbertauern Tunnel to East Tyrol and Carinthia. The baroque parish church (1756) has a seventeenth-century painting on the high altar by A. Mascagni. In Felben, south-east of the town, there are old wooden houses as well as a tower dating from 1332, and the church of St Nikolaus dates from 1479 with an early baroque high altar from 1631. High above the town is Schloß Mittersill which originates from 1180 and today is a hotel. Across the river bridge, past an old, black steam engine, Route 161 to the left goes over the Thurn Pass to Kitzbühel. Follow Route 168 to the right, past the turn to the Felbertauernstrasse, toward Zell-am-See.

At Uttendorf (population 2,500) a signpost points southward to the valley of the Stubachtal, and the mountain hamlet of Enzinger Boden. At 75 miles the Lengdorf camp site is on the left, and the resort of Niedernsill (population 2,000) is a mile further. The road bypasses Piesendorf and at 81 miles turn right to Kaprun and the Kaprunertal.

THE KAPRUNERTAL

Kaprun (population 2,500) is an all-year resort and, with Saalbach and Zell-am-See, is part of the 'Europa Sport Region'. It has two youth hostels, and is a good centre for climbing. As the road passes the gigantic pipes of the power station to the cable car up to the Maiskogel (1,675m, 5,494ft), the concrete face of the Limberg dam comes into view. After a hairpin bend the road rises steadily, passing the small and still waters of the Klamm reservoir on the right, to the Kaprunertörl car park for the Gletscherbahn Kaprun cableway which rises in three stages via the Salzburgerhütte (1,897m, 6,222ft), then to the alpine centre (2,452m, 8,043ft), and on to the Bergstation (3,029m, 9,935ft) where there is a restaurant, and from which the summit of the Kitzsteinhorn (3,203m, 9,935ft) may be reached on foot in about 1^1/$_2$ hours. A mile further up the road is Kasselfall Alpenhaus (1,068m, 3,503ft). There is a free car park for private vehicles which are not allowed to go further. Buses then take visitors through steep, narrow tunnels to the Limbergstollen, an inclined open-air lift which gives wonderful views down the valley. A second bus goes up to the top of the Limberg dam where the hydro-electric installations may be visited.

Another bus goes 3 miles along the Wasserfallboden reservoir, which is retained by the Limberg dam, to the Mooserboden reservoir (2,100m, 6,888ft), at the upper end of the valley, which is formed by two dams. There is a restaurant with spectacular panoramas of the surrounding mountains and glaciers — including the north side of the Glockner group and the majestic Grossglockner (3,797m, 12,454ft) — and of the rock face of the Karlinger Kees. The Heathen's (*Heidnische*) Church was used by Protestants for secret prayer meetings during the counter-Reformation.

Returning down the Kaprunertal bear right through Kaprun to the junction with Route 168; and follow Route 311 to Zell-am-See, 100 miles from Strass via Mayrhofen.

Route 2g   Innsbruck to Kufstein (see map page 73)

From Innsbruck the valley of the river Inn runs for 46 miles between the Karwendel group, the Tuxer Alps, and the Kitzbüheler Alps to Kufstein. Then it becomes the international border for some 8 miles before forsaking the high country of Austria for the flat southern plain of West Germany. Here the river is a wide and fast flowing stream which was at one time navigated by horse-drawn barges and rafts as far as Hall-in-Tirol. Today the valley is traversed by a motorway (A12) as well as Route 171.

Leave Innsbruck eastbound on Route 171. Between Arzl (a mile north-east of the city) and Thaur, there is a nature reserve where the wild primrose and the *Anemone pulsatilla* grow in great profusion. Both villages have interesting churches and old Tyrolean houses. Six miles from Innsbruck the town of Hall-in-Tirol (population 13,000) lies mainly to the left of the road and is well worth visiting.

Hall-in-Tirol is a well preserved town with many period houses from the sixteenth and seventeenth centuries. The Stadtgraben, on the north and west side of the old town, is especially attractive. The Upper Town Square (Obere Stadtplatz) contains a fountain with a statue from 1776 and a sixteenth-century bronze waterspout. The Rathaus is fifteenth century, has a notable council chamber and a local history museum with Gothic and baroque decorations, and the account books of the local magistrate's court for 1411. The parish church of St Nikolaus is late Gothic, redecorated in baroque style in 1752, with ceiling paintings by Josef Adam Mölk (1752). On the black and gold high altar the painting of the Holy Mother is by Erasmus Quellinus, and there are beautiful fifteenth-century stained glass windows in the choir. A late Gothic wrought-iron screen encloses the Waldauf chapel (1494) which contains a large reliquary of the Knights of Waldauf. St Josef's chapel dates from 1698, and St Magdalena's chapel from 1330. The latter is now a chapel of remembrance. It contains notable wall paintings from 1400, and a fifteenth-century carved altar. On the south side of the square, in Fürstengasse, there is a mining museum which has collections including brine baths and other items relating to salt mining in the Hallertal, which began in 1280. The nearby Stubenhaus was built by the Knights of Waldauf in 1508 and has a beautiful façade and late Gothic entrance.

From the Obere Stadtplatz follow the Rosengasse to the Stiftsplatz where the convent dates from 1566. A statue in the square commemorates its founder Princess Magdalena, daughter of the Emperor Ferdinand I. The church organ was played by Wolfgang Amadeus Mozart in 1772 and is now in the parish church of Fügen, in the Zillertal. In the old town there are also the Franciscan church (1644), and the Salvator church (1406), as well as a statue of Josef Speckbacher, patriot and companion of Andreas Hofer.

Burg Hasegg, in the Lower Town Square (Untere Stadtplatz) was built for Count Siegmund in 1480 and was later used to mint coins from silver mined at Schwaz. On the first floor is St George's chapel which dates from 1515. The mint was transferred from Meran to the Münzerturm (Coiner's Tower), in the Münzergasse, when it became vulnerable to Turkish raids from the south. The word 'dollar' is said to be derived from the Austrian 'taler' coin which took its name from 'Inntal'. The Münzer Gate has notable stone carvings.

Leaving Hall-in-Tirol, Route 171 crosses to the right bank of the Inn. Immediately on the right-hand side is a small road which leads up to Tulfes. Just beyond the junction, on the left of this road, is the Servitenkloster, and ahead, the red and white walls of the notable

A locksmith's wrought-iron sign, Hall-in-Tirol

church of St Karl Borromäus (1650). The high altar (1767) and ceiling
paintings (1765) are by Martin Knoller. There are two beautiful side-
altars: that on the right has a wrought-iron screen (1682), and that on
the left has a *pietà* by Andreas Damasch (1694).

The main road then runs past a camp site to **Volders** (population
2,750). In the Middle Ages this was a centre for the manufacture of armaments and today it has the air of an industrial town. South of the town,
on a hill at the mouth of the Voldererbach valley, is the attractive Schloß
Friedberg (1268) which has a chapel with fine frescoes from 1600.
Wattens (population 6,000) is a centre for the manufacture of sheet
glass. The main attractions for visitors are the open-air museum and the
local history museum which contains many prehistoric and Roman
finds. Wattens is at the foot of the Wattenbach valley which runs southward to Wattener Lizum, a climbing and skiing village in the Tuxer Alps.

The road bypasses **Weer** (population 1,200) where the rococo
church of St Gallus (1778) has a high altar and paintings by Franz Anton
Zeiller. At **Pill** the Gothic parish church has frescoes by Christopher
Anton Mayr, as has the church of the Cross (1764) which stands beside
the road. The road runs alongside the Inn as it approaches the old town

of Schwaz.

Schwaz (population 11,000) dates from the Bronze Age and was once an important mining town. The fifteenth-century copper and silver mines employed 10,000 miners and financed the establishment of the Habsburg Empire under Emperors Maximilian I and Karl V. In the sixteenth century the township was three times its present size. The fifteenth-century parish church has one tower with a copper dome by Jakob Zwisel (1513), and another pointed tower, by Christopher Kessler (1516) with a roof covered by 15,000 beaten copper plates. Inside there is a representation of the Holy Mother and Child dating from 1430 on the altar, and a notable tomb of Hans Freyling by the Dutch sculptor Alexander Colin (1578). The church is richly decorated with stained glass, statues, and reliefs from the fourteenth to sixteenth centuries which reflect the prosperity of that period. In the two-storey chapel of rest (1505) there is a late Gothic panelled altar from 1511, and in the churchyard there is a Lantern of the Dead from 1518.

Also worth seeing are the Augustinian church of St Martin (1516) with frescoes by Christopher Anton Mayr (1746), and the Franciscan church and abbey (1514) which has a baroque interior (1735) by Jakob Singer of Götzens. The cloisters date from 1512 and have late Gothic paintings by the Franciscan monk Wilhelm von Schwaben which depict scenes from the Passion, and which are renowned for their representation of the wild faces of Austrian and Turkish soldiers.

Schwaz also has many period houses. The Fuggerhaus (1510) has pointed towers at its corners and an arcaded courtyard, as well as wall paintings by Christopher Anton Mayr (1750). The Kreuzwegerhaus (1525) has an attractive façade and a second-storey arcade at the rear. The Enzenberg palace (1700) is a baroque building with a painted façade. On the east side of the town is Schloß Freundsberg, a thirteenth-century castle with rooms with late Gothic paintings and one with hunting frescoes. It also has a chapel (1477) with an early baroque interior and two little chapels beneath it, one with frescoes by Christopher Anton Mayr, and a local history museum.

Beyond Schwaz Route 171 runs beside the Inn and it is worth turning left to visit **Jenbach** (population 6,000). The town itself is a busy working community with a fifteenth-century parish church. It lies at the entrance to the Achenbach valley and commands the road to the 5-mile-long, half a mile wide, Achensee. In its lovely setting between the Karwendel group nature reserve and the Rofan group, the lake is popular for fishing and watersports, and it has a regular boat service between Seespitz, Pertisau, and the village of Achensee at the northern end. It may be reached from Jenbach by cog railway or via Route 181, which goes on to reach the border with West Germany about 21 miles from Jenbach. At **Maurach** there is a cable car up to the Erfurterhütte (1,834m, 6,016ft). Jenbach is also the terminus of the steam railway

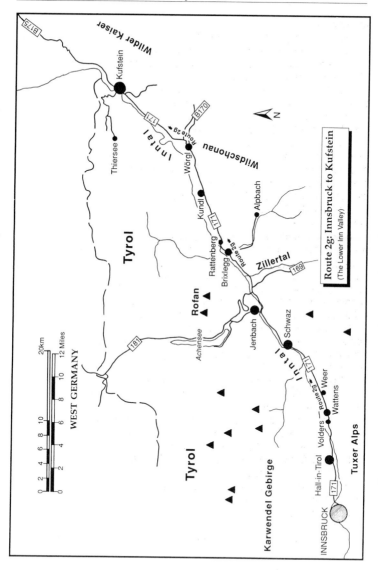

which runs up the Zillertal.

Some 2 miles west of Jenbach is Schloß Tratzberg, built in the sixteenth century on the site of a twelfth-century castle. It has many late

The terminus of the Achensee narrow-gauge steam railway at Jenbach

Gothic features, a collection of armaments, a hunting trophy room, and a Devil's Room (Teufelszimmer) from which it is said that a dishonest knight was taken by the devil himself. The late Renaissance Habsburg Room has a central pillar of red marble and rib vaulting, and a beautiful 45m-long (148ft) mural (1530) depicting 148 members of the Emperor Maximilian's family. In the rooms of the north and south wings there are many paintings, collections of globes and scientific instruments, and other items. The chapel (1502) has late Gothic carvings.

Continuing on Route 171, at **St Getraudi** the ruins of Schloß Kropfsberg stand to the left of the road. This twelfth-century castle was the meeting place, in 1417, of the brothers Friedrich IV (of the Empty Pocket) and Ernest of Styria, sons of Count Leopold of Tyrol, when they agreed to lay down their arms and so end their struggle to possess Tyrol. Alongside the road the little church of St Gertrude dates from 1680 and has a baroque altar from 1687. A short distance further along the road and Schloß Lichtenwörth comes into view, a Romanesque building with a Gothic chapel. This was one of the seats of the Knights of Freundsberg as was Schloß Matzen, less than a mile further on. Built in 1176 it has a massive Romanesque keep, medieval courtyards, and a three-storey, arched gallery.

Brixlegg (population 2,500) stands on the site of a Bronze Age settlement, and is now the location of an important copper-smelting works. The parish church dates from 1508 and has a baroque interior with a high altar by Kaspar Waldmann (1692), a crucifix (1765) by Franz Xavier Nißl on a side altar, ceiling decoration by Christopher Anton Mayr (1768), and a cruciform choir with frescoes from 1692. A small road to the south rises along the banks of the Alpbach to reach, after 5 miles, the typical Tyrolean village of **Alpbach** (population 2,000). The church of St Oswald is fourteenth century and has paintings by Christopher Anton Mayr, a carved figure of Joseph and Child, and another of Sts Anna and Maria, by Franz Xavier Nißl (1770). Alpbach is the home of the Austrian College, an international educational centre established in 1945 to bring people together from all over the western world for seminars on culture, politics and economics. It is a good base for walking via Inneralpbach to the Grosse Galtenberg (2,424m, 7,951ft).

Rattenberg (population 600) has many fifteenth- and sixteenth-century houses, and a late Gothic parish church of St Virgil which was built between 1473 and 1507 and redecorated in baroque style in 1737. The frescoes in the choir are by Simon Benjamin Faistenberger, those in the nave are by Matthäus Günther from 1735. The Augustinian abbey was founded in 1384 and its church was rebuilt in 1709 by Francesco Diego Carlone. It has notable ceiling paintings by Johann Josef Waldmann (1711), and stucco decoration in the chancel by Paolo d'Allio. The ruined castle above the roadway dates from 1254 and provides a good view over the town and across the valley. On the other side of the river the town of **Kramsach** (population 3,500) stands at the entrance to the Brandenberger valley and is a good base for walking in the Rofan group. It also has a well known glass and crystal works, and is the home of the Tyrolean farm museum.

Kundl (population 3,000) has a large pharmaceutical works. In the town centre there are typical old Tyrolean houses with painted façades, and the parish church (1736) has a richly decorated baroque interior. Kundl lies at the bottom of the Waldschönauer Ache which runs up to the Kundlalm at 1,320m (4,330ft) and provides good walking and climbing. **Wörgl** (population 8,500) is 37 miles from Innsbruck. Here there have been extensive archaeological excavations and many Bronze Age items have been found. The baroque parish church dates from 1740 and beside it is a heroic statue to commemorate those Tyrolean patriots who died on 13 May 1809 fighting the French invaders.

Continue on Route 171 past the junctions with Routes 170 to Kitzbühel and 312 to St Johann. At Kirchbichl, an interesting detour may be made by turning left then left again at Niederbreitenbach to reach **Mariastein** after about 4 miles. The mighty keep of Schloß Mariastein, built by the Freundsbergs in 1361, stands on a high rock. There are several notable rooms, with sixteenth-century decorated ceilings and old rafters, and a treasury of sacred and secular items. The chapel of the Holy Cross (1550) has a rococo altar, and the chapel of Mercy has a carving of the Holy Mother and Child (1470) on the high altar.

Route 171 joins Route 173 from the right before entering Kufstein, 46 miles from Innsbruck.

Kufstein (population 13,000) is a border town dominated by the Geroldseck fortress which testifies to ancient battles with invading Bavarians. With the exception of two short periods, it has been part of Austria since 1504 and today is a busy all-year-round tourist centre easily reached by road and rail.

The fortress (*Festung*) allows views across the Inn valley to the Kitzbüheler Alps to the south, and on clear days to the Stubai Alps to the west. Guided tours of the castle take about $1^1/_2$ hours. Built in the twelfth century, it became in 1205 the seat of the Bishops of Regensburg. The huge Emperor's Tower with walls up to $4^1/_2$m ($14^1/_2$ ft) thick was erected in 1522 and its rooms, and a vaulted gallery, surround an enormous central pillar. The cells on the third floor were in regular use from 1814 to 1867 when the fortress held political prisoners. The Deep Well (Tiefer Brunnen) dates from 1546 and goes down 68m (223ft) to the level of the Inn. The Burgher Tower contains the famous Heroes' Organ (Heldenorgel), installed in 1931 to commemorate those who died in World War I. Recitals are performed at 12 noon every day and it can be heard 4 miles away. The chapel has a stucco ceiling in baroque style. In the barracks (Schloß Kaserne) there is a local history museum.

In the Upper Town Square (Obere Stadtplatz), the late Gothic parish

The town centre, Kufstein

church of St Veit dates from 1707. It has modern wall and ceiling paintings by Rudolf Stolz (1931), and, on the south wall, a sculpture from 1493. The chapel of the Holy Trinity is fifteenth century and has a rococo altar with gilded figures. The coats of arms on the external walls date from the sixteenth and seventeenth centuries. A tablet commemorates the life of Anton Kink (1820-68), a former mayor, who founded the Austrian cement industry. In the Lower Town Square (Untere Stadtplatz), and in the romantic Römerhofgasse, there are many old houses — including the Batzenhäusl, the oldest wine bar in the Tyrol — which typify the architecture of the Inn valley. In Kienberggasse there is a statue of Josef Madersperger (1768-1850) who invented the sewing machine, and on the Kalvarienberg, on the east side of the town, there is a statue of Andreas Hofer.

Kufstein is a good centre for touring, walking, climbing, and skiing. It has chairlifts to the Stadtberg (1,140m, 3,739ft), the Duxer Alm (900m, 2,952ft), and on to the Jahnhügel (1,260m, 4,133ft), and from the Brentenjoch to the Steinberggraben (1,232m, 4,041ft).

An enjoyable excursion from Kufstein follows the steep and winding road out of the west side of the town via Morsbach to the village of Thiersee, between the little lakes of the Hechtsee, Pfrillsee, and Längssee — where there are easy walks around the banks — and proceeds to the triple village of **Vorderthiersee**, **Thiersee**, and **Hinterthiersee**. Since 1799, as a protection from the ravages of war, the villagers have enacted a Passion Play of the life and death of Christ. Although

Kufstein fortress

repeatedly prohibited by the church authorities, the people persisted in performing their plays. Formerly held at 10-year intervals, since 1970 they have been presented every 6 years. The original wooden hut was replaced in 1801 by a theatre which today seats an audience of 1,000. Like the Oberammergau Passion Play, this Lent production is spectacular, but it is memorable especially as evidence of the strong and unfailing Christian faith of the people of Thiersee. The road goes on through several gorges before turning north to cross the Ursprung Pass to Bayrischzell in West Germany.

Another village Passion Play has been enacted since 1633 at **Erl**, 13 miles north of Kufstein via Ebbs (Route 175) and Niederndorf (Route 172). It too is now presented in a modern theatre at intervals of 6 years (from 1985). Route 172 leads via the picturesque village of **Walchsee** (population 1,300), on the north shore of the lake of that name, to **Kössen** (population 3,200), a village with many decorated houses. The border with West Germany is just 2 miles to the north at the Klobenstein Pass, and also 3 miles east on Route 176 to Reith-im-Winkl. To the south Route 176 winds for 13 miles to St Johann through the scenery of the Wilder Kaiser where, according to folk tales, there are caves inhabited by giants and sleeping princes.

North of Kufstein the border runs along the west bank of the Inn which then enters West Germany.

Route 2h   Wörgl to Zell-am-See

THE BRIXENTAL

From Wörgl the road to Kitzbühel (Route 170) rises steeply up the Brixental past the thirteenth-century Schloß Itter, now a hotel, on a high rock partly hidden by trees. **Hopfgarten** (population 5,000), is a popular winter sports centre with attractive old houses and an impressive twin-towered baroque parish church. Its location at the bottom of the Kelsauer and the Rettenbach valleys makes Hopfgarten a good centre for exploring the Kitzbüheler Alps to the south, as is **Westendorf** (population 2,800) where the parish church has a carved figure of St Nikolaus from 1500. **Brixen-im-Thale** (population 2,500) is a busy working town with an unusual parish church with two green cupolas and a painted ceiling by Josef Schöpf of Telfs (1795). Then the road winds down past farmhouses to **Kirchberg-in-Tirol** (population 3,500). Kirchberg has winter sports facilities and is a base for touring as well as walking in the Spertental. The Gothic parish church dates from 1511 and has a remarkable ceiling by Simon Benedict Faistenberger (1739). A cablecar goes up to the Fleckalm (1,795m, 5,888ft). After 17 miles the Schwarzsee lies on the left, and nearby is fifteenth-century Schloß Münichau, now a hotel. One mile further and the road enters Kitzbühel.

Kitzbühel (population 8,000), formerly a silver and copper mining centre, is now a fashionable resort at the foot of the busy road over the

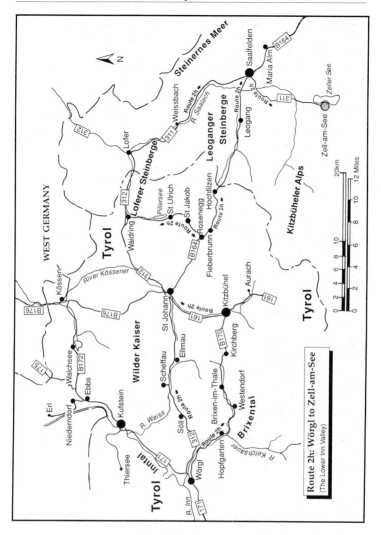

Route 2h: Wörgl to Zell-am-See
(The Lower Inn Valley)

Thurn Pass. From the south the pedestrianised Vorderstadt is entered through the Jochberger Tor, a fifteenth-century town gate. In the town centre many old houses are decorated in traditional style. On the left is a local history museum, and, on the corner with the Hinterstadt, the fourteenth-century St Katharine's church which has a winged altarpiece from 1520. At the north end of the Vorderstadt is the parish church of

The parish church and the Liebfrauenkirche, Kitzbühel

 St Andreas (1506). Its baroque interior is elegant, from the high altar (1663) to the organ gallery (1665), both by Benedict Faistenberger,

The Wilder Kaiser Mountains from near St Johann

whose son Simon painted the picture of the *Three Kings* (1724) in the nave, as well as the frescoes in the chapel dedicated to St Rosa of Lima. The relief on the tomb of the mine-owning Kupferschmied family was carved in 1520 by Hans Frosch of Hall-in-Tirol. In the churchyard there is a late Gothic Mount Olive chapel, with frescoes from 1600, and a Gothic Lantern of the Dead from 1450. The bell tower of the adjacent Liebfrauenkirche dates from the fourteenth century. This church has two storeys, the lower church dating from 1373. In the upper church there are ceiling and wall paintings by S. B. Faistenberger (1739), who also executed the paintings (1727) in the Johannes Nepomuk chapel on the west side of the site.

The Faistenberger family played an important role in the creation of religious art treasures in Kitzbühel, their home town. Benedict Faistenberger, who died in 1693, had seven sons all of whom were artists and sculptors, as were many of his grandchildren. Their exquisite work may be seen in many of the churches in the surrounding area. Simon Benedict Faistenberger (1695-1759) was the outstanding baroque artist of the Tyrol.

Kitzbühel, with St Johann and Kirchberg, is one of the foremost ski centres in Austria with many cable cars, chairlifts, and skilifts up to the Hahnenkamm (1,655m, 5,428ft) and the Kitzbüheler Horn (1,998m, 6,553ft). There are many enjoyable walks in the vicinity (eg up to the waterfall on the river Schleier, south of the town). To the north is the sixteenth-century Schloß Lebenberg, now a hotel, and, to the south, is

Schloß Kaps which has a Gothic chapel. At Aurach, about 3 miles south off Route 161, there is a wildlife park with Tibetan yaks and fallow deer.

To the south from Kitzbühel Route 161 goes 18 miles over the Thurn Pass to Mittersill. Instead turn northward along Route 161 to reach **St Johann** (population 6,500), 6 miles from Kitzbühel, a delightful old town which has attractive houses with painted façades, balconies and bay windows, and carved gables. The baroque parish church has ceiling paintings by S. B. Faistenberger, and his brother George Faistenberger carved the figures of Sts Peter and Paul on the high altar. The paintings (1740) on the marble side altars are by Jakob Zanussi of Salzburg.

St Johann enjoys a crowded winter holiday season. A funicular railway rises to the Angereralm (1,295m, 4,248ft) and gives spectacular views, and a cable car goes up to the Harschbichl (1,600m, 5,248ft). There is also a *Sommerrodelbahn* — a concrete slope down which little toboggans on wheels carry courageous passengers who control their flimsy vehicles by means of a small brake and the banked sides of the runway. St Johann is known for its international mountain climbing school which offers a varied programme of walking and climbing tours throughout the Tyrol from spring to autumn. Two miles east of the town there is a small private airfield from which sightseeing flights are available. Visitors are entertained by events such as the World Classic Grand Prix Cross Country Skiing Championships in February; the Corpus Christi procession in the spring; Senior Citizens World Cup Cycling Race in August; Alm Festival Weeks in September; and the Dumpling Festival in September when noodles stretch the whole length of Speckbacherstrasse!

St Johann can also be reached from Wörgl via Route 312, which avoids Kitzbühel and gives superb views of the Wilder Kaiser range to the north. At **Söll** (population 2,700) the parish church has ceiling paintings (1768) of scenes from the lives of Sts Peter and Paul by Christopher Anton Mayr. Three miles further, on the right, there is a cable car up to the Brandstadl (1,649m, 5,409ft), and on the left a small road goes up 5 miles through **Scheffau** (population 1,000) to the Hintersteiner See in the Wilder Kaiser nature reserve. At **Ellmau** (population 1,800) there is a funicular railway up to the Hartkaiser (1,524m, 4,999ft) which affords a panorama of the High Alps as far as the Grossglockner. After Going (population 1,000) the road runs down alongside the Reither Ache to reach St Johann, 19$^{1}/_{2}$ miles from Wörgl.

THE PILLERSEE AND THE THREE CHURCHES

From St Johann take Route 164 up the Pillersee valley. At Rosenegg, a detour can be made along a small road to the left, which winds up a narrow defile, heavily wooded on both sides, beneath a railway viaduct. Soon the brown steeple and ochre tower of **St Jakob** come into view. This is the first of three churches in this peaceful glen. The parish church of St Jakob was built in 1689. It is a simple church with a painting (1710) of the Resurrection by Ignaz Faistenberger. About $2^1/_2$ miles further the fifteenth-century Gothic parish church of St Ulrich appears. This is larger than St Jakob, with some decorated pews and a larger altar. The ceiling is covered with paintings (1746) by S. B. Faistenberger. The village of **St Ulrich-am-Pillersee** (population 900) is a health resort with hot baths for the treatment of asthma and neuralgia. It enjoys a pretty setting amid meadows and mountains, and beside the shallow Pillersee which has facilities for boating, sailing, and fishing. The easy walk around the lake takes about 3 hours. Just beyond the end of the lake stands the little pilgrimage church of St Adolari which dates from 1013. Even the visitor sated with church architecture will find delight in the simple elegance of its interior. The rustic grey pews and panelling provide a perfect backdrop for the richly furnished eighteenth-century rococo high altar and two side altars, the decorated vaulting, and the magnificent paintings of scenes from the life of St Adolari over the choir. The latter forms a hexagonal semi-circle around the back of the high altar which bears a *pietà* from 1420. Amongst all the jewels in Austria's crown of beautiful churches St Adolari is a notable gem!

The road goes on through a narrow gorge to **Waidring** (population 1,500) where the parish church of St Veit has a seventeenth-century carved figure by George Faistenberger, and there is a wood carving school. At the junction with Route 312 turn right down the Strubtal, across the border into Land Salzburg, to **Lofer** (population 1,700) after 15 miles. Lofer is a small resort on the river Saalach, a centre for touring and walking with good skiing facilities. Here Route 312 goes north over the Steinpass into West Germany where Bad Reichenhall is 16 miles away. To reach Zell-am-See turn right at Lofer onto Route 311 on which the busy traffic runs alongside the river Saalach. On the right is the entrance to the Lamprechtsofenloch caverns, a system of grottoes, domed caves, underground waterfalls and lakes, which are open to visitors. Fifteen miles from Lofer the road reaches Saalfelden.

ROSENEGG TO SAALFELDEN

Back on the main route at Rosenegg, continue on Route 164 to **Fieberbrunn** (population 4,000), an unspoilt village with a parish church dating from 1455, and a chapel of Johannn Nepomuk which has notable frescoes from 1762. The village was given its unusual name — which means 'fever spring' — by Princess Margarethe Maultasch who found a cure in the local spring water. At Hochfilzen the road crosses the Grießenpaß at 967m (3,172ft) and the border into Land Salzburg. Along the Leoganger Ache there are good views of the Leoganger Steinberge (up to 2,634m, 8,640ft). The craggy peaks dominate the small town of **Leogang** (population 2,700) where the parish church of St Leonhard (1323) has ceiling paintings by Christopher Anton Mayr.

Windsurfing on the Pillersee

Saalfelden-am-Steinernen Meer (population 11,000) is 23 miles from St Johann, at the foot of the Steinernes Meer — 2,600m-high

The chapel of Johannes Nepomuk, Fieberbrunn

(8,528ft) mountains to the north-west which form the border with West Germany — in a broad basin in the Saalach valley. It is an old market town where horse sales are a speciality. The parish church has a late Gothic panelled altar from 1530. About a mile to the south is the Ritzensee, a small bathing lake, and Schloß Ritzen which was restored in 1975 and now houses the Pinzgauer museum. Its collection of Christmas nativity cribs is the largest in Austria. On the west side, just off the road to Leogang, is the sixteenth-century Schloß Dorfheim, and 1¹/₂ miles to the north-east is the thirteenth-century Schloß Lichtenberg overlooking the valley. From the castle a pathway leads up to St George's hermitage at 1,004m (3,293ft) which dates from 1675 and is said to be the only inhabited rock hermitage in Europe. Three miles east is **Maria Alm** (population 1,500) where the steeple of the parish church (1500) is 90m high (295ft). The interior is baroque with frescoes by Christopher Anton Mayr (1757), and some of the tombstones are from the fifteenth century. In the chapel there are frescoes from 1638.

From Saalfelden the busy Route 311 runs up the gently rising valley to Zell-am-See, 33 miles from St Johann.

3 THE GROSSGLOCKNER HOCHALPENSTRASSE AND EAST TYROL

The journey from North Tyrol to East Tyrol is most readily made through the Felbertauern Tunnel but no visitor should miss the opportunity to travel over the highest and most spectacular public road in Europe—the Grossglockner Hochalpenstrasse. In this chapter that road is described together with Lienz and East Tyrol.

PART 1   THE GROSSGLOCKNER HOCHALPENSTRASSE

Route 3a   Zell-Am-See to Lienz

Leaving Zell-am-See Route 311 skirts around the lake towards the resort of Bruck. Following the Grossglockner Hochalpenstrasse sign-post, the road sweeps to the right to enter the Fuschertal, and the mountains ahead promise splendid panoramas to come.

The road rises gently up the steep-sided valley, hugging the little river on the left as it tumbles over a weir, to the village of **Fusch** (population 730) with its pretty *pensions* and unusual, stepped church tower. A road to the left leads to **Bad Fusch**, where the hot baths are fed by radioactive spring water.

Soon the road rises more steeply, past a signpost warning of Z-bends for the next 23km (14$^1/_2$ miles), through the Barenschlucht Gorge. At Ferleiten it levels off, the valley briefly opens out, and the Walcherbach Waterfall appears on the right. This is the start of the historic track over the Hohe Tauern via the Trauner Alm (1,520m, 4,986ft) into the Mölltal and Carinthia. Nearby there is a game park extending over 30,000 acres and open to the public. The toll booth marks the beginning of the Grossglockner Hochalpenstrasse.

The road then winds upwards and at 12$^1/_2$ miles reaches the first hairpin bend (note that the hairpin bends are numbered from this side). Over the next 8 miles there are thirteen more hairpin bends and the road rises 1,269m (4,162ft). The road is excellent, well surfaced and wide, so that the bends are easily negotiated, but engines may need to be allowed to cool at one of the frequent stopping places on both sides of

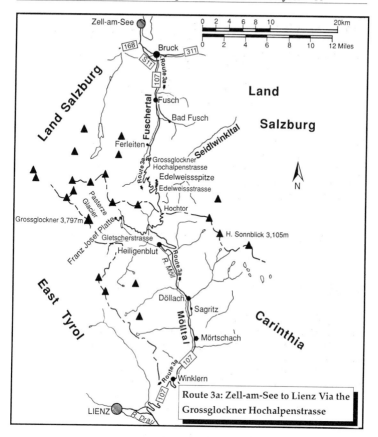

Route 3a: Zell-am-See to Lienz Via the Grossglockner Hochalpenstrasse

the road. Drivers and their passengers may also wish to stop to admire the magnificent views of the Grosse Wiesbachhorn (3,570m, 11,710ft), its glaciered companions, and the many waterfalls across the valley.

After the Rasthaus Hochmais the trees are left behind and shortly the road curves left up to Nassfeld, passes through the wilderness of the Hexenküche (Witches' Kitchen), and, at 2,407m (7,895ft), reaches the car park of the Dr Franz-Rehrl-Haus restaurant, 20 miles from Zell.

From this saddle between the Fuschertal and the Seidlwinkltal the achievement of the highway engineers who built the Grossglockner Hochalpenstrasse can be appreciated. It was constructed between 1930 and 1935 under the direction of Fritz Wallack. It extends for $13^{1}/_{2}$ miles at an altitude of over 2,000m (6,560ft) via twenty-six hairpin bends with a maximum gradient of 12 per cent (1 in 8). At its highest point (at

View north from the Edelwießspitze on the Grossglockner Hochalpenstrasse

the entrance to the Hochtor Tunnel) it reaches 2,506m (8,222ft). It is normally open from May to October inclusive depending upon the season. Its importance as a commercial route has diminished since the opening of the Felbertauern Tunnel and more recently, the Tauern *Autobahn*, both of which are open all year round. It is, however, one of the most spectacular roads in Europe and a journey over it is an unforgettable experience. Alternatively there are many coach excursions from both sides of the Hohe Tauern as well as a regular bus service.

THE EDELWEISSSTRASSE

At the northern end of the Dr Franz-Rehrl-Haus restaurant car park the Edelweissstrasse, once forbidden to cars, rises 161m (528ft) in a distance of just over a mile. The steep (14 per cent, 1 in 7), narrow, block surfaced, stack of six very tight hairpin bends affords a formidable test for engine cooling systems on the way up, and for braking systems on the way down. Driving skills also need to be adequate for the task. At the top, the Edelweissspitze car park provides a haven for overheated vehicles while drivers and passengers enjoy the hospitality of the Edel-

Snow-clad peaks viewed from the Hochtor

weisshütte (accommodation and restaurant). The fabulous view from
the tower is said to include thirty-seven peaks over 3,000m (9,840ft)
high, and nineteen glaciers. To the north the Zeller See, Steinernes
Meer, Tennengebirge, Berchtesgaden Alps, and Dachstein group may
be seen; to the east, the Ankogel and Sonnblick groups; to the south,
the Schober group; and to the west and south-west, the Glockner
group. Ample reward on a clear day for the intrepid motorist.

The Edelweissspitze also provides a superb overview of the rugged
landscape of part of the Hohe Tauern National Park which lies on either
side of the Grossglockner Hochalpenstrasse. The park is a conservation area of alpine fastness with unique flora and fauna, as well as man-
made pastures, meadowlands, and forests, now protected for the
benefit of future generations.

Back on the Grossglockner Hochalpenstrasse, the road continues
in a long loop around the flagged peak of the Fuschertörl (2,420m,
7,938ft) to the Glockner restaurant where another car park affords excellent views including the summit of the Grossglockner itself. Then the
road runs through barren screes which are not so picturesque, as the
road snakes up between the Fuscher lake and its *Alm*, through the short
tunnel at the Mittertörl, through hairpins Nos 16 and 17, and beneath the
Hochtor, to emerge into Carinthia. Here there are excellent views of the
mountains of the Schober group, which rise to the Petzeck (3,283m,

10,768ft), and, to the left, the Goldberg group which includes the Hohe Sonnblick (3,105m, 10,184ft) with a weather observatory on its summit.

From the Hochtor the excellent road winds down the mountainside. The hairpin bends are easily negotiated, albeit with low gears and heavy braking. After the nineteenth hairpin the road passes the Wallack Haus, the Schareck chairlift, and the Romerhütte. On the long descent, through alpine pastures and flocks of sheep, to the twenty-fifth hairpin, the Mölltal and the Heiligenblut basin appear ahead. At 30 miles the road reaches the Guttal fork. Heiligenblut is signposted left but a diversion to the right, up the Gletscherstrasse, should not be missed.

THE GLETSCHERSTRASSE

The Gletscherstrasse passes the Rasthaus Schöneck with its large car park and, rounding a corner, the Grossglockner (3,798m, 12,457ft), the highest mountain in Austria, comes into glorious view, black as coal, with a bright, white glacier draped over its left shoulder. Shortly afterward the Karl Volkert Haus, the Glocknerhaus and the Pasterzenhaus are passed, and the Margaritzen lake comes into view in the gorge below left. After climbing up six hairpin bends (gradients up to 12 per cent), and 35$^1/_2$ miles from Zell, the road ends at the Franz Josefs Platte (2,369m, 7,770ft). The complex of buildings comprise the Alpenhotel Kaiser Franz Josefs Haus, the Gletscherestaurant Freiwandeck, a bank, shop, and toilets, and a multi-storey car park as well as open parking spaces.

From the highest platform of the Freiwandeck the view is breathtaking. On the left the Grossglockner, flanked by the Kleinglockner (3,764m, 12,346ft) and the Johannisberg (3,460m, 11,349ft), seems near enough to reach out and touch, and ahead the Pasterze glacier, a 6-mile-long river of ice, flows from the head of the valley down to the Margaritzen lake. It is said to be the best view in Europe.

From the Freiwandeck a funicular railway (the Gletscherbahn) affords easy access to the cold and slippery surface of the glacier (May to September inclusive, 8am to 4pm daily), and the Gamsgruberweg footpath (signposted 'Zur Hofmanus und Oberwalderhütte') leads to a viewpoint for the Wasserfall Winkel (2,548m, 8,357ft). The pathway is in fact a ledge above the glacier and ascends fairly gently. The round trip takes about 90 minutes.

HEILIGENBLUT TO LIENZ

Returning to the Guttal fork (41 miles), the road to Heiligenblut drops down the mountainside with the Mölltal deep below on the right. At the Kasereck and the Rossbach huts there are car parks with superb views. At the toll booth, tickets are checked and cancelled. The twenty-sixth hairpin bend (not counting those on the Edelweissstrasse and the Gletscherstrasse) is followed by the sign 'Wilkommen Heiligenblut'.

From this point the lovely tree-lined road descends through a final, un-numbered hairpin bend. The famous view of St Vincent's church greets the visitor to the village of **Heiligenblut**, 47 miles from Zell.

In the tenth century, according to tradition, Briccius, a Dane in the army of the Emperor Leo, brought from Byzantium the flask from the high altar of St Sophia containing the Sacred Blood which had run from a picture of Jesus Christ. At Heiligenblut he was caught in a snowstorm. Fearing that robbers might steal the Sacred Blood, he cut a deep wound in his leg and hid the tiny phial inside it. In the bitter cold of that night he died. By morning the storm had ended and the sun shone. Peasants coming up the track were astonished to find three blades of wheat sprouting through the snow and when they dug them up they found the body of Briccius. They loaded the body onto an ox-cart but the oxen refused to move, so they buried Briccius where they had found him. The very next day they observed a leg sticking up from the grave and found the phial of the Sacred Blood. The Archbishop of Salzburg built a pilgrimage church which the present church replaced. The phial of the Sacred Blood is now preserved in the Sacrament of the Holy Blood in the crypt of St Vincent's church.

Nestling at the head of the Mölltal, beneath the high peak of the Grossglockner, and enjoying the sunny, south-facing slopes of the Schareck (2,604m, 8,541ft), Heiligenblut (population 1,300) is a flower-decked village surrounded by trees and alpine pastures. It is a noted winter sports resort with many chair- and ski-lifts. It has indoor tennis and squash courts, a swimming bath, and equitation hall. Walkers can choose from 20 miles of marked pathways in winter, and 150 miles in summer. Anglers may fish for brown trout in the river Möll. The world-famous climbing school operates from the Franz Josefs Hohe in summer when the climax of the course is the ascent of the Grossglockner. An unusual attraction is gold panning in the streams of the nearby Goldberg mountains. Visitors may hire panning equipment or join one-day excursions. Mineralogists can find plenty of interest in the rocky outcrops of the Pasterzental (the museum at Döllach has a collection of items associated with local mining and minerals).

The Gothic church of St Vincent was built by the monks of Admont abbey and took over a century to complete, the nave being finished in 1490. The altar is 35ft high and is panelled in the style of Michael Pacher so that its twelve paintings can be folded to make alternative displays. The tabernacle, in the choir, and the Veronika altar, in the north aisle, date from about 1490, and the carved *Madonna Enthroned with Child* from about 1400. The little churchyard girdles the church with a garland of fresh flowers and wrought-iron memorials.

The village has accommodation ranging from a youth hostel to first-class hotels. There are two camp sites, one 10 minutes' walk from the centre of the village, and the other about $1\frac{1}{2}$ miles away at Pockhorn,

The Pasterze glacier from the Freiwandeck at Franz Josefs Platte

on the bank of the Möll and close to the 130m-high (426ft) Jungfern-sprung Waterfall. There is no railway up the Mölltal but there is a regular

The village square at Heiligenblut and the Grossglockner beyond

bus service over the Hochalpenstrasse and to Winklern and beyond.

Leaving Heiligenblut the road winds down the valley, beside the sparkling river Möll. At **Döllach** (population 1,520) there are sixteenth- and seventeenth-century houses and, in Schloß Grosskirchheim, a gold and silver museum as well as a local history museum with collections of statues, musical instruments, paintings, etc. A small road from Döllach runs north-eastward past a waterfall and up the Zirknitztal to the Kegelsee and Grosssee where footpaths lead to the Brettsee and Weisssee. Döllach is a good centre for climbing in the Schober group. At **Sagritz** the choir of the church of St George contains paintings by C. Brandstatter the Younger (1840) and fragments of sixteenth-century frescoes in the vaults and on the external walls.

Beyond Mörtschach, with its late Gothic church, the road passes the pilgrimage church of St Maria-in-der-Au (1806) then the massive, rugged outline of the Lienzer Dolomite mountains comes into distant view. At 60 miles from Zell, Winklern (population 2,500) boasts a medieval watchtower. The road avoids the centre of the village, going left down the lower Mölltal via Obervellach to Spittal, and ahead via the Iselsberg Pass to Lienz.

After a hairpin bend the road climbs high on the hillside affording lovely views over Winklern and in both directions along the Mölltal. Another hairpin bend leads to the crest of the pass and, entering East Tyrol, the road begins to descend between woodlands, the stark outline of the Dolomites now dominating the view ahead, through Iselsberg. The descent into the valley of the Drau is steep and there are several sharp bends, but the road is good. At the bottom it forks left to Spittal and right to Lienz. The centre of Lienz is reached after 71 miles from Zell-am-See.

PART 2   THE VALLEYS OF EAST TYROL

Looking at a map of Austria, East Tyrol (Öst Tirol) appears to be an anomaly. Separated from the main area of North Tyrol by the High Alps, its foaming rivers and sunlit valleys running down to the Carinthian basin and on to Yugoslavia and the Adriatic Sea, there would seem to be every natural reason to associate this area with Carinthia. Indeed over many centuries East Tyrol has often been forced into an administrative association with Carinthia. But in 1919, when the Habsburg Empire was being broken up, the people of East Tyrol saw their cultural, historical, and social affinities with the people of the Tyrol and voted to remain part of that province rather than unite with Carinthia or with Italy. In neighbouring South Tyrol the plebiscite resulted in the transfer of that area to Italy, and so East Tyrol was cut off from the Inn valley. The construction of the Felbertauern Tunnel in the 1960s was significant in opening up all-year road communication and in bringing closer together the inhabitants of the two Tyrols. East Tyrol exists for the good reason that its people want it that way.

East Tyrol is bounded on all sides by high mountains. To the north the Venediger and the Glockner groups form the boundary with the province of Salzburg. On the eastern side the Schober group, and on the southern side the rugged Lienzer Dolomites extend along the border with Carinthia. To the west the Lasörling and Deferegger Mountains, and the Carnic Alps form the border with Italy. These high peaks are furrowed by many verdant glens but there are seven principal valleys: Drautal, Iseltal, Tauerntal, Virgental, Defereggental, Kalsertal, and Pustertal. The latter has two side valleys: Villgratental, and the Tyroler Gailtal. The warm climate south of the High Alps and the lush pastures of the valleys and hillsides encouraged settlement in this area many thousands of years ago. Today tourism is the main source of income and the market towns and farming villages open their doors to visitors from all over the world who come in all seasons to enjoy the peace and quiet and the great natural beauty of this ancient landscape, as well as the friendly hospitality of its peoples.

When the fragrant meadows of summer have faded then East Tyrol turns into a winter wonderland. Sparkling powder snow transforms the landscape and attracts both the novice and the expert skier. There are seventy-one cable cars, chairlifts, and ski-lifts; over 130 miles of high- and low-level cross-country ski trails; countless toboggan runs, skating and curling rinks; ski schools and ski kindergartens; free ski buses; as well as many miles of snow-free walks; indoor tennis and squash courts, swimming pools, and horse riding halls. Near Lienz the skiing is conveniently located at Zettersfeld, Hochstein, Leisach, and Haidenhof. Excellent facilities are also to be found at Matrei, Kals, Prägraten, St Jakob, Sillian, Kartitsch and Obertilliach. When the summer season is over then East Tyrol prepares to welcome the crystal clear days of sunshine and snow and its winter guests.

LIENZ
Lienz is a small town with unique charm. Located at the confluence of the rivers Drau and Isel, it commands the upper Drau valley and the road westward to Italy; the Felbertauern road northward to the Tauerntal and Innsbruck; the Iselsberg Pass to the east via the Grossglockner road to Salzburg; and the road down the Drautal to Villach and on to Klagenfurt. This strategic position, together with the fertile soil of the broad valley, made it an obvious site for settlement. Both the Celts (400BC) and the Romans (15BC) found it congenial, and relics of their early occupation can be seen in the town's museums. Lienz today is a market town which bustles throughout the year with the many visitors who find it an excellent centre for exploring the valleys and mountains of this beautiful region and, especially for walking, climbing — particularly rock climbing in the Lienzer Dolomites — and for winter holidays.

Lienz is easily reached by road or rail and there is a small private airfield 7 miles down the Spittal road. The town — and the whole of East

The Lienzer Dolomites from Grafendorf, near Lienz

Tyrol — is well served by the post-bus system. At the west end there is a chairlift to the Hochstein (1,500m, 4,920ft), and at the other end a cable car up to Zettersfeld (1,820m, 5,970ft). The town provides a full range of accommodation including a youth hostel, two camp sites in the town and four more within easy reach.

A decorative fountain in Lienz

The **parish church of St Andrä** is located on the north bank of the Isel. The present Gothic structure stands on the site of a fifth-century Christian chapel and an early thirteenth-century Romanesque church. Worth noting are the four fifteenth-century sculptures on the parapet of the organ; the wooden crucifix dated 1500; the altarpiece by Anton Zoller, and the ceiling fresco by Josef Adam Mölk, both from 1761; and *St Anne with Mary and the Child Jesus* (1515). Under the organ gallery two red marble tombstones by Christopher Geiger are dedicated to Leonhard, Count of Görz-Tirol, dated 1506, and to Michael von Wolkenstein and his wife Barbara von Thun, dated 1509. In the octagonal crypt a Crucifixion group dates from 1510, and there is an early fifteenth-century *pietà*. In the arcaded churchyard the memorial chapel (1925) by Clemens Holzmeister contains murals by Albin Egger-Lienz as well as his tomb. Nearby, in the Beda Weber Gasse, the small St Michael's church has net vaulting. Although building started in the fifteenth century, the onion dome on the north tower was only completed in 1713. A short walk away, in the Kärnterstrasse, is the oldest house in the Tyrol dating from 1400.

On the south bank, the **Franciscan church** in the Muchargasse was originally part of a Carmelite nunnery endowed by Countess Euphemia of Görz in 1349. It contains fifteenth-century frescoes behind the altar, and a Gothic *pietà*. From the Neuer Platz the Schweizergasse, which contains beautiful old houses, leads to the Dominican **Klosterkirche**, parts of which date from 1243. Opposite the church is the Klosterle Schmiede, a 500-year-old smithy. The south side of the Hauptplatz is dominated by the sixteenth-century **Liebburg**, with its twin, onion-topped towers, which now houses government offices. At the east end the **Antoniuskapelle** is also sixteenth century. The north side of the square is arcaded and alleyways lead to the Südtiroler Platz through the Hotel Post, formerly the residence of the Burggrafen of Lienz.

On the western outskirts of the town, **Schloß Bruck**, with its large keep, was the thirteenth-century home of the Counts of Görz whose estates extended from the Tauern as far south as Istria, on the Adriatic Sea. It was purchased by the town in 1943 and adapted to house the **East Tyrol local history museum** (Östtiroler Heimatmuseum). The keep, chapel, and gatehouse were part of the original building; the barbican and round tower date from the sixteenth century. On the second floor the Great Hall is decorated in period style with flags and weaponry. In the two-storey gatehouse chapel notable paintings can be found in the round apse, by Nikolaus Kentner (1452), and on the walls, by Simon von Taisten (1490), to whom is also attributed the Görz altar (1490) on the upper floor. The lower altar is styled after Michael Pacher. The museum contains archaeological finds from Celtic and Roman times, from *Aguntum* and Lavant. There are also folk and natural history collections, and paintings by local artists including Franz von Deferegger, Paul Troger, and Albin Egger-Lienz.

Around Lienz

Also worth visiting, 3 miles outside the town on the road to Spittal, are the excavations of the Roman town of *Aguntum* which include a temple, tower, town walls, and a mosaic-floored house. Half a mile further and a turn to the left leads into the village of **Dölsach**. Its Romanesque parish church was built in 1857. The painting on the 'Holy Family' side altar is by Franz von Deferegger. The sister church of St Margarethe, like the ruined Schloß Wallenstein, in nearby **Stronach**, is thirteenth century. Also at hand is the Gothic St George's church (1425) at **Gödnach** where the stone figure of St George dates from 1400.

Shortly after the Dölsach turn, a road to the right leads to the village of **Lavant**. This was the location of a first-century Celtic temple. In the fifth century the Bishop of *Aguntum* built a refuge around it but a century later both lay in ruins. The site was excavated in 1948 and many finds are on display in Schloß Bruck. Higher up the hillside the church of St Ulrich was refurbished in 1770 by Thomas Mayr but the older parts of

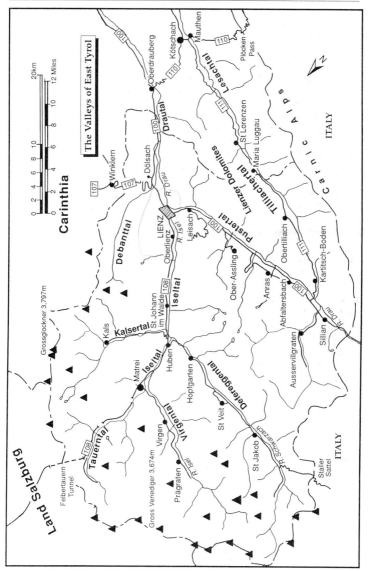

The Valleys of East Tyrol

the building date back to 855. Beneath the sharp red spire the beautiful arched doorway with its marble relief leads into a baroque interior. The

The Tauerntal near Matrei-in-Östtirol

high altar has two statues by Johann Paterer (1750). Even higher up the hillside is the church of Sts Peter and Paul (1485), built of stone from the ruined Schloß Lavant (1200). Fragments of Roman stones and tablets have also been discovered. It has three panelled altars dating from 1450, 1510 and 1530.

THE FIVE VALLEYS

Lienz is the gateway to five of the seven valleys of East Tyrol. Route 108 runs north-west of the town through the Iseltal, past the Kalsertal and the Defereggental to reach Matrei-in-Östtirol after $17^{1}/_{2}$ miles. From Matrei the Tauerntal lies to the north and the Virgental to the east.

Matrei-in-Östtirol (population 4,300) is a small market town in a picturesque setting, cupped in the hand of the mountains. Its beauty is enhanced by house paintings and mosaics by Virgil Rainer, Fritz Tiefenthaler, and others. It is famous for its mountain guides who ensure the safety of climbers on the surrounding peaks, including the Venediger group, in which the Grossvenediger rises to 3,674m (12,051ft). Walking, tennis, horse riding are readily available and there is a camping ground on the south-western side of the village.

There are three churches in Matrei. The impressive parish church of St Alban (1780), with a fourteenth-century Gothic tower, was first mentioned in 1170. The ceiling frescoes are by Franz Anton Zeiller (1783) and the sculptures by Johann Praterer (1784). St Florian's chapel (the Bachkapelle) has a decorative baroque altar, and the little

The river Isel

Klaunzkapelle has a simple beauty. A mile to the south-west of the
village stands the church of St Nicholas which dates from the thirteenth

century. External frescoes are fourteenth century and St Christopher dates from 1530. The tower contains two choirs with Romanesque frescoes (1226). The upper choir has a wooden figure of St Nicholas (fifteenth century), and the lower choir has a figure of the Madonna and Child dating from 1400.

North of the village, on the road to Prossegg, there are two famous roadside shrines. The Schützenstöckl was erected in 1809 to commemorate the deaths of two French soldiers. The figure of St Sebastian, by Gottfried Feutsch of Virgen, is sheltered by a pitched roof supported by wooden pillars. A short distance further along the way is the Kreutzbühel-Stöckl. The exquisite proportions of the slender little steeple are in perfect unity with the body of the shrine. At Prossegg and Prossegg-Klamm there are excellent walks, the Steiner Waterfall, and St Anna's chapel.

Half a mile from the Kreutzbühel-Stöckl, east of the Prossegg road, stands Schloß Weissenstein, perched high on a lonely rock. Built in the twelfth century, and at one time the property of the Bishop of Salzburg, the castle is now a local history museum. Another collection of local artefacts is housed in the town hall.

On the south side of Matrei the Hildenweg provides lovely views across the valley; about 2 miles down Route 108 stands the Trattnerhof with its sixteenth-century chapel; and a short distance further is the 'Brühl', a moorland nature reserve of interest to birdwatchers and nature lovers. At **Bichl**, about a mile from Matrei, there is a Roman tomb dating from 200BC.

North of Matrei the main road rises rapidly to reach the toll booth for the Felbertauern Tunnel (5,304m, 17,397ft long) after 10 miles. About 2 miles earlier a road to the left leads to Matreier Tauernhaus (1,512m, 4,959ft), a starting point for mountain walking and climbing. Further along this narrow valley are Aussergschlöss and Innergschlöss, and the 'Tauernhöheweg' track which starts in the Zillertal.

West of Matrei the river Isel runs along the beautiful Virgen valley. The road rises steadily for 4¹/₂ miles to reach **Virgen** where the Gothic parish church (1516) contains an eighteenth-century altar dedicated to Sts Virgil and Rupert, and baroque figures by Johann Paterer. Nearby is the twelfth-century ruin of Burg Rabenstein with a chapel containing early Gothic frescoes. At **Göriach**, there is a chapel with Romanesque planform and Gothic figures. West of Virgen, at **Obermauer**, the pilgrimage church was rebuilt in 1456 but the tower is thirteenth century. Its beautiful reliefs, notable frescoes by Simon von Taisten, altars and statues from the fourteenth and fifteenth century are worth seeing. Welzelach is the site of Iron and Bronze Age settlements and excavation uncovered many prehistoric remains now on display in the Landesmuseum Ferdinandeum in Innsbruck.

Beyond Virgen the road rises again to **Prägraten** (population

The Kalsertal, the village of Kals and the Zolspitze

1,300), at the foot of the Grossvenediger mountain (3,674m, 12,051ft). The Gothic parish church (1500) has sixteenth-century frescoes in the choir. The road ends at the hamlet of Hinterbichl. Nearby is the Gumpach Waterfall, and it is only half an hour on foot to the 'Grossvenedigerblick' with its splendid panorama of the surrounding peaks. There are camping grounds at both Prägraten and Hinterbichl.

At Huben, south of Matrei, a side road rises via hairpin bends into the Kalsertal, and after 8 miles, reaches **Kals**, at the foot of the Grossglockner (3,797m, 12,454ft), where the Glocknerblick cableway goes up to 1,950m (6,396ft). It has two churches and a folk museum. The parish church is fifteenth and sixteenth century and has St Sebastian's chapel on the second floor of the tower, as well as frescoes from 1520. St George's church is fourteenth-century Romanesque/Gothic. Nearby is a fifteenth-century ruined castle, and the village has many old houses. It is a good starting point for wandering in the Grossglockner group, providing good access to the Kaprunertal and the Stubachtal. Kals is one of the principal ski resorts in East Tirol.

On the west side of the Iseltal from Huben lies the Defereggental, the valley of the river Schwarzach. At **Hopfgarten** steep footpaths to the south lead up to the Regenstein (2,891m, 9,482ft), and the Bockstein (2,805m, 9,200ft) peaks, and to several mountain lakes. **St Viet in Defereggen** has a late Gothic church and **St Leonhard** has a church (1464) with paintings by Simon von Taisten. At **St Jakob** (population 1,000) the parish church is fifteenth and sixteenth century but the

The parish church of Obertilliach in the Lesachtal

paintings in the dome and the stained glass windows are by Hans Oberkofler (1935). At the fork, the road to the right follows the Schwarzach river up to the Patscher Hütte (2 miles) and good walking country. The road to the left climbs up to the Staller Sattel Pass and the Italian border, 21 miles from Huben.

Beyond Huben Route 108 runs swiftly down the valley alongside the Isel, affording a panorama of the craggy peaks of the Lienzer Dolomites to the south-west. The clear waters of the river are a temptation to a flyfisherman. The road passes the ruined twelfth- and thirteenth-century Burg Kienburg before reaching **St Johann-im-Walde** which has a late Gothic parish church (1500). **Oberlienz** is 16 miles from Matrei and has a parish church with external frescoes from 1450, and an open-air museum. Lienz is just 1¹/₂ miles away.

THE PUSTERTAL

West of Lienz Route 100 follows the upper reaches of the river Drau, rising, at first gently then more steeply, to reach Sillian after 20 miles of the lovely scenery of the Pustertal. Some 3 miles further the road crosses the border with Italy.

At **Leisach** the church of St Michael has a winged altar by Josef Bachlechner (1923). It is also the beginning of the old mountain road — the Pustertaler Höchenstrasse — now designated as a 'gastronomic' route with twelve recommended eating places. A side road (toll) rises through hairpin bends to the Hochsteinhütte (2,057m, 6,747ft) which affords a wonderful view of the Lienzer Dolomites. Just beyond Leisach the road passes, on the right, the ruined Lienzer Klause with a late Gothic tower.

At **Thal** the fifteenth-century church of St Korbinian stands on a lonely hill above the valley. The high altar dates from 1660, and there are frescoes, a Gothic crucifix, and a fifteenth-century Madonna. But the main feature of the church are the three side altars. The Magdalenenaltar (1498) and the Korbinianaltar (1480) are by Friedrich Pacher (1440-1508). The Passionsaltar (1440) is attributed to the Brixen school and has an especially beautiful centre panel. The nearby church of St Ulrich was erected in the fifteenth century and refurbished in the baroque style in 1680. The side altar dedicated to St Paul is by Josef Adam Mölk (1762). From the middle of Thal a road leads north-west about 3 miles to **Oberassling** where there is a deer park.

Beyond Thal a small road to the right leads to the charming little baroque church of St Justina, sited on high ground in a small valley, which was built about 1500. The fresco of St Christopher, on the tower, dates from 1513, and the altar is early fifteenth century. At **Anras** the old parish church, now a baptistry and war memorial, was built about 1250, and has a winged altar from 1513, and a sixteenth-century bell tower. The newer church of St Stephan was built in 1755 by Franz de

Paula Penz and has frescoes by Martin Knoller and a rococo high altar by Anton Zoller (1755).

At **Abfaltersbach** there is an eighteenth-century parish church, and at **Abfaltern**, higher up on the right hand side of the valley, there is a beautiful Gothic church (1441), rebuilt in baroque style in 1765. The interior of the dome was painted by Josef Anton Zoller in 1769. The road rises steeply for the next 2 miles to reach **Strassen**. Here the church of St Jakobus (1460) has lovely frescoes in the choir and sanctuary by Master Leonhard of Brixen. The nearby Holy Trinity church dates from 1763 and was built by Thomas Mayr. The frescoes in the dome are by Franz Anton Zeiller (1768), and the high altar is by Johann Mitterwurzer, of Brixen (1778). There is also a Gothic church (1471) at Tessenberg with late fifteenth-century frescoes. At Strassen there is access to the 15-mile-long Pustertal high-level ski trail, and there is a folk theatre.

Beyond Strassen the village of **Panzendorf** has two churches. The baroque St Antonius is seventeenth century, and St Peter's (1331) is Gothic, with frescoes by Simon von Taister and a gilded and enamelled monstrance (1591) by Heinrich Egolf of Constance. Just after the village a road to the right leads up the delightful Villgratental with gradients up to 20 per cent (1 in 5). At the entrance to the valley is the ruined Schloß Heimfels which was built by the Count of Görz in the thirteenth century.

Sillian (population 2,000), 20 miles from Lienz, is a summer and winter resort. The parish church was originally Gothic (1435) but is now baroque (1760). The dome was painted by Josef Adam Mölk, and the twelve statues of the apostles are by Johann Paterer (eighteenth century). The figure of Mary and the Child Jesus on the high altar dates from 1450. Sillian also has a hang gliding school.

THE TILLIACHERTAL AND THE LESACHTAL
The road from Sillian to Kotschach-Mauthen is part of the Karnische Dolomitenstrasse which goes on down the Gailtal toward Villach. It follows Route 111, first up the short valley of the Gailbach, which discharges into the Drau, then over the watershed and down the upper valley of the Gail, which is known as the Tilliachertal, and down the Lesachtal.

The road rises steeply out of the Pustertal via hairpin bends which achieve a maximum gradient of 18 per cent (1 in 5). Six miles from Sillian it reaches **Kartitsch-Boden** with a Gothic church of St Leonhard (1386).

Enthusiastic walkers will be interested in the Karnischer Höhenweg 403 which extends for over 50 miles, close to the border with Italy, connecting ten mountain huts and refuges (up to 2,350m, 7,708ft) of the Carnic (Karnische) Alps. This highway begins near Wetlanbrunn Arnbach, a mile west of Sillian, may be accessed from various points along the Tilliachertal and the Lesachtal, crosses the Plöcken Pass, and ends at Nassfeld Pass. Walking time from the valley floor up to the nearest refuge varies from 1 to 3 hours. Refuge accommodation is usually available from about the end of June to the end of September. This well defined — red/white/red markers — pathway offers many opportunities for short walks, or the whole length may be covered in 7 to 9 days. The scenery amongst the high peaks is spectacular from dawn to dusk. In July and August look out for the heart-shaped base leaves and steel-blue flower heads of *Eryngium alpinum* near the Plöcken Pass, and the long spikes of slender purple flowers of *Wulfenia carinthiaca* near Nassfeld. Full details of Höhenweg 403 can be obtained from the tourist office in Kartitsch.

A saddle (1,525m, 5,002ft) is reached about $2^1/_2$ miles beyond Kartitsch and the road then runs down to **Obertilliach** (1,450m, 4,756ft). This pretty little village of wooden houses is a good starting point for walking in the Lienzer Dolomites. The parish church was built by Franz de Paula Penz (1762) on the site of a Gothic church of 1365. Anton Zoller and Josef Anton Zoller painted frescoes in St Ulrich's chapel (1764), and in St Nicholas' chapel there are frescoes by Simon von Taisten (late fifteenth century). At 18 miles the road crosses into Carinthia and enters the Lesachtal.

The pilgrimage church of Maria Schnee, at **Maria Luggau** dates from 1520 but was decorated in baroque style with painted vaulting and stucco in the eighteenth century. The altar is by Paul Huber of Innsbruck. The *Miraculous Image* (1513) is clad in traditional brocade. At **Wiesen** the church of St Radegund on the roadside is fifteenth century and has an outside fresco of St Christopher. On the left a road leads up to **Tuffbad** where the waters are said to be good for rheumatism and diabetes. **St Lorenzen** stands on a plateau high above the river and colourful paintings on the walls of the local farmhouses enhance the natural beauty of its setting. The Gothic parish church (1474) has frescoes and three carved figures of saints dating from 1500.

From St Lorenzen the road twists and switchbacks down the left-hand side of the valley above the Gail with the Lienzer Dolomites towering to the north and the Carnic Alps to the south. Gradients reach 18 per cent (1 in 5), the road is at times extremely narrow and should be driven with great care. Gothic/baroque churches may be seen at **Liesing**, **Kornat**, **Birnbaum**, and **St Jakob**. Thirty-six miles from Sillian the road reaches the market town of Kotschach-Mauthen, at the crossroads of Route 111 down the Gailtal, and Route 110 from Lienz via Oberdrauberg via the Plöcken Pass to Italy.

4 CARINTHIA

Carinthia (Karnten) is surprisingly undiscovered for the majority of English-speaking visitors to Austria. The most southerly of the eight provinces of Austria is a warm and sunny region, protected from cold northern air by the High Alps, and sharing the benefits of anticyclones over Italy. It extends for 100 miles along the borders with Italy and Yugoslavia and is separated from them by the southern limestone Alps — the Carnic Alps and the Karawanken group — with their unique alpine flora. Its 3,681sq miles consist largely of the central basin of the river Drau and its tributaries, notably the Möll, the Gail, the Gurk and the Lavant, which provide some of the best white-water canoeing in the world. It has some 200 lakes in which the waters reach summer temperatures in excess of 24°C (75°F). The larger of them — Wörther, Ossiacher, Millstatter, Weissen and Faaker — provide recreational activites for guests at the many resorts on their shorelines, yet those who look for peace can readily find it.

On the west side, the Lienz Dolomites provide awesome rock faces for the expert climber, and, to the north of them, Carinthia pushes out a finger along the Möll valley, between Salzburg and East Tyrol, to reach into the mountains of the Glockner group beyond Heiligenblut where all climbers can find challenge and satisfaction. On the east side the more modest Saualpe and Koralpe Mountains form the boundary with Styria.

The half-million people of Carinthia have a strong affinity with the Slavs who inhabited this area for many centuries. Today there is a significant minority who speak Slovene and in the schools of Carinthia Slovene is taught together with German. Carinthians give their allegiance to Austria while taking fierce pride in their own culture and traditions. As well as conserving their religious and artistic heritage, they also seek to protect the natural flora and fauna of the province — some of which is unique — and its beautiful landscape. Abbeys, cathedrals, and churches such as those at Gurk, Klagenfurt, St Paul, Millstatt, St Andrä, Thörl-Maglern, and St Leonhard in Lavanttal, are filled with a thousand years of artistic gems. Museums at Klagenfurt, Villach, and many smaller towns and villages, record the settlement of these warm valleys in prehistoric and Roman times, as well as the rise and fall of progress during the Middle Ages. Nature reserves and zoological and botanical gardens, such as those at Klagenfurt, Rosegg, and in the Villacher Alps, indicate a keen appreciation of nature.

The Romans, protecting their trade routes to the north, built many towns and military camps at strategic points in the region, and they often formed the nucleus for later settlements. After the end of the Roman Empire in 476 the Slavs, driven westward by the Avars, settled here and joined forces with Bavarians to drive off their oppressors. In the eighth and ninth centuries noble Saxons and others created an upper class which founded many religious houses and which developed into a number of ducal families. In 1335 rule over the region passed to the Habsburgs. At the end of the fifteenth century Hungarians and Turks made incursions into Carinthia and inflicted much damage; many churches were fortified, many were destroyed and had to be rebuilt. Trade and industry — especially coal mining, iron working and arms manufacture — developed under Empress Maria Theresa and her son Emperor Josef II.

St Veit an der Glan was the capital of the province until 1518 when Klagenfurt assumed that role. Of Carinthia's population of about 525,000, some 85,000 live in the capital. The city is known for its elegant architecture and for the wealth of cultural and historical resources contained in its churches and museums — especially notable are the cathedral, the Landhaus and the Landesmuseum — and in its long established theatre. Klagenfurt is easily reached by rail, road, and air and is an excellent centre for touring the lovely valleys and mountains, rivers and lakes, towns and villages of Carinthia.

Route 4a Lienz to Klagenfurt

Klagenfurt is 90 miles east of Lienz. Route 100 follows the river Drau to Villach where the A2 motorway provides a swift passage to the provincial capital of Carinthia. More enjoyable alternatives are available, however, if time and inclination permit, crossing the Gailtaler Alps and driving down the Gail valley to Villach.

THE LESACHTAL

Leaving Lienz on Route 100, signposted Spittal, the market town of **Oberdrauberg** (population 1,400) is reached after 13 miles. The fifteenth-century baroque parish church of St Oswald contains paintings by Brandstätter the Elder (1809). The church of St Leonhard at **Zwickenberg**, 2 miles to the north, has a beautiful panelled altar with paintings by Simon von Taisten.

Instead of going ahead on Route 100, take Route 110 to the right, signposted Kötschach. Ten easy hairpin bends take the tree-lined road up 362m (1,187ft) to the Gailberg Sattel with superb views back over the

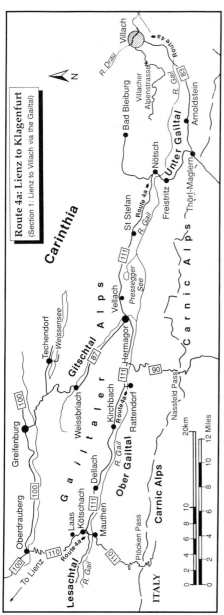

Route 4a: Lienz to Klagenfurt
(Section 1: Lienz to Villach via the Gailtal)

Carinthia

Drau valley. The road then descends with the high peaks of the Carnic Alps outlined ahead. A left-hand hairpin, followed by a right-hander, takes the road downhill, past the bus stops, to the village of **Laas**. Here, on the roadside, is the church of St Andreas (1535) with notable vaulting and a fragment of an external fresco of St Christopher (1520).

At 23 miles the road reaches **Kötschach-Mauthen** (population 3,600) at the head of the Ober Gailtal. This market community, and terminus of the railway from Villach, comprises the villages of Kötschach, on the north bank of the river, and Mauthen, on the south bank. In Kötschach the parish church of Our Lady is built on the site of an earlier edifice which was destroyed by the Turks. The net vaulting, executed by B. Firtaler in 1527, is remarkable. There are also late Gothic frescoes, baroque ceiling paintings, a classical high altar (1833), and rococo side altars. Mauthen is located on the site of _Loncium_, which was a staging post on the Roman road over the Plöcken Pass. The Romanesque parish church of St Mark, de-

A carved wooden drinking fountain in Carinthia

stroyed by the invading Turks, was rebuilt in 1478 and refurbished in baroque style in 1742. Of principal interest are the external frescoes which date from 1514.

THE OBER GAILTAL

Route 110 goes on to Italy via the Plöcken Pass. Route 111 (the Karnische Dolomitenstrasse) crosses it and runs alongside the railway track down the Gailtal. Follow the signpost Villach/Hermagor on Route 111 through **St Daniel**, a small resort with a late Gothic parish church. The valley ahead opens out between the Carnic Alps to the south and the Gailtaler Alps to the north, and the villages cling to the warmer

A frescoed roadside shrine, or Bildstück, *typical of southern Austria*

northern side of the valley. At **Dellach-im-Gailtal** there are remains of
the Celtic-Romano settlement of *Gurina*. Discoveries from the eighth
century BC have been made, including the site of a Roman temple

A mile further and the black onion dome of the sixteenth century
church at **Grafendorf** appears on the left of the road which goes on to

pass Gundersheim and reach **Reisach** at 32 miles. The nearby Schloß Schönberg is sixteenth to eighteenth century. At **Kirchbach** the parish church of St Martin stands alongside the road. It dates from 1296 and has late baroque stucco decoration and ceiling paintings. Beyond Kirchbach the road continues gently down the left bank of the river Gail past pretty *Gasthöfe* and through Treßdorf, Waidegg, Jenig — across the river from Rattendorf — to the junction with Route 90 at 39 miles. Route 90 crosses the railway and the river to Tröpolach and then ascends to the Nassfeld Pass and into Italy. Five miles further and Route 111 reaches Hermagor.

Hermagor (population 5,400) is a pleasant little town and a convenient centre for walking holidays. The parish church, dedicated to Sts Hermagoras and Fortunatus, dates from 1484. The keystone painting of 1485, in the nave, depicts Christ supporting the church. The altars are baroque, the figures on the main altar being by Johann Paterer (1749). The panelled altar in the south chapel dates from 1510, and there are fourteenth-century murals in the choir. The Gailtal local history museum is located in Schloß Möderndorf, 2 miles to the south, and has prehistoric finds, as well as a Martin Luther Bible from 1541. There are five camp sites in the vicinity of Hermagor.

THE GITSCHTAL AND THE WEISSENSEE

An enjoyable excursion from Hermagor takes the road (Route 87) up the Gitschtal and alongside the small river Gösseringbach past farm land and orchards. After Moschach the road passes the ruined castle Grünburg, and reaches **St Lorenzen-im-Gitschtal** where the parish church has notable fourteenth-century frescoes. About 2$^1/_2$ miles further along the scenic road lies the village of **Weißbriach** with its two churches. The evangelical church stands on a hill on the east side and dates from 1782. The little late Gothic church of St Johann (1520), on the west side, has an idyllic setting amongst the meadows, and contains frescoes from the seventeenth century. Weißbriach is a health resort with steam and mud baths. It is also a beautiful location for a holiday.

Beyond Weißbriach the road winds up (gradients up to 12 per cent, 1 in 8), out of the Gitschtal, to Kreuzbergseehohe at 1,077m (3,533ft), then descends rapidly. About 4$^1/_2$ miles from Weißbriach a road to the right leads to the **Weissensee** (930m, 3,050ft). In its lovely setting between low hills, the long (7$^1/_2$ miles), narrow (half-mile) lake is very beautiful. Along the north side, in Praditz, Oberdorf, Gatschach and Techendorf, there are many small hotels; on the south side, across the road bridge, there is a large camp site. The lake provides for boating, fishing, and swimming. It is also a good centre for walking and touring. Beyond Techendorf the road ends at **Neusach**.

Return to Route 87 and turn right. The road twists downhill (gradients up to 15 per cent, 1 in 7) through Weisach to **Greifenburg** (population 2,000), 17 miles from Hermagor, on Route 100 from Lienz to Spittal. This market town is a good centre for walking and touring in the Kreuzeck group and the Gailtaler Alps. It has interesting sixteenth- to eighteenth-century houses and a late Gothic parish church (1521).

THE UNTER GAILTAL

Below Hermagor Route 111 continues down the valley. At **Vellach**, a road on the right goes down to the Pressegger See, a small lake popular for swimming in its warm waters. The lake road rejoins the main road before **Köstendorf** which has a late Gothic church. At **Nötsch** a road on the left leads past Schloß Wasserleonburg (fourteenth to sixteenth century), 6 miles up to **Bad Bleiberg**, a health resort in the Fuggertal with its seventeenth-century parish church of St Florian. There a track to the south leads up to the highest pilgrimage church in Europe, the church of Mary on the Holy Rock on the Dobratsch (2,166m, 7,104ft), in the Villacher Alps. Route 111 crosses the Gail to **Feistritz** which has a late Gothic church with fifteenth-century frescoes.

The road bends sharply out of Feistritz. About $3\frac{1}{2}$ miles later take the right fork onto Route 83, to **Thörl-Maglern**, a mile from the border with Italy. Turn right onto the main road then immediately left to cross the fields to the parish church of St Andreas which contains wonderful wall paintings dating from 1470-80 by Thomas von Villach. They depict, in dramatic and colourful form, figures of the saints and Biblical scenes.

Return to Route 83 and continue across the junction with the A2 motorway to **Arnoldstein** (population 6,000). The church of St Lambert is late Gothic. It has notable headstones in the graveyard, and the chapel of the Cross has sixteenth-century frescoes and a stone crucifix from 1517. On the edge of the town are the ruins of a former Benedictine abbey which was damaged by the Turks in 1476 and destroyed by fire in 1883. There is also a local history museum in the town.

VILLACH TO KLAGENFURT (see map page 125)

At 74 miles, after recrossing the motorway, the road enters **Villach** (population 53,000), second largest town in Carinthia. Evidence has been found of Stone Age settlement on this site, and its importance as a crossing point on the river Drau brought the Romans here. It achieved town status in 1240, and today is a bustling urban community.

The centre of the town is the Hauptplatz which contains notable sixteenth-century houses — including the one-time residence of the famous Doctor Theophrastus Bombastus von Hohenberg, known as Paracelsus (1493-1541) (see Salzburg) — and a plague column from 1739. At the southern end, elevated above the Hauptplatz, is the fourteenth-century Gothic church of St Jakob. The 95m-high (312ft) tower on the west side is linked to the body of the church only by an archway. The interior is spacious, the ten round, red pillars rising to

The lakeside promenade at Velden on the Wörther See

ornate vaulting and a beautiful baroque ceiling. The high altar is decorated in stucco (1748) and has a Gothic crucifix (1502) bearing a life-size figure of Christ. On the south wall of the choir there is a late fifteenth-century fresco of St Christopher. In the three fifteenth- and sixteenth-century side chapels there are tombs, frescoes and stained glass. The red marble tomb of Balthasar von Weissbriach (1484) is by H. Valkenauer of Salzburg.

Around the corner from St Jakob (through the narrow alleyways with their little shops) in Widmanngasse, is the municipal museum which contains collections from Bronze Age and Roman periods, and historic art works, including paintings from the fifteenth century by Friedrich von Villach and Thomas von Villach. South of St Jakob, off 10-Oktober

Strasse in Schiller Park, there is a relief model of Carinthia constructed on a scale of 1:10,000 which provides a bird's eye view of the province.

The twin-towered church of St Peter is the only Italianate, domed church in Carinthia. It was rebuilt in 1738. The interior is baroque with a notable high altar. The altar of the chapel of the Holy Cross has a wrought-iron screen from 1774.

Some 2 miles south of the town centre is **Warmbad Villach**, a health resort, close to the Ossiacher See, Faaker See, and three other smaller lakes. Regular boat services operate on the river Drau, from Villach, and on the Ossiacher See, from St Andrä. The Villacher Alps, to the south-east, also provide summer and winter activities for the visitor. The Villacher Alpenstrasse toll road leads up to the Dobratsch

Schloß Hallegg on the road from Krumpendorf to Wölfitz

(2,166m, 7,104ft) ridge. At Parkplatz 6, at 1,500m (4,920ft), there is a clifftop alpine rock garden with a superb collection of about 800 species including the very rare *Wulfenia carnathiaca*.

The A2 motorway provides rapid transit from Villach to Klagenfurt, but take Route 83 for a more leisurely pace. About $7^1/_2$ miles out of Villach at **Rosegg** (south of Route 83) there is a nature park with monkeys, red deer and birds. **Velden** (popuation 7, 500) is 10 miles from Villach, at the western end of the Wörther See. It is a delightful resort, its streets lined with chestnut trees, and has a lakeside promenade. The lake provides opportunities for swimming, sailing, windsurfing, cruising, and fishing. A regular boat service connects nine landing stages along both the north and south shores of the lake and terminates at Klagenfurt. Shore-based entertainments include tennis, walking and a casino. Velden is a good centre for touring and for relaxing holidays. Close to the water's edge is the Renaissance Schloß Velden, built in 1590 by B. Khevenhüller and now a hotel. It has a notable entrance gateway and four hexagonal towers. North of the town, in a game park, is Schloß Mageregg which originates from 1590 but was redesigned in 1841.

From Velden Route 83 runs alongside the railway track. At **Pörtschach** (population 2,500) there is also a waterside promenade and the Renaissance Schloß Leonstein is now a hotel where a statue commemorates the fact that Brahms was a guest. Pörtschach is the venue for sailing regattas, waterskiing, and tennis tournaments.

At 20 miles the road reaches **Krumpendorf** (population 2,500). The parish church of St Ulrich is Romanesque and has a beautiful archway over the door. In the centre of the town there is a *Schloß* (1740) set in lovely parkland.

After 29 miles the road enters the provincial capital Klagenfurt.On the road around the south side of the Wörther See the picturesque resort of **Maria Wörth** stands on a small peninsula. The parish church of St Primus has a remarkable altar from 1658 with a figure of the Virgin Mary dating from 1420. The altar panels in the side chapel are also notable and date from 1470. The nearby Rosenkranz church is Romanesque and has lovely eleventh-century frescoes.

KLAGENFURT

Klagenfurt means 'ford of lament', a reminder of times when travellers risked life and limb crossing the treacherous marshes and the river Glan at the eastern end of the Wörther See. It became the site of Celtic and Roman settlements and grew into a fortified town until, after a treaty with Napoleon in 1809, its walls were pulled down and its moat filled in to create an inner green belt. The city suffered badly from air raids during World War II but was soon restored to become a modern city, and to continue its role — which it has had since 1518 — as the administrative, economic, and cultural centre of the province of Carinthia, and the seat of the Bishop of Gurk.

Klagenfurt is a city of arcades, alleyways, and courtyards; of wide squares and gardens, old houses, churches, and markets. It is linked to the Wörther See by the Europa Park, a triangle of entertainments including a promenade and bathing beach. At the heart of the Carinthian basin, it is surrounded by lakes, which help to cool the hot summers. It is easily reached by road and rail, and there is an airport on the north-east edge of the town. Demand for accommodation is high during trade fairs and exhibitions. All kinds of sports are catered for and there is a nearby nature reserve with 40 miles of marked footpaths. It is a convenient centre for touring eastern Carinthia.

The tourist information centre, in the **Rathaus** on the west side of the Neuer Platz is a convenient starting point for a walking tour. Originally a Renaissance palace of the counts of Rosenberg, the Rathaus dates from 1650. In the courtyard there is a statue of a fisherman (1606) which commemorates the old fish market. The spacious Neuer Platz, lined by tall trees, was originally a place of execution; now it is a pleasant resting place where the life of the city passes by. In its centre is the unusual Lindwurm (1605), the city's symbol, a stone dragon confronting a man with a large club. At the east end of the square is the **Maria Theresa monument** of 1873. Around the perimeter of the square the old buildings are mostly seventeenth century, notably No 4 with an arcaded courtyard; No 9, an old pharmacy with stucco ceilings; No 10, Longo House, with Khevenhüller coat of arms; and No 13, Porcia palace, former home of Prince Porcia.

Leave Neuer Platz on the north side via Dr Lemisch Platz where there is a fountain and statue of Duke Bernhard of Spannheim (1205-56), the city's founder. Bear left into the pedestrianised Kramergasse which leads into Alter Platz. Here there are many old houses. No 30, **Goess palace**, from 1738, has a column façade, coat of arms, a staircase and grill, and a stone balustrade. No 31 is **Golden Goose House**, which appears on records dated 1489, where, in the arcaded courtyard, there is a relief of a centaur with women, probably sixteenth century. No 1, the **old town hall**, formerly the Weizer palace but now the Rosenberg palace, has a coat of arms above a columned portal, and on the left of the doorway, a standard measuring rod for the market traders.

In the corner of the Alter Platz, between Nos 30 and 31 is the courtyard entrance to the **Landhaus**, one of the most important buildings in the city. It was built in 1574, by H. Freymann and J.A.Verda in the German Renaissance style. The two large towers with double onion domes are very powerful. The large Hall of Arms (Wappensaal) is magnificent, with 665 gilded and colourful coats of arms creating a brilliant spectacle alongside the ceiling paintings by Joseph Ferdinand Fromiller (1740), and in the small Wappensaal there are another 298 coats of arms by the same artist. The provincial parliament meets in the Landhaus, and concerts and plays are presented in the courtyard.

On the north side of Alter Platz a passageway runs from No 34 through a three-sided courtyard to 20 Pfarrplatz and the **parish church of St Ägyd**. The original thirteenth-century church was destroyed by an earthquake in 1690. The onion-topped tower (1733) is 92m (302ft) high and the city's tallest building. It contains a notable painting in the choir by Fromiller, an altarpiece by Anton Cusetti (1761), and ceiling paintings by Joseph Mölk (1761).

Leave the Pfarrplatz via Theatergasse and at the end turn right to the **city theatre** which dates from 1808 although there has been a theatre on this site for over 250 years. The programme of events extends throughout the year. Across the plaza is the **Stadthaus** with its classical three-cornered gable, and along Radetzky Strasse is the art gallery.

From the theatre turn left into the busy Ursulinengasse, pass Herrengasse on the left, and walk to Heiligen Geist Platz, which is the bus station. On the north side is the **church of the Holy Ghost**. This Gothic church, first mentioned in 1355, has a font dating from 1623, altar panels from 1635 by Lorenz Glaber, and stone reliefs of six coats of arms including those of the Abbot of Ossiach. Cross Ursulinengasse to return to Neuer Platz via Wiesbaden Strasse. Note the entrance archway to the Renaissance house at No 3 and its arcaded courtyard. Gurk House, at No 5, was built in 1756 as a town house for Gurk abbey and the coat of arms of the chapter appear on the gateway.

Go ahead along the north side of the Neuer Platz into Burg Gasse.

Springtime in the Neuer Platz, Klagenfurt

No 8 was built in 1586 by J.A.Verda. During the seventeenth and eighteenth centuries it was the town residence of the Burggrafen. The courtyard is surrounded by two-storeyed arcades, and in the chapel (1734) there is a fresco by Fromiller. On the first floor is the **Carinthian gallery** (Kärntner Landesgalerie) which has a collection of about 750 paintings, 2,500 sketches, and 100 sculptures by nineteenth- and twentieth-century Carinthian artists.

From Burg Gasse turn into Domgasse and walk three blocks to Domplatz. The **cathedral of Sts Peter and Paul** was built in 1578-91 as a Protestant church. In 1604 it was acquired by the Jesuits, and in 1787 became the cathedral of the prince-bishopric of Gurk. The interior is said to be the earliest example of a pilastered hall in Austria, and has three arcaded galleries which, together with the vaulting, create an impression of great space. The baroque high altar (1752) has fine paintings by Daniel Gran, and the Christuskapelle side chapel has a painting by Paul Troger (1726). The ceiling paintings are by Fromiller, and the walls of the choir bear frescoes by Suitberg Lobisser (1928). In the galleries the stucco decoration is by K. Pittner (1725).

Adjacent to the cathedral is the **diocesan museum**, a rich collection

Coats of arms in the Wappensaal of the Landhaus, Klagenfurt

of religious art from the twelfth to eighteenth centuries. From the west door of the cathedral, cross Karfreit Strasse and turn left into Lidmansky

Gasse. No 8, on the left, is **Golden Fountain House**, part of the former Jesuit barracks. Go ahead into Benediktiner Platz where there is a large fruit and vegetable market. House No 3 has a beautiful inner courtyard.

It is a short walk along Kaufmann Gasse to Neuer Platz and the end of the double-circular walking tour.

Around Klagenfurt

Two miles west of Neuer Platz, along Villacher Strasse, another tourist information centre is located alongside a triangular entertainment complex called **Europa Park**. At the apex, in the famous Minimundus, more than 150 models (on a scale of 1:25) of well known buildings from all over the world, as well as a model ship and a miniature railway, make up a mini-world in which the Statue of Liberty stands alongside the Taj Mahal. In July and August there are folk concerts each Wednesday evening at 8pm and the exhibition is floodlit.

Adjacent to Minimundus is the reptile zoo which has a collection of mambas, cobras, rattlesnakes, crocodiles, giant turtles, as well as an insectarium with flying spiders, black widows, etc, and a 'House of Horror'. On Wednesday and Saturday, 3pm is feeding time for the piranhas. Nearby is a planetarium. Note that, about a mile to the south, along Wörthersee Südufer Strasse, there is a **nature park** with deer, ocelots, wild sheep, and pony rides.

Across the road from Minimundus there are formal gardens, sculptures, fountains, grassland, a small lake with swans, and open space. On the bank of the **Wörther See** there are boat houses, jetties, a marina, a promenade, restaurants, a camp site, and the largest public beach in Austria. This is Klagenfurt-on-See!

About half a mile north-west of Neuer Platz, along Radetzky Strasse, are the **botanical gardens** and the **Bergbaumuseum** which is housed in a World War II air-raid shelter tunnelled into the rock face. They are on the edge of the wooded Kreuzbergl Park which offers walking and riding, an observatory, a bear zoo, and a baroque church with a high altar by Fromiller.

To the south of the city, some $3\frac{1}{2}$ miles along Rosentaler Strasse, is the Cistercian abbey of **Viktring** which was founded in 1142, by Bernhard von Spanheim, and dissolved in 1786. The abbey church, a late Romanesque, pillared basilica, is notable for its beautiful stained glass windows over the choir which date from 1400.

Route 4b   Klagenfurt to Spittal

KLAGENFURT TO FELDKIRCHEN

The quickest road from Klagenfurt to Spittal is via the A2 and A10 motorways, or alternatively, Routes 83 and 100 are fast principal highways.

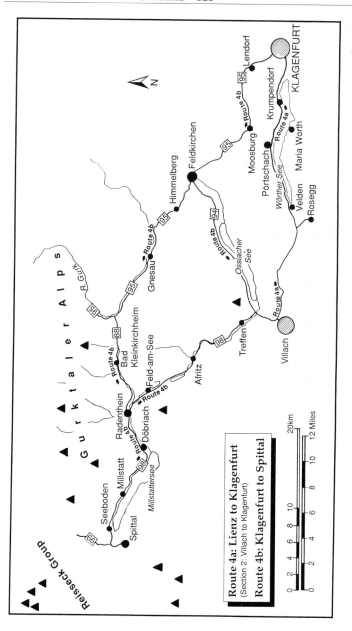

Route 4a: Lienz to Klagenfurt
(Section 2: Villach to Klagenfurt)

Route 4b: Klagenfurt to Spittal

Minimindus, Klagenfurt

A more leisurely journey can be made via Feldkirchen and Millstatt.

Leave Klagenfurt on Route 95 to **Lendorf** where the Romanesque-Gothic church has Roman statues and reliefs. On the east side of the village is the nineteenth-century Schloß Mageregg. This area abounds with castles. At Wölfnitz the road to the left, toward Krumpendorf, leads to Schloß Hallegg (thirteenth to sixteenth century) and Schloß Seltenheim (restored in 1848). The road to the right leads to Schloß Pitzelstätten (1529) and Schloß Ehrenbichl (seventeenth century). Five miles further on is Schloß Ratzenegg, from the fourteenth century, on a rocky outcrop.

Moosburg, 10 miles from Klagenfurt, is an old town. The *Schloß* stands on the site of a ninth-century palace in which the future Emperor

Faded frescoes on the little church at Faning, near Moosburg

Arnulf of Carinthia was born. The ruin of a tenth- and eleventh-century tower stands on a nearby hill. The interior of the parish church of St Michael was redesigned, and redecorated in baroque style, in 1769. The altarpiece may be the work of J.F. Fromiller. There are notable Roman stones let into the outer wall, and a Carolingian tracery stone in the west wall of the churchyard. There are also remarkable coats of arms on the tombs. Two miles north of Moosburg, in the hamlet of **Tigring**, the church has fourteenth-century frescoes. Half a mile east from Tigring there are footpaths through protected woodland around a small lake — the Strussnig See, and at **Faning** there is a delightful little church with a fading fresco and a sundial on the south wall.

Beyond Moosburg the road runs alongside the river Glan and after 16 miles arrives at **Feldkirchen** (population 10,000). The parish church of the Assumption is Romanesque with a Gothic choir. It has thirteenth-century frescoes, a sixteenth-century crucifix on the high altar, and a Gothic winged side altar (1510). In the Hauptplatz there are some fine sixteenth-century houses and a Mariensäule of 1760 as well as a seventeenth-century fountain.

From Feldkirchen there are two possible routes to Radenthein: Routes 95/88 via Gnesau and Bad Kirchenheim, or Routes 94/98 via the Ossiacher See and Afritz.

FELDKIRCHEN VIA GNESAU TO RADENTHEIN

Two miles out of Feldkirchen on Route 95 is the village of **Pichlern**. Its late Gothic church has a lovely winged altar from 1520. The road then rises through rolling upland country before descending into **Himmelberg**. Here Schloß Piberstein was the residence of the Lodron family. Paris Lodron became Archbishop of Salzburg in 1662. The Lodron coat of arms can be seen on the parapet of the organ gallery of the parish church which is eleventh-century Romanesque and has baroque frescoes.

After Himmelberg the road rises through several sharp hairpin bends into the upper Gurktal and, 25 miles from Klagenfurt, reaches **Gnesau**, a village of old farmhouses. The parish church of St Leonhard is Gothic and was formerly fortified, with gun-slits in the walls of the churchyard. From Gnesau the road follows the river up the valley passing the white buildings of the former Carmelite convent of Zedlitzdorf. At 30 miles, at Patergassen (1,065m, 3,493ft), Route 95 goes ahead through Ebene Reichenau and over the steep Turracher Höhe Pass (1,783m, 5,848ft) to Predlitz. The road to Radenthein, Route 88, goes to the left.

The road now climbs out of the Gurktal and drops into another valley. Shortly, it passes a golf course and enters **Bad Kleinkirchheim** (population 1,800). This attractive village is a popular health resort and ski centre. The thermal springs feed a modern complex of baths and treatment rooms, and the waters are said to be good for rheumatic and nervous complaints. It is also a good centre for walking on the Nockgipfel (up to 2,331m, 7,646ft). With St Oswald, $2^1/_2$ miles to the north, it is the largest winter sports centre in Carinthia. There are eighteen ski-lifts, and two chairlifts. The parish church of St Ulrich (1743) is baroque. At the west end of the village is the pilgrimage church of St Katharine-im-Bade which is fifteenth century, and is built over a thermal spring in the crypt. It has a winged altar from 1510. The late Gothic church of St Oswald has frescoes from 1514 and an altar from 1678.

Following the river, the road descends rapidly into the market town of **Radenthein** (population 7,000) and the junction with Route 98, 23 miles from Feldkirchen.

FELDKIRCHEN VIA AFRITZ TO RADENTHEIN

Alternatively, follow Route 94 in a south-westerly direction from Feldkirchen. After Steindorf the road runs along the north bank of the Ossiacher See for 6 miles passing through Bodensee and Sattendorf. About

14 miles from Feldkirchen turn right onto Route 98 to skirt the foot of the Kanzehöhe (1,489m, 4,884ft) to **Treffen**. The parish church of St Maximilian has a Romanesque-Gothic tower and a fifteenth-century choir. Nearby Schloß Grottenegg was built in 1691.

At **Afritz** there is a fifteenth-century Gothic church after which the road descends gently past the Afritzer See. From the top end of the next lake — the Feld See — there is a lovely view of **Feld-am-See**. This is an excellent resort for both summer and winter holidays. In addition to water activities there are facilities for tennis, archery, keep-fit, fishing, and walking up to 2,100m (6,888ft) on the Nockberge. Accommodation includes — with Afritz — five camp sites. Just 2$^1/_2$ miles beyond Feld-am-See, and 27 miles from Feldkirchen, the road reaches Radenthein and joins Route 88 from Patergassen.

Radenthein (population 7,000) is a market and industrial town with a large magnesite works alongside the road. The seventeenth-century parish church of St Nikolaus is Romanesque-Gothic and has a splendid eighteenth-century high altar.

RADENTHEIN TO SPITTAL

Route 98 then bypasses Döbriach at the eastern end of the Millstatter See. Along the north bank of the lake there are lovely views and the road reaches Millstatt, 8 miles from Radenthein.

Millstatt (population 2,000) is tucked into the foot of a partly wooded bluff which runs the whole length of the Millstatter See, with the resorts of Delach, Presenthein, and Techendorf clinging to the edge of the lake. Behind it runs a terrace, perhaps a mile wide, which bears the pleasant little villages of Matzeldorf, Sappl, Gortschach, Lammersdorf, Granitsch, Ober-Millstatt, and Gössering. The northern boundary of this shelf is formed by the peaks of the Nockgebiet, which rise to 2,100m (6,888ft). On the south side, the lake is separated from the Drau valley by low hills. To the north-west, beyond Spittal, the rugged mountains of the Reisseck and Kreuzeck groups can be seen.

This summer resort is enjoying increasing popularity. Around the former Benedictine abbey the town extends down to the tranquil waters of the lake. A wide range of accommodation includes two camp sites. There are schools for sailing, windsurfing, and water skiing; facilities for riding, fishing, tennis, and mini golf; and courses in painting and sketching. Music plays a very important part in the life of the community. A programme of concerts by Austrian and international artistes starts in March and continues until October. Millstatt is also a convenient centre for exploring Carinthia.

The abbey was founded in the eleventh century and dissolved in 1469. In the sixteenth century it was the residence of the Order of the Knights of St George who built towers and walls to keep out the Turks. The beautiful cloister is twelfth century, has intriguing fragments of frescoes, and notable columns and capitals carved to depict demons in human and animal form. Carolingian guilloche stones, from the ninth century, depicting pagan symbols, have been set into the walls of the gateway from the lovely arcaded courtyard of the abbey to the church.

The abbey church is an eleventh-century pillared basilica of generous proportions. On the churchyard gate there are large Gothic frescoes from 1490. The twin towers of the west front were built in 1170, and in the porch there is a Romanesque doorway. The side chapels contain the sixteenth-century tombs of the Grand Masters of the Order of the Knights of St George, and, in the right-hand side chapel the fresco of the *Last Judgement* is by U. Görtschacher of Villach. It is one of the most significant works of Renaissance art in Austria.

From Millstatt the road runs along the lake 2¹/₂ miles to **Seeboden** (population 5,000), an attractive resort with a park leading down to the Millstatter See and a lakeside promenade. Beyond the town Route 98 meets Route 99. Turn left to Spittal which is 14 miles from Radenthein, and 53 miles from Klagenfurt via Gnesau, or 57 miles via Afritz.

Spittal-an-der-Drau (population 15,000) lies at the confluence of the Lieser and the Drau rivers. Little remains of the original twelfth-century town but the Hauptplatz is bounded by elegant sixteenth- and seventeenth-century houses, including, at No 9, a late Gothic arcaded house. On the corner of the Bogengasse is the notable Petzlhaus which has a late baroque façade from 1780. At the western end of the Hauptplatz, on a corner of the town park, is Schloß Porcia which was built from 1530 to 1600 for Count Gabriel von Salamanca, who was treasurer to the Archduke Ferdinand. It is famous for its beautiful arcaded courtyard, with its graceful stairs and balustrades, where a programme of dramatic arts is presented each summer from July into September. On the second floor is a local history museum which has a collection of memorabilia associated with life in the palace from 1550 to 1900. To the south of the town a cable car goes up to the Goldeck (2,142m, 7,026ft) which provides skiing in the winter and hang-gliding in the summer. The Lieser river, along with its tributaries, has a high reputation for whitewater canoeing and is the annual venue for international competitions.

Route 4c   Spittal to Neumarkt

(see maps pages 131 and 135)

Leave Spittal via the Neuer Platz and take Route 99 northbound, signposted Salzburg. The road winds up the Lieser valley through successive basins and gorges with the A10 motorway high above. After 9¹/₂ miles bear left into **Gmünd** (population 2,500). The town centre is reached over a narrow bridge over the river Malta and through an archway in one of four defensive towers. In the delightful town square

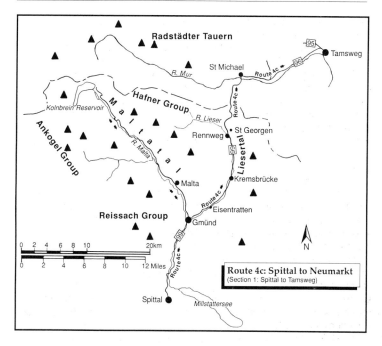

Route 4c: Spittal to Neumarkt
(Section 1: Spittal to Tamsweg)

houses from the fifteenth to eighteenth centuries surround a Trinity column of 1690. There are two castles. South-east of the town is the New Castle (Neue Schloß), of 1654, once owned by Count Lodron. In the gardens there are a pair of heraldic lions in stone which he brought from Schloß Mirabell in Salzburg. There is also a bust of Ferdinand Porsche who resided in Gmünd, and whose achievements are com- memorated in the Porsche automobile museum. The Old Castle (Alten Schloß) was built in 1506 by Archbishop Leonhard von Keutschach of Salzburg and today houses a local history museum. Pankratiuskirche, in the Hintere Gasse, is thirteenth century and has a lovely thirteenth-century arched window in the south wall. Adjacent is the Pancras Tower (1488) which is late Gothic and bears the coat of arms of the Habsburgs. Nearby is the fourteenth- and fifteenth-century Antoniusspital which   has frescoes from about 1400. North of the town square the church of Maria Himmelfahrt (1339) has a beautiful choir with rib vaulting and a Gothic nave. The painting on the baroque high altar is by Jakob Zanussi (1722). The life-size figures of Sts Peter and Paul, beside the altar, and the figures on the walls of the choir are also remarkable. The two side altars and the pulpit are eighteenth century.

THE MALTATAL

For an exceptionally scenic excursion take the road which runs north-west of Gmünd up the Maltatal. The road follows the river through meadowland between the wooded sides of the valley with occasional glimpses of snow-clad peaks. On the left is the 'Diana' wildlife park and zoo which has lions, tigers, monkeys and birds. In the village of **Malta** (838m, 2,749ft) the parish church has notable fourteenth-century paintings and a thirteenth-century charnel house. After the hamlet of Brandstatt the valley is rock-strewn and narrows rapidly, and the lovely Fallerfall is followed by the Schlierfall and a series of waterfalls. Shortly the road reaches the toll booth where a footpath alongside the Gasthaus Falleralm leads to another waterfall.

After the toll booth the road is a marvellous feat of engineering. On two tunnels there is one-way passage controlled by traffic lights. The road goes through a hairpin bend inside one of the tunnels! Gradients are up to 13 per cent (1 in 7.5) but neither cars nor coaches have any difficulty. The cliffs and boulders of the ravine create wild scenery of a kind rare even in Austria. At the top of the valley the Kölnbrein dam contains a reservoir surrounded by the peaks of the Ankogel and the Hafner groups which rise up to 3,360m (11,021ft) (Hochalmspitze, to the south). The lake is at 1,920m (6,298ft) which is 1,180m (3,870ft) above Gmünd, 20 miles away.

At the dam there are car parks and a rotund hotel with two restaurants. There are eighteen marked footpaths, but the walking is most suitable for experienced mountaineers. On the return journey refreshments can be obtained at several places such as the excellent Gasthof Almrausch.

THE LIESERTAL

Back on Route 99 the road runs alongside the river Lieser and below the motorway viaducts. Over on the right appears the red onion top of the church at **Eisentratten**, which derives its name from the iron works that once stood there. The valley is steep-sided and narrow at Leoben, and the road winds through **Kremsbrücke** where the first blast furnace in Austria was built in 1541. The little church of St Johannes dates from 1465 and has a late Gothic painting (1513) in the west gallery. At **Rennweg** the valley opens out into a wide basin. The parish church of St Peter is late Gothic with a beautiful baroque interior. About a quarter of a mile off the road, on the right, is **St Georgen** with its attractive church on the hillside. The hamlet is filled with the sound of mechanical saws cutting planks from slender tree trunks. The motorway disappears into a tunnel over on the left but Route 99 sweeps to the right and rises steadily (gradient 15 per cent, 1 in 7) as the mountains close into what seems to be a dead end. At 23 miles, leaving the Liesertal behind, the road reaches the Katschberghöhe (1,641m, 5,382ft) and the border

Waterfall in the Malta valley

between Carinthia and Land Salzburg.

The road then descends steeply (gradient 16 per cent, 1 in 6) with good views of the Lungau, and of the limestone peaks of the Radstädter Tauern, to cross the river Mur to **St Michael-im-Lungau** (population 3,000), a summer resort at the foot of the Speiereck (2,411m, 7,908ft). There has been a market here since 1416 and the Romanesque parish church was first mentioned in 1147. In the portico there is a Roman tombstone and three busts. It has beautiful frescoes in the choir from the thirteenth and fourteenth centuries. The high altar dates from 1908 and the baroque side altar from 1731. The two-storeyed, octagonal, domed Wolfgang chapel in the churchyard is a fourteenth-century ossuary. The town of **St Martin** has Roman origins and excavations have revealed fragments of a wall with a tomb from the second century AD.

A mile beyond St Martin turn right off Route 99 onto Route 96 to **Tamsweg** (population 5,000) (see map page 135). The history of the town goes back to 1160. The sixteenth-century houses in the market place are reminders of the prosperity which derived from trade in iron and salt. The parish church dates from 1741. The interior is rococo, and the large altar has paintings by Gregor Lederwasch. In the Barbaraspitalkirche there is a magnificent baroque altar from 1702, and a late Gothic figure of a saint from 1520. The Lungauer local history museum has a folklore collection and Roman relics. South-west of the town is the church of St Leonhard, founded in 1433, which is one of the most important pilgrimage churches in Austria. In a sequence of stained glass windows (1430-50) the famous Gold Window, which depicts the Apostles, is magnificent. The baroque high altar dates from 1660; the frescoes on the choir wall from 1433; and the lovely carved choir stall in the south chapel from 1450.

Leave Tamsweg on Route 95 across the bridge over the Mur and turn left at the junction. The road rises onto the right-hand side of the valley and passes through wooded country with the river Mur glistening on the left below. At Madling the little valley of the Thomatal goes off to the right. Burg Finstergrün appears on the right ahead and a mile later the road reaches **Ramingstein** (population 1,500) where there is white-water canoeing. Burg Finstergrün was built in the twelfth century, restored in the Gothic style in 1901, and today is a youth hostel.

The road continues down the wooded valley, crosses from Land Salzburg into Styria, and enters **Predlitz** (population 1,200). In the parish church there is a painting by Gregor Lederwasch. Here Route 95 goes to the right and up to the Turracher Höhe Pass via Ebene Reichenau and Gnesau to Feldkirchen. Take Route 97, to the left, to follow the Murtal.

Stadl has a fifteenth-century church, and the nearby Renaissance Schloß Goppelsbach was built in 1595. Here the road crosses the river onto the left-hand side of the valley. At **St Ruprecht** the fourteenth-century Gothic parish church has eighteenth-century altars and a beautiful seventeenth-century organ loft. At **Bodendorf** barrages in the river create a succession of ponds which fish may be seen rising to feed on the surface insects. At **St Georgen-ob-Murau** the fifteenth-century parish church has a winged altar (1524) with a painting by Konrad von Friesach (1450). At 61 miles the road enters Murau.

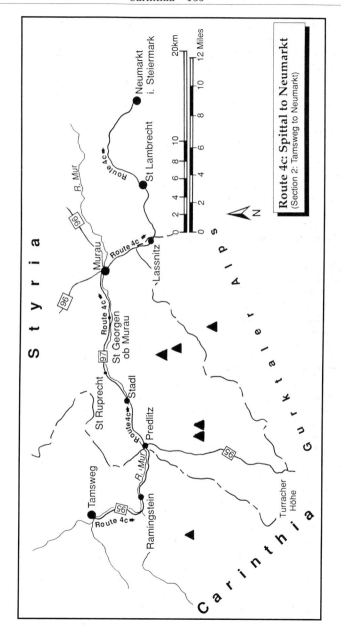

Route 4c: Spittal to Neumarkt
(Section 2: Tamsweg to Neumarkt)

Murau (population 3,000) is an old market town with a delightful central square. The parish church of St Matthäus was founded by Otto von Liechtenstein in the late thirteenth century. It has a large central tower with a stubby black spire. Before the Gothic doorway there is a 'Lantern of the Dead'. The high altar (1654) has figures from 1500; there are fourteenth- to sixteenth-century frescoes, and a decorated fifteenth-century sacristy. The town is overlooked by the Renaissance Schloß Obermurau (1648) which has an arcaded courtyard and a chapel with an altar from 1655. The church of St Leonhard (1450) has a beautiful high altar (1640) with late Gothic statues of Sts George, Florian, and Eustachius from 1520. In the church of the Capuchin abbey there is a notable altar painting by Gregor Lederwasch. The abbey, which is in Grazerstrasse, also houses a local history museum. Murau is a good centre for climbing in the Murtal and Rantenbachtal, and on the Stolzalpe (1,817m, 5,960ft). In winter there is good skiing on the Frauenalpe (2,000m, 6,560ft) to the south-west of the town.

From Murau the main road — Route 96 — follows the Mur to Scheifling whence Route 83 runs south to Neumarkt-im-Steiermark. Instead follow the signpost to St Lambrecht past the railway station (*Bahnhof*) — from which there are steam train excursions — and up a steep little hill with a lovely view to the left over the Murtal. Five miles from Murau the road runs along the border through the village of Laßnitz, one half of which is in Carinthia and the other half in Styria. The road swings left into Styria and, 5 miles later, reaches the market town of **St Lambrecht**.

The Benedictine abbey was founded in the eleventh century and dissolved in 1786. The gateway leads into a rectangular formal garden bounded on the west side by a high wall surmounted by a line of statues, and on the east side by the abbey buildings with the twin towers of the abbey church at the far end.

The church was first consecrated in the eleventh century, but its present form dates from 1645 when it was re-designed by Domenica Sciassia. The fabric of the twin towers which flank the west door is sadly in need of repair, but the great beauty of the façade is undeniable. In the portico there is a fourteenth-century wooden crucifix and a figure of the Virgin Mary from 1642. The interior is illuminated only by windows high on the north wall, the south wall being devoted to two very large frescoes. The lower of them is about 10m (33ft) wide and 4m (13ft) high and depicts the scene on the hill at Calvary. Above it is a painting, about 3m (10ft) wide and 5m (16ft) high, of a brown-skinned Polynesian man in a grass skirt, and black-and-white feather cape, carrying in his right hand a long stave topped with green leaves, and on his left arm a baby, presumably the Baby Jesus. In the dim light this fresco is both striking and intriguing. The high altar is baroque and the carvings are by Christopher Paumgartner, of Neumarkt, who, in the seventeenth century, also made the pulpit and the choirstalls. The paintings in the chancel are

West façade of the abbey church of St Lambrecht

by Balthasar Prandstätter, of Judenburg, and date from 1731.

Outside the north wall of the church, and reached through an archway, is the round ossuary chapel which dates from the twelfth century. The chapel is on the upper floor, has twelve windows, and may have been dedicated to the twelve Apostles. The seventeenth-century abbey buildings, designed by Sciassia, are generously decorated. The ceiling of the Kaisersaal was painted by Melchior Mayr in 1645; in the baroque Konklavesaal there are portraits of Emperor Francis II and of Empress Maria Theresa; in the refectory the ceiling painting depicts the *Feeding of the Five Thousand* and is by Leonhard Fez (1654). In the abbey museum there are collections of paintings and sculptures from the thirteenth to the nineteenth centuries, and a remarkable collection of birds. Behind the west wall of the gardens is St Peter's church (1424) which has a high altar from 1515, and, in the left side chapel, a Gothic winged altar from 1435 with notable paintings.

Leaving St Lambrecht the road descends through a large timber yard and passes small, simple, undecorated houses typical of Styria. At Maria Hof there is a large rail junction. A signpost points left to Teufenbach. Take the right turn, then sharp left across a gated railway crossing to follow the Neumarkt signpost. After descending through a lovely open valley bounded by rolling hills, at 79 miles the road joins Route 83 at **Neumarkt**. The town is overlooked by the thirteenth-century Schloß Forchtenstein, and the late Gothic church has beautiful eighteenth-century altars.

Route 4d Neumarkt to Klagenfurt

South of Neumarkt Route 83 follows the river Olsa through its deep, heavily wooded valley. At Wildbad Einod there are thermal springs, and beyond Durnstein the road enters Carinthia. Nine miles from Neumarkt the road arrives at the old fortified town of **Friesach** (population 7,000) tucked into the base of the right-hand hillside. The town is a thousand years old — probably the oldest in Carinthia — and was owned by the Archbishop of Salzburg until 1803. Remnants of the town walls (1131), a moat, and two castles can still be seen. The parish church of St Bartholomäus is a twelfth-century Romanesque, pillared basilica with lovely stained glass in the choir, and a pretty altar from 1679. On the north side of the church is a lapidarium which includes Roman stones in its collection. Behind the church is the higher ground of Petersberg with St Peter's church, a late Carolingian building with Gothic and baroque styling, and the remains of the eleventh- and twelfth-century Burg Petersberg. There are attractive old houses in Bahnhofstrasse, off the Hauptplatz, including several with arcaded façades. West of the Hauptplatz is the church of the Sacred Blood (twelfth century) which has a high altar from 1681, and a Gothic Madonna dated 1420. In Neutorgasse the Dominican monastery has the longest (80m, 262ft) church (1265) in Carinthia, which contains the *Friesacher Madonna*, a sandstone figure. In the Fürstenhof there is a plague column from 1732, and in the Fürstenhofgasse is the municipal museum. Friesach is a town full of historical interest and a good base for touring.

Beyond Friesach the road runs down the Metnitztal through Micheldorf and Hirt. Fifteen miles from Neumarkt it passes Schloß Pöckstein (1782), once the residence of Johann George Hagenauer, Bishop of Gurk. The castle overlooks the junction of Route 93 signposted Gurktal. The Metnitz here runs into the river Gurk and the road crosses and re-crosses the meandering river as it scurries southward to the right fork onto Route 94 to reach St Veit-an-der-Glan at 26 miles.

St Veit-an-der-Glan (population 12,500) was, until 1518, the capital, and residence of the Dukes of Carinthia. Today it is a busy town which attracts many visitors. In the long Hauptplatz there are interesting eighteenth- and nineteenth-century houses, a plague column (1715), the 'Key Fountain' (Schlüsselbrunnen) (1566) with miner's statue, and

The town hall, St Veit-an-der-Glan

the Florianibrunnen (1676) with a bronze of the poet Walther von der Vogelweide (1960). The Rathaus (1468) has a baroque façade (1754) and a three-storeyed, arcaded courtyard with graffito decoration. There are elegant old houses in the surrounding streets, such as the Untere Platz and the Burggasse. The local history museum, at No 9 Burggasse, has a collection of costumes and uniforms of the Trabant Guard from the thirteenth century. The lapidarium has a collection of statues and Roman stones.

The parish church of the Holy Trinity was built in the twelfth century and there are many Romanesque features but the interior furnishings are mainly baroque. Over the Romanesque doorway the tympanum relief depicts the Lamb of God and symbols of the Evangelists in late Gothic style. The high altar is by Johann Pacher (1752). In the Romanesque ossuary a Carolingian stone let into the wall suggests that there was a ninth-century church on this site. The work of Johann Pacher can also be seen in the high altar (1734) of the Klosterkirche, and in the church of Maria Loretto, on the north-west side of the town.

In the area around St Veit there are a dozen castles and ruins. Schloß Frauenstein, 2 miles north-east, is a picturesque, early sixteenth-century castle with an arcaded courtyard, and the chapel (1521) has a baroque altar. Burg Hochosterwitz, 5 miles to the east (turn off Route 82) is one of the most impressive castles in Austria. First mentioned in 860, the present buildings were constructed by Prince George von Khevenhüller, from 1570 to 1586, on an impregnable 160m-high

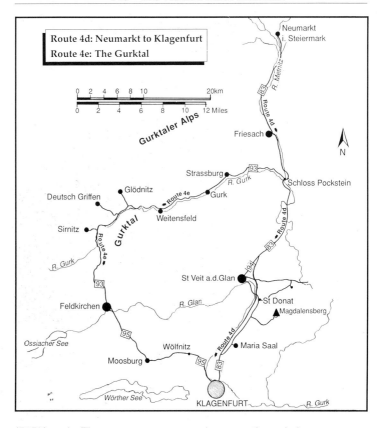

Route 4d: Neumarkt to Klagenfurt
Route 4e: The Gurktal

(525ft) rock. The steep entrance road passes through fourteen gate-houses linked by walls which are wrapped around the rock. On the first gate — the Fähnrichstor — is the coat of arms of the Khevenhüllers (1575); the three-storeyed Khevenhüllertor — gate No 7 — contains a marble relief of the prince; near the thirteenth tower there is a church dating from 1586 with a notable choir and a baroque altar from 1729. In the keep there is a lovely arcaded courtyard with a deep well, and in the east wall is St Nikolaus chapel (1568) which has paintings from 1576. There are conducted tours of the apartments and the museum with collections of arms, paintings, and documents including a letter from Empress Maria Theresa. The views from the castle are splendid.

South-east of St Veit, through St Donat (baroque church with late Gothic Madonna from 1500), and St Michael-am-Zollfeld, some 9 miles distant, at the end of a narrow, winding road, is Magdalensberg

Burg Hochosterwitz

(1,059m, 3,743ft). Much evidence of Celtic and Roman settlements, including a Roman temple and other buildings from the first century BC, has been uncovered by excavating the mountainside, and these finds are exhibited in an open-air museum. The church of Sts Helena and Magdalena is further up the steep little road and is worth a visit. The high altar is said to be one of the most beautiful winged altars in Carinthia, and the Gothic and baroque furnishings are notable. The panoramic view from the terrace is spectacular!

From St Veit take the road through St Donat to **Maria Saal** (population 3,000). The pilgrimage church is the oldest in Carinthia, dating from 750. Until 1072 it was the seat of the bishop. The late Gothic style of the present church dates from the beginning of the fifteenth century, the walls being constructed to keep out the Turks and the Hungarians in the latter half of that century. In the west front façade, and on the south wall, there are Roman stones, including a remarkable relief of a Roman wagon drawn by two horses. The red marble Keutschacher epitaph on the south wall dates from the early sixteenth century and is by H. Valkenauer of Salzburg. Above the south door is a fifteenth-century Romanesque relief of Christ. The centrepiece of the baroque high altar (1714) is the late Gothic miraculous image of the Madonna and Child

Roman carving on the wall of the church at Maria Saal

(1425). On the left of it is the Magi fresco from 1435, which was found in 1884. In the north choir is the Arndorfer altar from 1515 by the Villach school of artists. The baroque chancel is by Johann Pacher. On the south side of the choir is St George's altar (1526), a late Gothic winged altar. The Modestus altar, in the Sachsen chapel (1451), is a simple table on six columns and came from the original church on this site. The relics of St Modestus are contained in a Roman child's sarcophagus beneath the altar. The pulpit and organ are baroque, and the many painted panels in the vaults of the nave are late Gothic (1490), as is the *Last Judgement* on the front of the triumphal arch. In the north tower hang the 'Maria Saalerni' bells which, at 6,600kg (6.5 tons) are the heaviest in Carinthia. Outside the ossuary, which is a Romanesque, octagonal, two-storeyed building, there is a 'Lantern of the Dead' dating from 1497.

On the east side of the town there is a plague cross with late Gothic frescoes (1523). About 3 miles to the north, at **Zollfeld**, is the site of the Roman town of *Virunum*, which was the capital of the province between the first and fifth centuries AD. Finds from the excavations are displayed in the Landesmuseum in Klagenfurt. In the centre of Zollfeld is the Kärntner Herzogsstuhl, a mighty throne made from Roman stones, which dates from the eighth and ninth centuries, and was used by the Lords of Carinthia as a symbol of their power, to make proclamations, and to receive homage. A similar Fürstenstein ('prince's stone') is located near Karnburg, 2 miles west of Maria Saal.

Also at Maria Saal is the Carinthian open-air museum (Freilichts-museum) with its delightful collection of thirty-five country dwellings and farm buildings which illustrate the development of rural architecture in the province.

From Maria Saal it is a short journey into Klagenfurt, 39 miles from Neumarkt-im-Steiermark.

Route 4e The Gurktal (see map page 140)

The river Gurk rises in the Gurktaler Alps, close to the Turracher Höhe, on the border between Styria and Carinthia, then flows south, north-east, then south again to join the river Glan just east of Klagenfurt. The Gurktal is that middle length of valley which starts at Schloß Pöckstein, on Route 83, extends upriver through Gurk and beyond Sirnitz, and is traversed by Route 93. Travelling south on Route 83, turn right 15 miles from Neumarkt onto Route 93, signposted Gurk/Straßburg.

The Gurktal is a lovely valley with meadowland broken by copses of tall trees and the river Gurk, a babbling stream on the left-hand side. After 10 miles, across the river, the domed church of St Stefan hides behind the trees; ahead the white Burg Straßburg appears high on a hill and the road enters the small medieval town of **Straßburg** (population 3,000). The parish church of St Nikolaus dates from the fifteenth century and has notable late Gothic rib vaulting and a baroque organ loft (1743). On the high altar, by V. Erhard (1747), the carved figures are by Balthasar Prandstätter, and the painting is by Josef Ferdinand Fromiller. The superb double tomb, in red marble, of Bishops von Schallermann (died 1453) and von Sonnenberg (died 1469) is by H. Eybenstock.

Constructed in 1147, Burg Straßburg was the residence for the Prince-Bishops of Gurk until they removed to Klagenfurt in 1787. Only the two keeps and the chapel are original, the rest of the building having been added over the centuries following damage from fire, earthquakes, and wars. Especially striking is the two-storeyed arcaded courtyard by Johann Payr (1689). The stables are connected to the main building by an arcaded passage by J.A. Verda (1584). The knight's hall is now a hunting museum, and another room houses the diocesan museum. In the town there is a Gurktal museum as well as a local history museum. The Romanesque chapel of St Mauritius is twelfth century and was converted to the baroque style in 1685.

Leaving Straßburg on the west side, past the ochre walls and red roof of the old schoolhouse, the picturesque church of the Holy Ghost stands half a mile to the right on a low hillside. It has a notable arched Gothic doorway and wall paintings from 1330.

Two miles beyond Straßburg the onion-topped towers of Gurk cathedral come into sight. Turn left into the market town of **Gurk** (population 1,500) the cathedral is one of the most beautiful Romanesque churches in Austria. Building began under Bishop Roman I in about 1140, and was completed by 1220. The external appearance of the cathedral is the more impressive for its simplicity. Twin towers (1680) embellish the plain, high walls of the basilica which are decorated only at the east end by a carving of a lion symbolising Christ the warrior.

Inside the west porch the wall paintings from 1340 depict scenes from the Bible, and there are twelve medallions depicting Christ and the apostles on the wall around the doorway. The wooden door dates from 1200 and is magnificently carved.

In the south tower a stairway leads up to the bishop's chapel which contains the frescoes *The Creation of Man,The Virgin Mary on King Solomon's Throne*, and others by Meister Heinrich of Gurk (1230). The stained glass windows are also notable, and from the same date. The high altar was dedicated in 1200; the present masterpiece is by Michael Hönel, of Pirna, and dates from 1632. It incorporates seventy-two statues and eighty-two angels in its great proportions and is very powerful. During Lent the high altar is covered by a 9sq m (97sq ft) cloth, decorated with ninety-nine scenes from the Old and New Testaments, by Master Konrad of Friesach, dating from 1458. The paintings in the two side altars are by Johann Seitlinger (1638). The crypt is quite remarkable, containing 100 columns and the sarcophagus of Countess Hemma who, in 1043, founded a convent on this site, and was canonised in 1938. Note the four heads supporting the tomb.

The altar, in the nave, is bounded by lead figures which were executed by G.B.Donner, as were the lead reliefs on the pulpit. Also notable, on the north stairway to the crypt, is the tympanum relief which dramatically depicts Samson's victory over the lion. There are many more remarkable features in the cathedral such as the frescoes in the west gallery, and, in the south nave, reliefs of the life of St Hemma which date from 1515. A visit to Gurk cathedral is a great spiritual and cultural experience. Note that it is currently being extensively restored.

Return to the main road. Along the upper reaches of the valley note the unusual, picturesque, farm outbuildings in which the window openings are filled with a lattice-work of terracotta bricks. Five miles after Gurk the parish church of **Weitensfeld** has fifteenth-century frescoes. Austria's oldest stained glass windows (1170) came from the sister church of St Magdalena and are now in the diocesan museum in Klagenfurt. About a mile further along the road, on the right, is St Ämilian, the parish church of **Altenmarkt**, which has a remarkable fresco of the Virgin Mary protecting supplicants under her cloak, probably by Thomas von Villach (1470). About 8¹/₂ miles from Gurk, a road on the right leads to **Glödnitz**, fifteenth-century Schloß Kirchenburg, and the parish church of St Margaret with a beautiful baroque altar. One mile further and another road on the right leads to **Deutsch Griffen** where the church of St Jakob the Elder has Gothic frescoes from 1430 and a baroque high altar from 1640. Twelve miles from Gurk yet another right turn leads to **Sirnitz** and a small lake as well as an early Gothic, fourteenth-century church and a fifteenth-century ossuary.

The road then leaves the Gurktal through a pass and descends via Poitschach into Feldkirchen, 30 miles from Schloß Pöckstein, or 45 miles from Neumarkt.

5 STYRIA

Styria (Steiermark) is the second largest province in Austria with an area of 16,386sq km (6,330sq miles), and a population of 1.2 million people. To the south it is bounded by Yugoslavia and Carinthia, to the west by Land Salzburg, to the north by Upper Austria and Lower Austria, and to the east by Burgenland and Hungary. Almost all of its surface area is covered by mountains drained by the main catchments of the rivers Mur and Enns, and the smaller rivers Raab and Lafnitz to the east, all of which discharge eventually into the Danube. The mountains are highest in the north and west where they include the bare crags of the Hoher Dachstein (up to 3,004m, 9,853ft) and the Totes Gebirge groups. In the south and east the slopes are easier and covered by forests, mostly coniferous and spruce but with some beech and oak. Styria has been called 'The Green Heart of Austria' and frequently proclaims the joy of rambling in the cool and silent air of its woods. In the south-east corner, beyond the Styrian hills, the landscape changes to the plain flatlands which extend across Hungary to the Carpathian Mountains.

Historical evidence of early settlement in Styria has come from the 150,000-year-old Palaeolithic cave dwellings in the middle Mur valley. Artefacts from the Bronze and Iron Ages have indicated widespread habitation throughout the region and especially in the west. Incursions by the Romans were resisted until 15BC by which time almost the whole of Styria had become part of the Roman Empire, and then enjoyed its benefits until it ended in AD476. For almost three centuries the region was occupied by the Slavs until the Bavarians came to liberate them from the oppression of the Avars. From Salzburg the Bavarians brought Christianity, and made large land grants to the church and to noble families. From 895 to 955 Styria suffered successive assaults from Hungary which led to the creation of 'marches' or landed lordships to provide a front-line defence along the border. In 1180 the Emperor Frederick I (Barbarossa) made Styria a duchy, and so it remained until 1918. From 1192 it was held by the Babenberg family, then for a short time by King Ottokar of Bohemia, and from 1276 to 1918 by the Habsburgs.

The fourteenth and fifteenth centuries were especially difficult for Styria. Rivalry between the noble families, together with incursions by Hungarian and Turkish armies, caused much destruction across the land. Infestations of locust brought famine, and the black plague

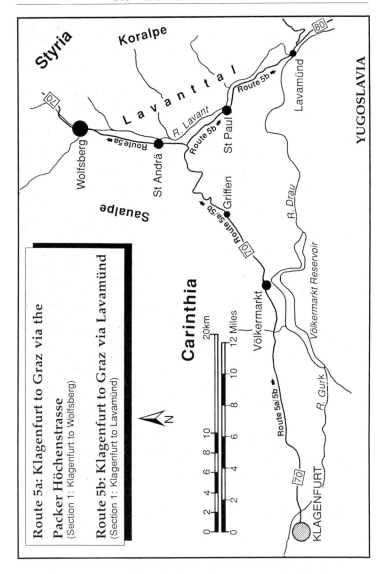

Route 5a: Klagenfurt to Graz via the
Packer Höchenstrasse
(Section 1: Klagenfurt to Wolfsberg)

Route 5b: Klagenfurt to Graz via Lavamünd
(Section 1: Klagenfurt to Lavamünd)

brought death on a large scale. A period of great cultural achievement
in more fortunate lands was for Styrians a time of struggle for survival.
The Turkish threat continued for 200 years until finally defeated in 1683.

Except for the invasions of the Napoleonic Wars between 1797 and 1809, the eighteenth and nineteenth centuries allowed the development of roads and railways and the establishment of industries so that the economy of the region improved. In World War II industrial installations were bombed and fighting on the ground in the eastern section caused great damage. Since 1945 Styria has shared in national recovery and in economic and technological development.

Styrian climate varies, like the landscape, from north to south. In the high country of the north the climate is typically alpine, being influenced by the proximity of mountain chains and deep valleys and gorges. It can be delightful but it is local and changeable. In the lower, more southerly sector the climate is almost Mediterranean and supports fruit and tobacco growing, market gardening, and wine production. In addition to timber from the northern forests, Styria's resources include high grade iron ore from the Erzberg, brown coal from Köflich and salt from Bad Aussee. Styrian hops and the clean waters of the Mur river support Austria's principal breweries at Graz (Puntigamer) and at Leoben (Göss).

Until the advent of the motorway and the 5-mile tunnel under the Gleinalm, roads followed the valleys and crossed mountain passes which today serve the more remote habitations and provide scenic routes for intrepid visitors. Travelling from Tyrol through Carinthia and on into Styria, the differences between the people, the architecture, and local customs becomes progressively more noticeable. The flower-decked wooden houses of alpine Tyrol contrast with Styria's modest, stone buildings; the gentle, Bavarian features of people north of the High Alps contrast with the striking Slav faces of the people of Styria.

The cities, towns, and villages of Styria are strung like pearls along the valleys and gather in the few large basins. The capital of the province is Graz, in the lower valley of the Mur river. It is far from the geographic centre of Styria, being less than 30 miles from Yugoslavia and 100 miles from Bad Aussee at the western end of Styria. Nevertheless, Graz is the political, social, and cultural centre of Styria. Its old town, its opera house, theatre, museums, its old buildings, cathedral and churches, and the respect of its citizens for its long traditions are reminiscent of Vienna. It is an excellent centre for the visitor to Styria.

Route 5a   Klagenfurt to Graz via the Packer Höchenstrasse

The most direct road link between Klagenfurt and Graz is via Route 70 over the Packsattel. Leaving Klagenfurt's one-way road system and following the Route 70 Graz signposts, the road bypasses **Völkermarkt** (population 11,000), a twelfth-century trading town, and continues eastwards. It is a good highway through rolling farmland and at times traffic may be heavy. Two miles after Völkermarkt bear left to stay on the main road via **Griffen**, where there is a thirteenth-century abbey. After 30 miles the main road curves to the left toward Wolfsberg, passing the smaller road on the right signposted Lavamund/St Paul which is the start of the alternative route to Graz described in the next section.

Two miles further along Route 70 the road reaches **St Andrä** (population 2,500), one-time seat of the Bishops of Lavant (1228 to 1859). The parish church of St Andrä is a pillared basilica, partly Romanesque and partly Gothic. The high altar is neo-Gothic and the side altars are baroque. There are fragments of fifteenth- and sixteenth-century frescoes in the baptistry, a relief of the Virgin Mary, dating from 1480 in the portico, and many tablets and tombs commemorating former bishops. In the pilgrimage church of Maria Loreto (1687) there are baroque statues and beautiful altar paintings.

About 27$\frac{1}{2}$ miles from Klagenfurt, on the Lavant river, is the busy town of **Wolfsberg** (population 12,000). The long, narrow Hohe Platz, in the middle of the town contains some interesting fifteenth- and sixteenth-century houses and a baroque Pestsäule (1718). The parish church of St Mark is a Romanesque basilica which dates from the thirteenth century. The altar painting of St Mark is by Kremser Schmidt (1777), and the fifteenth- and sixteenth-century tombs are notable. Opposite St Mark's is St Anna's chapel, which has a late Gothic panelled altar. Also worth seeing is the church of the Holy Trinity at the north end of the town. The old castle of the Bishop of Bamberg overlooks the town on the east side. In 1846 it was purchased by Count Henckel-Donnersmarck who converted it into the style of an English country house.

At **Twimberg**, 7$\frac{1}{2}$ miles from Wolfsberg, Route 78, on the left, goes 4 miles up the Lavanttal to Bad St Leonhard, an old health resort, with one of the best Gothic churches in Carinthia. This fourteenth-century basilica is especially noted for its stained glass windows, and also has a large, baroque high altar (1640), a panelled altar dated 1513, and late Gothic and Renaissance tombstones built into the walls both inside and outside the church. The little town also has interesting old houses in the Hauptplatz; old town walls; the fourteenth-century Schloß Ehrenfels; an arcaded house, restored after bomb damage in 1945; and two other churches: St Kunigunde and the Spitalskirche, both Gothic. As well as the ruined fourteenth-century Gomarn castle, at the west end of the town, the Renaissance Schloß Lichtengraben (1564) and the ruins of the fifteenth-century Painhof castle are 1 mile to the north. Bad St Leonhard provides a worthwhile diversion from Route 70.

The Packer Höchenstrasse begins at Twimberg. The road climbs steeply through a series of hairpin bends via Waldstein to Preitenegg and on through Hebalpe to the Packsattel at 56$\frac{1}{2}$ miles. From this saddle between the Packalpe to the north-west and the Hebalpe, to the

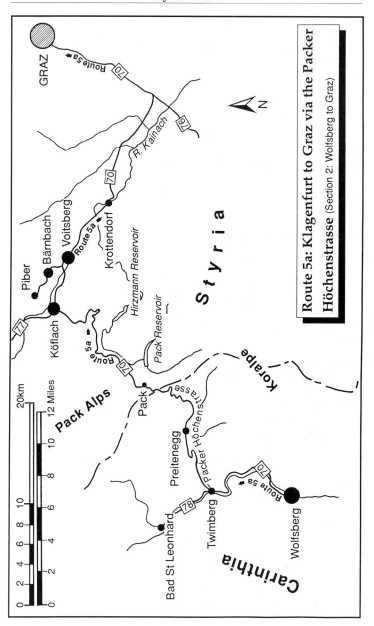

Route 5a: Klagenfurt to Graz via the Packer Höchenstrasse (Section 2: Wolfsberg to Graz)

south-east, the views are spectacular. The border between Carinthia and Styria crosses the road at this point, and there is a link road to the A2 Klagenfurt-Graz motorway which passes through a tunnel beneath the Packsattel.

The road then descends via the hamlet of **Pack** (church and castle — now the priest's house — both eleventh century), passes on the right the little road up to the Packer Stausee, goes through Edelschrott then winds downward through the heavily wooded — and very scenic — hills to **Köflach** (population 13,000) at 70$^1/_2$ miles. The deposits of brown coal in this area are the most important in Austria, and extensive workings can be seen around the town. The church of St Magdalena was built in 1649 by Domenico Sciassia and contains frescoes by Josef Adam Mölk (1777). Just over a mile to the north is the village of **Piber** which is the home of the world famous Lipizzaner stud farm (see Graz). The farm itself is immaculate and the sight of these graceful animals — the white mares with their (surprisingly) black foals — in the most beautiful sylvan countryside is delightful.

From Köflach Route 77 goes north to Judenburg while Route 70 turns eastward to reach, after a further 5$^1/_2$ miles, **Voitsberg** (population 11,000), an industrial town and a holiday resort. In the town centre there are picturesque old houses from the fifteenth to eighteenth century and a baroque Pestsäule. There are three churches. The late Gothic church of the Sacred Blood was built in 1509; St Michael's was built in the thirteenth century; and the parish church of St Josef dates from 1395 and has a beautiful baroque altar. The ruined Obervoitsberg castle (1183) provides a splendid view over the town. Schloß Greisenegg (1443) stands on the opposite bank of the Kainach river. To the north of the town, 3 miles away, the other side of the village of Bärnbach, is Schloß Alt-Kainach (1548) which has a pretty arcaded courtyard, a baroque chapel, and an interesting museum which provides a historical perspective of all of the important castles in Styria.

From Voitsberg the road runs down alongside the Kainach river. After less than a mile the stately ruins of Krems castle (twelfth century) may be seen on the right. Another 3 miles and the road passes through Krottendorf where it crosses the river to pass sixteenth-century Schloß Hohenburg, on the left. Some 3$^1/_2$ miles further, also on the left, Schloß Großsoding (1563) precedes the village of Söding, and, at 86$^1/_2$ miles, the road reaches Lieboch. Here the road turns left toward the north-east, passes the junction with Route 76, from Deutschlandsberg, then runs through low hills before reaching Graz after 96 miles.

Route 5b Klagenfurt to Graz via Lavamünd

(see maps page 146 and 151)

For an alternative, more leisurely journey from Klagenfurt to Graz, turn

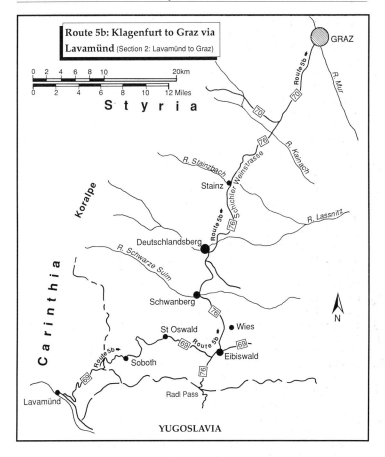

Route 5b: Klagenfurt to Graz via Lavamünd (Section 2: Lavamünd to Graz)

GRAZ

Styria

Koralpe

R. Stainzbach

Stainz

Schichler Weinstrasse

R. Kainach

R. Lassnitz

Deutschlandsberg

R. Schwarze Sulm

Carinthia

Schwanberg

St Oswald

Wies

Soboth

Eibiswald

Lavamünd

Radl Pass

N

YUGOSLAVIA

right off Route 70 at 30 miles, following the Lavamünd/St Paul signpost. The narrower road swings to the south, and at 36 miles reaches **St Paul-in-Lavanttal**. The river Lavant runs through the middle of this lovely little village with rows of horse-chestnut trees on both banks. The Benedictine abbey perches in a most picturesque setting on a small hill. It was founded in 1091 and is a very active community with a large working farm and gardens as well as the abbey school. The church (1264) has relatively little decoration but is very beautiful with Gothic vaulting, richly carved capitals on the columns, and a baroque pulpit. It is said to be the finest Romanesque church in Carinthia. The delightful, small, gilded altar has a tabernacle from 1720, and reliefs and statues from the fourteenth to sixteenth centuries. In the right-hand chapel the skull of St Clement is displayed in a glass case. In the left-hand chapel there are interesting frescoes from the thirteenth to fifteenth centuries, and, on a wooden doorway, a painting of a shroud bearing the face of Jesus Christ. In the vaults there are the tombs of fifteen members of the Habsburg family from 1281 to 1386 but they are not open to the public. The abbey museum houses a magnificent collection of treasures including ecclesiastical utensils in silver and gold, porcelain, glass, and paintings including *The Adoration of the Shepherds* by Rubens.

After St Paul the road runs down the right-hand side of the valley between gently sloping woodlands on both sides, and alongside ploughed fields and large plots of maize. At the bottom of a hill (12 per cent; 1 in 8), at $56^1/_2$ miles, the road enters **Lavamünd** which has two churches. The parish church dates from 1193 and has a fortified tower and baroque altars and pulpit. The market church of Johannes der Täufer is baroque. Bear left out of the village through the middle of a timber yard, and after a mile a signpost indicates Yugoslavia ahead. Turn left up the narrow, winding hill toward Graz/Eibiswald (Route 69).

The $6^1/_2$-mile climb out of the Lavanttal is steep (up to 15 per cent; 1 in 7), there are four hairpin bends and many more sharp curves, and the road is sometimes narrow. But it is also very beautiful, often tree lined, and affords splendid views to the left over the Lavanttal and the broad river Drau wending its way 200 miles into Yugoslavia to keep its rendezvous with the river Danube. At $61^1/_2$ miles the pretty little church alongside the road on the right, in its lovely hillside setting, is St Magdalene's which has a baroque altar (1710). The top of the pass is reached at 64 miles, at the Kögler Eck (1,349m, 4,425ft) which is an excellent viewing point and picnic area. On a clear day there is a very fine view of the peaks of the Staualpe range to the south-west.

The road starts to descend swiftly (13 per cent; 1 in 8) and soon enters Styria (Steiermark). After winding through large tracts of forest and over two viaducts, the road reaches **Soboth**, a holiday resort with good skiing and walking. Two miles further on the road curves to the right to cross the bridge over the ravine at Krumbach. After a long, gentle run downhill the parish church of **St Oswald-ob-Eibiswald** appears ahead and to the left on a hillside. A short length of very narrow road leads into the centre of the village at $75^1/_2$ miles. The broad village square leads to an excellent *Gasthof* and, with the unpretentious church, village hall, school, and few scattered houses, provides a peaceful, rustic setting for relaxing and restful holidays.

THE SCHILCHER WINE ROAD

The road then runs steadily downward to bypass the straggling village of **Eibiswald** at $82^1/_2$ miles. This is one end of the Schilcher Wine Road, one of four in Styria. Alongside the road there are frequent vineyards of

Eibiswald on the road from Lavamünd to Graz

Müller-Thurgau and Traminer grapes. At 84$^1/_2$ miles a turn to the right leads into the little village of **Wies**, a summer resort. The church (1782) has magnificent frescoes in the dome which was restored in 1982. In one corner St George may be seen thrusting his lance down the throat of a green dragon. The nearby Burgstall castle is fourteenth century.

From Wies continue on to Route 76. In autumn the next 6$^1/_2$ miles are punctuated by the sight of women in the fields harvesting pumpkins and, sitting amongst the crop, preparing them for market by removing the seeds. The road rises and falls gently between stands of tall trees as it runs down the open valley to **Schwanberg** (population 1,500). A health resort, its mud baths are said to be good for rheumatism, heart and circulatory conditions, and women's complaints. The parish church is thirteenth-century Romanesque with a Gothic choir and a very unusual shrine to the apostle Thadeus. On a height overlooking the town is the seventeenth-century St Josef's church which has one of five baroque stone carvings of Christ the Passion. In the very pleasant town square there is a Mariensäule of 1717. On the west side of the town is Schloß Schwanberg (1581) which has a baroque interior, a lovely arcaded courtyard, and a chapel (1778) with a late baroque altar. About a mile to the south is Schloß Limberg, a seventeenth-century castle, which has three towers from 1664, a double staircase from 1720, and a knight's hall with stucco decoration.

The road continues down the valley past fields of maize, sunflowers, and yellow rape, past orchards and vineyards. A road to the left rises to the attractive Schloß Hollenegg (1576), at 97 miles, a Renaissance castle with two fine arcaded courtyards. The interior is decorated with French tapestries, stucco, frescoes, and includes a grand hall with ceiling paintings by Carl Laubmann (1750). The church of St Ägydius, in the south courtyard, has an elliptical nave and side altar panels by Laubmann (1753).

Return to the Graz road and at 100 miles turn left off the main road to enter **Deutschlandsberg** (population 5,300), a summer resort and a convenient centre for exploring the Koralpe Mountains to the west. In the town square there is a Mariensäule (1712), an eighteenth-century burgher's house, and the town hall has a baroque façade from 1797. The parish church (1701) is baroque. The nearby Landsberg castle, now in ruins, dates from the middle of the twelfth century. Three miles to the north is fourteenth-century Schloß Wildbach.

Back on Route 76 the road passes through a rolling landscape of meadowlands and trees and, descending a long hill, at $107^1/_2$ miles, the picturesque Schloß Stainz, a former Augustinian abbey (1230) comes into distant view. The building was secularised in 1785. In 1840 it came into the possession of Archduke Johann, and today it is owned by the descendants of the Duke of Meran. The twin-towered church is thirteenth century, later refurbished in baroque style. The dome frescoes date from 1686 and the high altar from 1689. The altar painting *The Martyrdom of St Katharine* is by Hans Adam Weissenkirchner. The castle has picturesque courtyards, and delightful garden pavilions (1730) on the east side. **Stainz** (population 2,400) is an important market town in east Styria set in beautiful surroundings of orchards, vineyards, and forests with many marked footpaths.

The Wine Road here goes left to Gundersdorf and as far as Krottendorf while the main road continues north-eastward across the A2 motorway to join Route 70 and so to reach Graz after a journey of 120 miles.

GRAZ

Graz (population 250,000), the capital of Styria, is the second largest city in Austria, and sprawls along the banks of the Mur river. Although a Roman road crossed the Mur at this point, the location was not popular with early settlers — perhaps because the land was liable to flooding by the swollen river — who preferred more southerly sites such as Liebnitz. The city dates back to the twelfth century. Its geographical location, at the edge of the Holy Roman Empire, ensured a sustained onslaught from the east. For more than 200 years, from 1469 to 1683, it suffered repeated attacks by Turkish armies, and both extensive fortifications and an armed citizenry were needed to keep the Turks at bay. A hundred years later, in 1784, Graz was occupied by Napoleon's troops who returned again in 1805 and 1809, and the fortifications were pulled down. Today its proximity to the Slav and Balkan countries and to

Turkey makes Graz a convenient venue for trade fairs and congresses, and adds spice to its very active cultural life. The highlight of a full year of art, music and literature is the Styrian Autumn Festival which is held each October. It is a city of courtyards and alleyways, and leafy parks — reminiscent of Vienna — and of museums, churches, castles and historic buildings.

Graz is easily reached by road, rail, or air. There are daily flights from Thalerhof Airport, 7 miles south of the city, to and from Vienna, Frankfurt, and Zurich. In and around the city there are bus lines as well as street cars which provide frequent services. Accommodation ranges from luxury hotels to reasonably-priced family hotels and *pensions*, as well as four camping sites and a youth hostel. Restaurants and entertainments are consistent with a cosmopolitan university city.

The tourist information office at No 16 Herrengasse is a convenient starting point for a circular walking tour of the city. The office is housed in the **Landhaus** (Styrian Parliament House) which was redesigned in its present form by Domenico dell' Allio, of Lugano, in 1565. The inner courtyard, arcaded and bounded on two sides by three-storeyed loggias, is a beautiful example of Italian Renaissance architecture. On the west side, outside the **Landstube**, is the lovely bronze fountain cast by Thomas Auer and Max Wening in 1590. The interior of the baroque Landstube was refurbished in 1741 and is truly magnificent. The stucco ceiling — as in the adjoining knight's hall — is by J. Formentini.

Next door to the Landhaus, in the Herrengasse, is the superb baroque doorway of the **armoury** (Ständische Zeughaus) built in 1642 by Antonio Solar. During the incursions by the Turks, in order to be able to mobilize the population at short notice, a central arsenal comprising three armouries was maintained in Graz. Today one of those three armouries is preserved in its entirety and houses a unique and spectacular collection of 30,000 items, mostly from the sixteenth and seventeenth centuries, including suits of armour, helmets, swords, muskets, cannon, and other artefacts of war.

From the armoury turn left along the Herrengasse (watch out for the streetcars!), which is the principal shopping street. Note at No 3 the **Painted House** (Gemaltes Haus) (1742) covered with dark scenes from mythology and events from the Turkish wars. At No 9 is **Palais Brenner**, a Renaissance house which has a good Renaissance court- yard and staircase. Napoleon Bonaparte lodged at No 13 in 1797.

At the end of the Herrengasse is the spacious Hauptplatz. The view from the front of the city hall (Rathaus) (1893) is picturesque. Surrounded by a small fruit, vegetable, and flower market is the monument to Archduke Johann (Erzherzog Johann Brunnen) (1878), the great benefactor and popular 'Prince of Styria' who established the Joanneum Landesmuseum. Beyond the bustling streetcars, to the right, at the entrance to the Sporgasse, are the old five- and six-storey **Luegg**

Houses with their baroque stucco façades and steep roofs. Houses No 16 (1650), No 4 (Renaissance), and No 5 (Gothic) are notable. Above them, in the background, can be seen the old citadel (Schloßberg) and the clock tower (Uhrturm) which is the symbol of Graz.

From the Rathaus go to the left across Schmiedgasse (in the Middle Ages a street of blacksmiths [*Schmiede*], gunsmiths and armourers, wheelwrights, and tinsmiths) into Albrechtgasse and almost immediately turn right into Neue Welt Gasse. The alleyway, passing the pretty Weißschen Haus at No 4, turns left then right to the **Franciscan monastery** and **church**.

The tower of the Franciscan church was built in 1636 as part of the city's fortifications. Its lower walls are 2m (6$^1/_2$ft) thick. The church was built in two sections, the Gothic nave being built about 1520 after the Franciscans had taken over from the minorites who built the choir in about 1350. The altar has a magnificent *pietà* of 1720 and the Antonius chapel has a baroque grille from 1650. From the right-hand aisle a side door leads into the cloisters, where there are impressive tombstones, and to Jakob's chapel (Jakobskapelle) (1330), which is an excellent example of Gothic architecture and contains a fine statue of St Anthony by Johann Jakob Schoy (1719).

Return to the Hauptplatz via Franziskanerplatz, turning right into Kaprunplatz, to see the rococo façades (1735) of the medieval houses, and the meat and sausage stalls of the Butcher's Quarter, before going ahead through the narrow Davidgasse. Then cross the square to the left-hand corner and enter the Sporgasse.

This winding, rising medieval lane is full of charm as well as fruit and vegetable and confectionery shops. Note the Gothic window at No 13, a simple *Burgher's* house which also has a fine courtyard, and the dragon's head gargoyles over a former inn. At No 22, on the corner with Hofgasse, is the **Deutsche Ritterordens Haus** (House of the Teutonic Order) with Gothic arches and a Renaissance courtyard. No 25 is the **Saurau palace** with baroque wrought-iron work over the Renaissance gateway. It is said that while the Turks were besieging the Schloßberg, having captured the town, their commander was dining on the top floor of this house when an Austrian cannonball carried his roast duck out of the window. The siege was not successful. On the left are the steps which give the seventeenth-century **Stiegenkirche** its name ('Church of the Steep Path'). At No 13 Paulustorgasse is the **Styrian folk museum** (Steirisches Volkskundemuseum) with collections of country artefacts, household utensils, and traditional costumes.

Turn into the Hofgasse and go ahead into Freiheitsplatz. In the centre is a bronze statue of Kaiser Franz II, the last emperor of the Holy Roman Empire of the German nation, by Pompeo Marchesi (1841). On the north side of the square is the former **St Lambrechts abbey**. On the south side is the **old university** (1609) which today houses the Styrian

The Painted House in the Herrengasse, Graz

archives. On the east side is the **theatre** (Schauspielhaus). The
original, built by Joseph Huger in 1776, was destroyed by fire on
Christmas Eve, 1823. It was reconstructed by Peter de Nobile and
reopened 2 years later. In 1952 it was closed down for safety until the
present theatre opened in 1964. The main auditorium can seat an
audience of 600 people and there are two additional stages. It is said
that a travelling company of English actors gave the first continental
performance of Marlowe's *Dr Faustus* in Graz in 1608.

At No 1 Bürgergasse the key to the **Barbarakapelle** can be obtained
from the porter. The little chapel is a baroque gem, the remarkable
frescoes being by Franz Christopher Janneck, of Graz.

At the end of the Hofgasse is the **cathedral of St Ägydius**. In 1174
it was a fortified church outside the city walls but it was refurbished and
extended in late Gothic style from 1438 to 1462 by Hans Niesenberger
under the direction of Kaiser Frederick III. His motto can be seen, with
his coat of arms, over the west door. It reads 'AEIOU' which stands for
'*Austria erit in orbe ultima*' — sometimes translated as 'Austria will
survive until the end of the world'. The church became a cathedral in
1786. Entrance is by the north door.

The interior of the cathedral is mostly baroque and of beautiful proportions having a spacious and lofty nave connected by an archway to a relatively narrow choir. The marble high altar of 1730 was created by Father George Kraxner, the sculptures being by Johann Jakob Schoy. Two side altars have paintings by Pietro de Pomis and sculptures by V. Königer. The four chapels have elegant seventeenth-century wrought-iron grilles. On either side of the triumphal arch of the high altar are the wedding chests of Paola Gonzaga, Duchess of Mantua. They date from 1475 and were made in Mantua by Andrea Mantegna. The ivory relief decorations depict Love, Innocence, Death, Fame, Time, and Eternity. In the vault, behind an iron grille, there are silver vessels which are said to contain the hearts of the Habsburgs buried there. One vessel also holds two fingers of an archduchess which were placed there 'because she was so good to the poor'! There is also a **diocesan museum** at Mariahilferplatz 3 containing Gothic works of art.

From the cathedral turn right to the Burgtor which is the older of the two surviving city gates, and leads to the **Burggarten** and the delightfully wooded **Stadtpark**. Next to it is **Frederick III's palace** — the Burg (1452). Little remains of the original structure but the Doppeltreppe, or double-spiral staircase (1499), which separates and reunites six times is a gem of Gothic architecture. It is located in the tower to the left of the archway which leads to the second courtyard.

Leaving the Burg behind proceed a short way down the Burggasse, enjoying the distant view of the dome of the **opera house**, then skirt around the south side of the cathedral. Note the fragments of the *Landplagenbild* (1485), a late Gothic fresco by Thomas of Villach which tells the story of the three scourges which ravaged Styria in those days: the Turks, the plague, and locusts. The lane leads to the front of the **mausoleum** of Emperor Ferdinand II, started in 1614 by Pietro de Pomis and completed in 1638 by Pietro Valnegro. It is considered the best example in Austria of mannerism — an exaggerated artistic style which pre-dated the baroque. Inside, the high altar of the church of **St Catherine** is the work of Fischer von Erlach who was born in Graz. In fact the sarcophagus in the tomb chapel contains only the remains of the Emperor's mother, Archduchess Maria.

Descend the steps from the mausoleum and turn left into Bürgergasse then right into Abraham-a-Sancta Clara Gasse then bear right into Glockenspielplatz. In the gable window of the house on the corner are two wooden figures of a Styrian couple which, at 11am and 6pm, dance to the tune of an old folk song. The **palace of Effans d'Avernas**, at No 5, has an impressive open staircase in its courtyard (1697). The house at No 7 has a splendid Renaissance arcaded courtyard.

Around the corner in the Mehlplatz, one of the prettiest small

squares in the city, are the **Inzaghi grand palace** (1720), No 4 with its
bas-relief of the Virgin Mary (1720), and the rustic gate of the former
town house of the Pöllau monastery in east Styria. The next square is
the Färbergplatz with lovely old houses. Continue to the left via
Prokopigasse, and return through the Mehlplatz to Glockenspielplatz,
then go ahead into Enge Gasse. On the left is the **bishop's palace**. This
was the site of the residences of the Bishops of Graz-Seckau from 1254
until the palace was badly damaged in World War II. In 1947-55 it was
rebuilt with an extra storey. Johann Kepler once lived at the house on
the corner with Bindergasse.

Now turn right into Stempfergasse which was a boundary of the
ghetto, abolished in the fifteenth century. No 6 has a Renaissance
courtyard. The lane winds down to its junction with the Herrengasse. On
the corner is the **Bärenapotheke** (1770) with its charming rococo
façade. And here the circular tour is completed.

A walk down Sackstrasse, off the north end of the Hauptplatz,
provides an interesting extension of the tour. The district bounded by
this street and the Sporgasse is the oldest part of the city. The Italian
courtyard of No 12, on the right-hand side, is worth a peep. Further
along on the same side is the **Herberstein palace** which houses, on the
second floor, the new gallery of the Joanneum museum (Neu Galerie
des Landesmuseums Joanneum). The palace was converted from
three large houses in 1602 and in 1754 the Duchess of Herberstein
remodelled it in rococo style. The new gallery includes the magnificent
room of mirrors (Spiegelsaal) (1754) and displays paintings, sketches
and sculptures by nineteenth- and twentieth-century artists.

Next door to the new gallery is the **city museum** (Stadtmuseum) in
the former Khuenberg palace. It has a seventeenth-century façade and
a baroque doorway (1710). A tablet in the entrance hall commemorates
the birth here, in 1863, of the Crown Prince Franz Ferdinand whose
death at Sarajevo, on 28 June, 1914 led to World War I. The museum
is used for temporary exhibitions. Across the street, at No 17, is the
largest and most beautiful of the city's palaces, the **Attems palace**. It
has a baroque façade from 1716 and a stairwell with ceiling frescoes
from 1706. Today it accommodates the archive section of the Joanneum museum.

Turn right into the Schloßbergplatz. On the right-hand side is the
Rainerhof, the oldest building in Graz dating from 1164. At the end of
the *Platz* is the rock staircase up to the Schloßberg. The less active
visitor will prefer to continue along Sackstrasse to Kaiser Franz Josef
Kai and to the lower station of the Schloßbergbahn funicular railway.
The 3-minute ride rises 108m (354ft) to the Schloßberg restaurant and
the nearby **bell tower** (Glockenturm) (1588). The large bell was struck
in 1587 by Martin Hilger. The **clock tower**, at the south end of the
Schloßberg, was built in 1556. The 'Poor Wretches Bell'

('Armensünderglocke') was used to announce public executions and the closing of the market and the city gates. The views across the city from the clock tower are splendid. Guided tours of the Schloßberg — the former citadel of Graz — start from the bell tower on the hour from 8am to 5pm during the summer months.

Return to the Hauptplatz from the Schloßberg either via the rock staircase into Schloßbergplatz, or down the more gentle gradients of the footpath into Paulustorgasse then turn right down the Sporgasse.

In his desire to share with others his delight in the world of arts and sciences, Archduke Johann donated his personal collections to establish the **Joanneum museum** in 1811. Today it is a major resource centre for educational, historical, and conservation studies. The old museum is housed in No 10 Raubergasse (from Schmiedgasse turn into Landhausgasse then left into Raubergasse) which was, from 1665 to 1674, the city palace for the Barons of Rauber, the chapter of St Lambrechts abbey for whom it was designed by Domenico Sciassia. It accommodates the departments of geology, palaeontology, and mining; mineralogy; zoology; and botany. Across a small park, at No 45 Neutorgasse, is the new museum which houses the department of industrial design and the art gallery.

Around Graz

Two miles west of the city centre is **Schloß Eggenberg** built in 1625 by Pietro Valnegro for Prince Ulrich of Eggenberg, counsellor to Ferdinand II. In 1742 the palace was acquired by marriage by the Herberstein family, and since 1938 it has been owned by the government of Styria. It is situated in a beautiful little wooded 'English' park full of deer, pheasants, and peacocks. Behind its imposing façade there is a large courtyard enclosed by arcades, and two smaller yards separated by a church, enclosed by four wings laid out in a square. On the ground floor is the department of pre- and early history of the Joanneum museum, containing many fascinating archaeological finds from all over Styria as well as the coin collection. On the first floor is the Styrian hunting museum which displays 150 pairs of antlers, and dioramas of Austrian fauna. The state rooms, on the second floor, are richly ornamented in stucco by Alessandro Serenio (1682) and are open to the public. The paintings in the great banqueting hall are by Hans Adam Weissenkircher (1685). On the south-east side of the park is the Roman relic collection (Römersteinsammlung) of the Joanneum comprising mosaics, statues, milestones, inscribed tablets, gravestones, altars and sarcophagi. Schloß Eggenberg can be reached from the city centre by Strassenbahn (streetcar) No 1.

For a contrast to the imperial opulence of the city's palaces visit the Austrian open-air museum at **Stübing** (Österreichische Freilichtmuseum Stübing). It is located about 9 miles from the city centre and

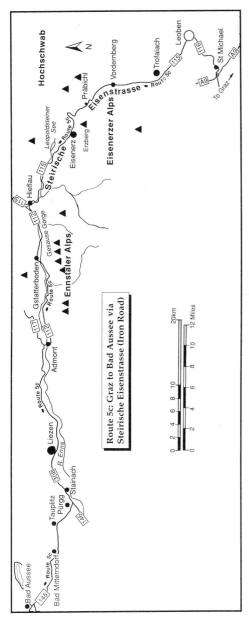

Route 5c: Graz to Bad Aussee via Steirische Eisenstrasse (Iron Road)

may be reached via the suburb of Gösting or by following the green road signs off the Salzburg motorway. Drivers should take care as the road is narrow and winding. Look out for the sharp double bend over the railway, and beware of oncoming heavy traffic. The entrance to the museum is unmarked. Park in either of the two parking areas and walk through the underpass beneath the railway to reach the administrative building and the ticket office. The museum comprises a superb collection of over sixty historic farmhouses, barns, cottages, water mills, smithies, a village shop, and other rustic buildings from all over Austria — many of them furnished — in the natural setting of a small valley. A visit will take about 3 hours.

Horse lovers will be especially interested in the stud farm at **Piber**, near Köflach, where the famous white Lipizzaner horses are bred and reared for the Spanish Riding

The Hauptplatz and Archduke Johann's monument in Graz

School in Vienna. Piber is some 27 miles west of Graz and a mile off Route 70 (see Klagenfurt to Graz via the Packer Höhestrasse). Exhibition presentations are held throughout the summer and early autumn on specific dates which vary from year to year. Up-to-date information can be obtained from the tourist information office in Köflach (Bahnhofstrasse 24, A-8580 Köflach; ☎ 03144 2520-70).

To the east of Graz there are numerous castles and fortresses: Schloß Stubenberg, Schloß Schieleiten, Schloß Herberstein, Schloß Freiberg, Schloß Kalsdorf, Schloß Feistritz, Schloß Welsdorf and Schloß Riegersberg. The latter, 30 miles south-east of Graz, is the most spectacular, being perched on a high basalt rock which made it impregnable. It dates from 1170 and includes a knight's hall, a decorative dining room, and a prince's room. Most of the present fortress was built in 1650 by Elisabeth von Galler — known as 'Wicked Leisel' for her ruthless treatment of her enemies. When the law failed to meet her demands then she resorted to force of arms. When the local priest denounced her she sent her men-at-arms to fetch him. Forewarned, the priest fled so Elisabeth took his cook and executed her. Here too lived Katharina Paltauf — 'the Flower Witch' — who, under torture, confessed to using witchcraft to make the flowers bloom in winter and, with

a dozen others, was hanged at Feldbach. Schloß Herberstein, north-

east of Graz, is also popular with visitors. It was built in 1230, and is surrounded by a seventeenth-century zoological garden. The two-storeyed living quarters adjoin a delightful arcaded courtyard with a well and a sundial dated 1561. There are two chapels, a knight's hall, an

ancestors' gallery, and a museum.

The portal to Schloß Eggenberg, near Graz

Route 5c   Graz to Bad Aussee via the Iron Road (Steirische Eisenstraße)

(see map page161)

Heading north from Graz several roads are available. One route which offers a combination of speed and leisure starts out by following the A9 motorway through the 5-mile-long Gleinalm tunnel. After 35 miles leave the motorway and turn to the right through St Michael i. Obersteiermark into **Leoben**, at 42 miles, an industrial town notable for the visit by Napoleon Bonaparte, in 1797, when he signed an armistice with the Emperor of Austria. A monument commemorating this event is outside St James' church, and the local history museum devotes a room to it.

Turn left onto Route 112 signposted Heiflau/Eisenerz. Travelling through the busy town the road passes several large iron and steel works and, after two sets of traffic lights, joins Route 115a which later becomes Route 115. Some 7 miles out of Leoben and the scene changes to lovely open country with steep wooded hillsides on either side. White-rocked peaks ahead create a dramatic skyline as the road winds up the valley through the villages of St Peter Freienstein and Trofaiach to **Vordernberg**, at 53 miles.

The market town of Vordernberg (population 2,100) has interesting historical exhibitions of local technology which include an early nine-teenth-century charcoal furnace, now a museum, and a steam engine museum. The town also has two churches: the baroque Maria Himmelfahrt, and the fifteenth-century St Laurentius. In the square before the Rathaus the wrought-iron fountain canopy (1668) is notable. Vordernberg is a good centre for walking and skiing in the surrounding hills.

After another 2$\frac{1}{2}$ miles the road crosses the iron-ore railway and rises through two long hairpin bends to a pass, and the village of **Präbichl**. This is a popular winter resort with a chairlift to the nearby Polster mountain (1,797m, 5,894ft) as well as several ski-lifts. It is also a convenient centre for walking and climbing in the Hochschwab group, to the north, and in the Eisenerzer Alps to the west.

As the road begins to drop down into the valley of the Erzbach river the views are fabulous. A high basin up on the left-hand side is enclosed in a ring of sharp, wooded peaks. Ahead the white escarpment of the Pfafferstein (1,871m, 6,137ft) overlooks the dark red terraces of the Erzberg. About 2 miles beyond Präbichl, at 57$\frac{1}{2}$ miles, an excellent picnic, and viewing park affords a spectacular view of the iron mountain.

The Erzberg has been exploited since the Middle Ages, initially by mines and small diggings, since 1870 by surface mining. The whole of the mountain comprises high grade iron ore which feeds not only the iron and steel works of Leoben and the Mur valley but also supplies 90 per cent of the needs of the whole of the Austrian iron and steel industry. The red mountain is now some 1,460m (4,789ft) high but its height has been reduced by about 70m (230ft) since mining began. Today thirty terraces, each 25m (82ft) high, cut into the hillside and, with the great excavators and crawling machinery, create a strange picture of a barren, dehumanised world. Guided tours are available from Eisenerz.

From the parking place the road runs quickly downhill around a long, long, left-hand curve and, at 60 miles reaches **Eisenerz** (population 11,000). In the old town there are several interesting sixteenth- and seventeenth-century houses including the old town hall which dates from 1548. The bell of the sixteenth-century 'Shift Tower' (Schichtturm) marked the start and end of shiftworking on the Erzberg. The parish church of St Oswald is the best preserved fortified church in Styria. In the school of mining there is a mining museum, and there is also a local history museum with an interesting collection of Christmas nativity cribs. Eisenerz is one of the principal winter sports centres in Styria.

From Eisenerz the road weaves down the narrow valley crossing and re-crossing the railway and the river. The quality of the road surface varies. A small road to the right, after $2^1/_2$ miles, leads to the Leopold-steiner See in its lovely setting below the rock face of the Seemauer. After 67 miles the road reaches the pleasant village of **Heiflau** where the Erzbach joins the Enns river to flow north to the Danube. Here Route 115 goes ahead to Altenmarkt; follow Route 112 which turns left into the Gesäuse Gorge. *Gesäuse* means 'roaring', and refers to the terrifying sound of the water of the Enns river as it tumbles roughly between the rocky walls, and over the rocks and falls, of the narrow ravine. Very narrow at first, with a pavé surface, the road soon improves and is very beautiful as it squeezes through tight gaps and over little bridges. After 6 miles it emerges into a long basin and runs alongside the broad river, on the left, into the village of **Gstatterboden**, a popular centre for climbing in the Gesäuse group. The river bed here is six times its low-water width to accommodate the torrent which comes down from the mountains after a storm. Crossing the railway line, then the river bridge, the sparkling white cliffs of the Hochtor (2,369m, 7,770ft) are high above. The road re-enters the gorge and follows $5^1/_2$ miles of corniches and bridges before the hillsides recede to form a wide valley of meadows and scattered houses around the village of **Weng**. At $81^1/_2$ miles the white, limestone peaks of the Haller Mauern group can be seen on the right and the twin spires of Admont abbey come into view.

The Benedictine abbey of **Admont** was founded in 1074 by the Archbishop of Salzburg. It became, in the twelfth and thirteenth centuries, one of the most prosperous and influential religious centres in Austria. In 1865 the extensive buildings — except for the library — were destroyed by fire and were rebuilt in neo-Gothic style. In the abbey church of St Blasius the embroidered hangings on the walls around the high altar are from the abbey workshops. Before the altar is a copy of the *Admonter Madonna* (1320). The original is in the Joanneum in Graz. The delightful gardens of the courtyard contain a fountain with a figure of Neptune by Franz Parnegger. The library claims to be the world's finest and largest baroque library. The magnificent, two-storeyed hall is 72m (236ft) long and there are two rooms on either side of an oval room with a dome decorated with frescoes by Bartholomeo Altomonte (1726), and eighteen sculptures by Josef Thaddäus Stammel (1760). The library stock comprises 145,000 books, 1,200 manuscripts, 500 pamphlets, and many other items on all subjects. There is also a natural history museum and an art history museum.

After Admont the road crosses the Enns river and at the junction Route 112 goes left toward Liezen, passing, on the right, **Frauen-**  **berg** where the seventeenth-century pilgrimage church contains notable frescoes and a very fine baroque altar by Stammel. At 95 miles the road reaches the industrial town of **Liezen** (population 6,500). The late Gothic parish church contains altar paintings by Kremser Schmidt (1777). Liezen is a convenient centre for climbing in the Warscheneck group.

Go ahead at Liezen onto Route 308 and, after 104 miles, at Neuhaus, turn right onto Route 145, the Salzkammergut Bundesstrasse, signposted Salzburg/Bad Aussee. On the left as the road rises through a ravine, are the high cliffs of the Grimming (2,350m, 7,708ft). After 2 miles turn right and about a mile off the main road is the little hillside village of **Pürgg** which is famous for the Romanesque chapel of St Johann (1160). The interior of the chapel is wholly covered with twelfth-century frescoes. The parish church of St George is late Gothic and also has interesting frescoes and a gallery.

The road then rises rapidly to the winter holiday village of **Tauplitz**. As well as a ski-lift there is a chairlift up to the Tauplitzalm (1,660m, 5,445ft) from which there are easy walks to the little mountain lakes of Steyrersee, Schwarzensee, and Grosssee. Just to the south is the hamlet of Klachau and the Kulmkogel (1,120m, 3,674ft) which boasts the world's largest ski-jump. Beyond Tauplitz the excellent road crosses the Hinterberg plateau to **Bad Mitterndorf** (population 2,600), another winter resort with several ski-lifts. The fourteenth-century parish church has an altar painting of *The Martyrdom of St Barbara* by Kremser Schmidt. There is also a local history museum.

At 123 miles from Graz the road reaches the old market town of Bad Aussee which will be described in the next chapter.

Springtime meadow in Styria

6 LAND SALZBURG AND THE SALZKAMMERGUT

PART 1 LAND SALZBURG
AND THE CITY OF SALZBURG

The province of Land Salzburg covers an area of 6,715sq km (2,762 sq miles) and extends to the borders with Tyrol in the west, Bavaria in the north, and Italy, East Tyrol, and Carinthia in the south. The south-eastern section reaches into the High Alps to touch Carinthia and Styria, and the northern portion stretches from the Salzach valley and the West German border to the Salzkammergut. The province is rich with heritage preserved in its churches, castles, and museums, and has great scenic beauty with lovely lakes, mountains and valleys. It is an active industrial province as well as a tourist region. As its name implies, its wealth originated from the presence of large deposits of salt. This attracted settlement as early as the Neolithic age and Celtic remains have been excavated at numerous sites. Today the population is about 438,000 making it one of the smaller of the nine provinces. The historical importance of Land Salzburg derived from the great power of the prince-archbishops of Salzburg in the Holy Roman Empire. Their wealth is evident in the majestic buildings of the city of Salzburg, the provincial capital.

In the chapter on the Tyrol routes from Innsbruck to Zell-am-See were described. This chapter is divided into three parts describing first the road from Zell to Salzburg, then the city of Salzburg, and, finally, the Salzkammergut.

Route 6a Zell-am-See to Salzburg via the Salzburger Dolomitenstrasse

Zell-am-See (population 8,000), enjoys a picturesque location on a narrow ledge beside the western shore of the Zeller See. The latter is about 2$\frac{1}{2}$ miles long, a mile wide, and up to 68m (223ft) deep. It is confined by the steep slopes of the Hahneckkogel (1,857m, 6,091ft) to the east, and of the Schmittenhöhe (1,965m, 6,445ft) to the west. The valley of the river Saalach lies to the north but the river rises in the

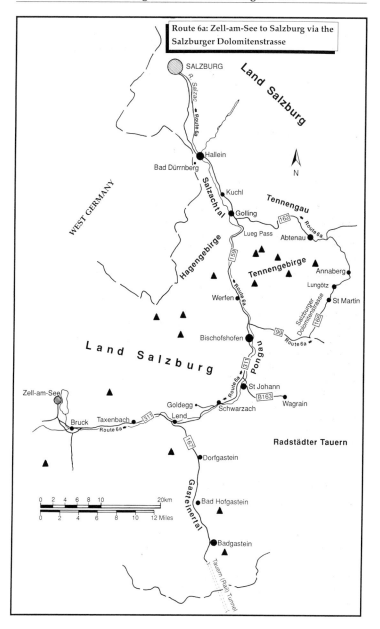

Route 6a: Zell-am-See to Salzburg via the Salzburger Dolomitenstrasse

Kitzbühler Alps and is not connected to the Zeller See. The lake discharges to the south into the river Salzach. The setting and the lake itself, with small hamlets around its edge, are very beautiful.

The town is a popular summer resort and an international centre for winter sports. It is the principal town in western Land Salzburg and is within easy reach, by road or rail, of Salzburg, the Salzkammergut, Innsbruck and the Tyrol, the Grossglockner Hochalpenstrasse, Lienz, and even Vienna is not too far away. The border with West Germany is 32 miles to the north. Downtown Zell is confined to a stubby peninsula which juts out into the lake. The pedestrianised town square is dominated by the massive Constable's Tower from the thirteenth century. The Romanesque parish church of St Hippolyt is very beautiful. The high altar is surprisingly simple with figures of Sts Virgil and Rupert from 1480. Recent restoration has revealed notable fragments of frescoes. The Madonna and Child in the north aisle is thirteenth century, and, in the anteroom, a bearded figure from the legend of St Katharine dates from the fourteenth century. In the choir there are beautiful frescoes of the apostles (fourteenth century) and of St John the Baptist (sixteenth century). The vaulting in the apse dates from the thirteenth and fourteenth centuries but the vaulting in the nave was destroyed by fire in 1770 and in 1898 was replaced by a flat wooden ceiling. The statues of Sts Hippolyt and Florian date from 1515. The crypt was closed in 1325 but has now been re-opened. The west gallery dates from 1515 and has a handsome balustrade. The silver-piped organ was installed in 1981 enabling regular organ and choral recitals to become a feature of the summer programme of entertainments.

The small streets of the old market town are full of character. There is a delightful promenade past the Grand Hotel and the marina, and the lake provides excellent facilities for sailing, boating, swimming, windsurfing, fishing for trout and zander, and boat excursions around the shoreline. To the west the land rises and many good *pensions* cling to the steep slope. From their balconies there are superb views eastward across the lake, and to the south loom the snow-capped peaks of the High Alps. The town hall is housed in the former Schloß Rosenberg (1583) where there is also a local history museum.

At Schmitten, 1 mile west of Zell, from mid-May to mid-September a cable car runs up to the Schmittenhöhe (1,965m, 6,445ft) where visitors may see the spectacular panorama, and enjoy the hospitality of the Berghotel. From mid-June to mid-October a second cable car goes up to the Sonnenalm, and from there a double chairlift goes up to the Sonnkogel (1,856m, 6,088ft). From the ski-school, at the top end of Gartenstrasse, a gondola lift operates from mid-June to mid-September up to the Mittelstation (1,360m, 4,461ft), where there is a restaurant. A cable car from Thumersbach, on the eastern shore of the lake, goes up to the Ronachkopfl (1,326m, 4,349ft) to allow splendid views across

The Constable's Tower and town square, Zell-am-See

the lake to Zell, to the Kitzbüheler Alps, and south to the Glockner group.

At the Bergstation a guide will advise visitors on the various marked routes they may follow. There are many opportunities to walk either along the Pinzgauer Spaziergang into the Kitzbüheler Alps, or down the slopes of the Schmittenhöhe. The post-bus services to and from the lower stations are a special feature of the timetable. For example, bus No 3404 leaves the post office in Zell early in the morning and goes to the lower station of the Schmittenhöhe cableway. From the top of the cableway go to the south, downwards following the signpost to the Pinzgauer Hütte. Then bear right through the high forest and across an open clearing to the Pillager Hütte where there are refreshments. A track leads down to the Einöd (Lonely) Alm. Soon the path crosses a brook and goes to the left-hand side and through the woods to Piesendorf. Then the pathway forks to the left to reach the meadows above the village of Fürth. The walk is not difficult and should take about $3^1/_2$ hours. From Fürth the post-bus (No 3430) runs an hourly service back to Zell.

Zell-am-See and Kaprun have co-operated to create a Europa Sport Region with facilities for all kinds of sporting activities, but especially for watersports and snowsports. Within the region there are fifty-one cableways and lifts providing access to 80 miles of prepared slopes and 75 miles of cross-country ski-tracks. Summer skiing is available on the high glaciers. At Zell there are indoor and outdoor tennis, yachting, rifle shooting, athletic, soccer, and riding facilities, an indoor swimming pool, and an 18-hole championship golf course at Limberg. In June there is a running competition, and in August triathlon and pentathlon, and show-jumping competitions.

The summer programme in Zell includes concerts in Elizabeth Park, in the town square, in the parish church, and in the school of music. Concerts, country-theatre, dancing, beer and wine parties, barbecues and fondue evenings, zither and torch-light evenings, garden parties, and fêtes take place in some of the larger hotels and are usually open to non-residents. In August there is a lake festival with a firework display. There are steam train excursions to Krimml on Tuesdays, Thursdays and Saturdays (check at the tourist office in Brucker Bundesstrasse).

 At the north end of the Zeller See is the sixteenth-century Schloß Prielau, and just north-east of Maishofen ($2^1/_2$ miles from Zell on Route 311) is Schloß Kammer which dates from 1711 and is now a hotel. At Maishofen a small side road runs westward up the Glammtal to **Saalbach** (population 2,400). This is an attractive summer and winter resort with a cable car to the Schattberg (2,018m, 6,619ft). The baroque parish church dates from 1719.

Leave Zell-am-See southward on Route 168 and after a mile bear left onto Route S11 to bypass Bruck and then join Route 311 eastbound down the bottom of the Pinzgau. After 13 miles the small market town of **Taxenbach** is known for its proximity to the Kitzloch ravine at the entrance to the Rauriser valley. At **Rauris**, 6 miles up the valley, there is a museum which has a collection of items relating to the local gold-washing industry. Gold panning excursions are available.

Beyond Taxenbach the traffic speeds alongside the Salzach to reach **Lend** (population 1,800) where there is an aluminium works. The parish church dates from 1674 and has a baroque and rococo interior. About a mile south-east, on the old road, there is a 63m-high (207ft) waterfall in the Gasteiner Klamm. The main road rises steeply (gradient 15 per cent, 1 in 7) and forks. The right-hand road — Route 167 — rises through a tunnel then runs up the Gasteinertal alongside the river and the railway. This road provides an interesting detour.

Five miles from Lend Route 167 passes, on the left, **Dorfgastein** (835m, 2,739ft) where it is a 30-minute walk up to Entrische Kirche, a 2-mile-long stalactite cave. Then the road continues gently upward to reach **Bad Hofgastein** (population 6,000) after 10 miles. This is a delightful health resort with a cable car up to the Kitzsteinalm (1,302m, 4,271ft) and a further cableway up to the Kleine Scharte (2,050m, 6,724ft). There are lovely old houses in the pedestrianised centre of the town and the late Gothic parish church has a notable altar from 1738.

As the mountain sides press in on the valley the road climbs steadily and at the outskirts of the town goes up a short hill (gradient 12 per cent, 1 in 8) to reach **Badgastein** (population 5,600) after 15 miles. This has been a fashionable health and winter sports centre since the nineteenth century. Its elegant hotels and shops stand in a semicircle around a woodland dell and the Gasteiner Ache spills its waters from the top of the slope through the very heart of the town. Overlooked by the peaks of the High Alps, Badgastein is a picturesque — and popular — all-year-round resort. The healing properties of its thermal springs are derived from the presence of radon in their waters, which is said to bring relief to those who suffer from rheumatism. The waters are supplied to more than 100 hotels and *pensions*, and is also available in disused mine workings above Böckstein. The resort was favoured by the philosopher Schopenhauer and the composers Johann Strauss and Schubert who wrote his *Gastein Symphony* in its honour.

The neo-Gothic parish church dates from the nineteenth century. Nearby is the unusual church of St Nikolaus which dates from 1410. The nave is built on a star-shaped plan around a central pillar, and on the baroque altars there are fragments of fifteenth- and sixteenth-century frescoes. The local history museum has collections of folk art, minerals and mining artefacts. An indoor swimming pool has been carved out of the rock and is filled with water from the hot springs. A cable car goes up in two stages to the Salesenwald (1,794m, 5,884ft) and on to the Stubnerkogel (2,231m, 7,318ft). Since 1971 the Nassfeldtal, above Böckstein, has been developed as *Sportgastein* with lifts onto the slopes of the Kreuzkogel (2,686m, 8,810ft). A cableway is under construction from the head of the Nassfeldtal up to the Schareck (3,122m, 10,240ft) where the views will be spectacular.

There are many good walks around Badgastein. For example, the Kaiser-Wilhelm-Promenade follows the Kötschachbach to reach the Hotel Grüner Baum after less than an hour of level walking. It affords

The Gasteiner Ache flows through the middle of Badgastein

views over the rooftops of the town and down the valley toward Bad Hofgastein. The latter may be reached on foot via the Gasteiner Höhenweg which clings to the right-hand side of the valley, away from the traffic of the main road. The Empress (Kaiserin) Elizabeth Promenade follows the river up to Böckstein and is also an enjoyable and easy walk.

About 3 miles above Badgastein Route 167 reaches the entrance to the Tauern Tunnel. The tunnel is over 5 miles long and cars are transported through it by rail to Mallnitz in Carinthia. The construction of the Tauern *Autobahn* (A10) and its new road tunnel has reduced the traffic through Badgastein.

THE PONGAU

To continue the journey from Zell-am-See to Salzburg take the left fork on Route 311 after Lend to enter the Pongau basin, and after 6 miles reach the market town of **Schwarzach** (population 3,500). The '*Salz-eckertisch*' in the town hall recalls the struggle of the Lutheran Church and the expulsion of Protestants from the Pongau in 1731. On the west side of the town is Schloß Schernberg, and $2^1/_2$ miles further is Schloß Goldegg, a fifteenth-century castle with notable decorations in its hall. It now houses the Pongau folk museum which has a collection of rural utensils and tools. The village of **Goldegg-im-Pongau** has a small lake and is delightful. A mile north of Schwarzach, **St Veit** has a lovely parish church with frescoes from 1460, and typical old Pongau houses.

Five miles beyond Schwarzach, 26 miles from Zell-am-See, turn right off the main road into the alpine town of **St Johann-im-Pongau** (population 7,700). The magnificent parish church of this summer and winter resort has two tall towers, is called the 'Cathedral of the Pongau', and is of considerable historical significance. The nearby, two-storeyed Annakapelle was once an ossuary and contains notable wooden carvings of Sts Heinrich II and Kunigunde on the lower altar. A small road to the south goes up the Großarltal for about 3 miles to the Liechtenstein Gorge (*Klamm*). This is a popular place to visit with an easy 45-minute walk over the suspension bridges to a rest area and viewing platform above the waterfall, and two large restaurants for refreshments. The road goes 13 miles further up the valley via Großarl to Hüttschlag. Also at St Johann are the Klingelberg excavations where 2,000-year-old Celtic graves are being uncovered. At **Wagrain** (population 2,500), 5 miles east on Route B163, Joseph Mohrs, who wrote the words of the Christmas carol *Silent Night*, is buried.

Route 311 now turns north following the river Salzach to reach **Bischofshofen** (population 9,500). This market town has three interesting churches. The parish church is Gothic, fourteenth and fifteenth century, and has baroque altars and frescoes, and a notable tomb of Sylvester, Bishop of Chiemsee who died in 1453. The Frauenkirche is also Gothic and has the oldest tabernacle (1618) in Land Salzburg. St George's church, now a church of remembrance, is Romanesque (1403) and has frescoes from 1230. St Rupert's Cross, in the priest's house, is said to date from AD800. The Gainfeld Waterfall is on the west side of the town.

Two miles north of Bischofshofen Route 311 goes north along the

Salzach, and Route 99 goes east along the Fritzbach. The visitor must choose here between proceeding along the main road via Werfen, or diverting eastwards to follow the Salzburger Dolomitenstrasse via Abtenau. These roads meet again at Golling.

Note here also the A10 toll motorway between Salzburg and Klagenfurt — the Tauern *Autobahn* — which is one of the most important roads across the High Alps. It passes through two tunnels — the 4-mile-long Tauern Tunnel, and the $3^1/_2$-mile-long Katschbertunnel — and its maximum gradient is $4^1/_2$ per cent (1 in 22). It is one of the newest and most scenic motorways in Austria.

THE SALZBURGER DOLOMITENSTRASSE

From Bischofshofen go north 2 miles on Route 311 then turn right onto Route 99 and, after 9 miles, turn left onto Route 166 which is the Salzburger Dolomitenstrasse. The road rises steadily past scattered houses and meadows and tall pines. At 12 miles the road passes through the hamlet of St Martin-im-Tennengebirge. Just $2^1/_2$ miles further, at **Lungötz**, with its pretty houses, the rugged peaks of the Tennengebirge Mountains are visible to the west and the Grosser Donerkogel (2,055m, 6,740ft) looms ahead. At $16^1/_2$ miles the road

crosses the river Lammer and goes right into the hamlet of **Annaberg-im-Lammertal**, a holiday resort with ski-lifts and marked footpaths, and a baroque parish church.

The road then rises through a succession of corniches, passes, and basins bordered by forests and meadows. At $22^1/_2$ miles Route 166 goes right to Gosau. Go left and ahead onto Route B162 signposted Golling. The road descends gently through a wide valley to **Abtenau**

(population 5,000). This is a good centre for walking and touring. There are several old houses with painted façades, and the Gothic parish church has a remarkably tall spire. It dates from the fourteenth century

and has a notable baroque high altar from 1675.

After another broad valley and another series of scenic ravines and basins the road passes the Lammeröfen Gorge which is worth a 30-minute stop. Four miles further and the road bypasses Scheffau-an-der-Lammer (population 1,000), and at **Unterscheffau** the sombre

black dome on the massive square tower of the late Gothic parish church may be seen to the right. It has an early baroque high altar from 1629 and Gothic stained glass windows from 1499. At 40 miles, as the road approaches the junction with Route 159, the view ahead is quite spectacular with the skyline formed by the conical top of the Kleiner Göll (1,753m, 5,750ft) and the adjacent peaks of the Hagengebirge on the border with West Germany. Go right onto Route 159 to enter Golling.

BISCHOFSHOFEN TO SALZBURG VIA ROUTE 159

From Bischofshofen go ahead on Route 159 down the Salzach valley to **Werfen** (population 3,000), a market town with the massive Burg Hohenwerfen (1077) on the north side. It is especially known for the Eisriesenwelt ('World of the Ice-Giant') ice caves to the north where conducted tours take about 2 hours. Of greater interest to spelaeologists are the Eiskogel caves at Werfenwang, to the east, where short conducted tours take 2 hours but more extensive tours, requiring insurance and the hire of proper gear, take up to 5 hours.

The road then goes over Pass Lueg, where there is a pilgrimage church, to reach Golling after 15 miles from Bischofshofen. **Golling** (population 3,500) is a market town and summer resort with old and colourful houses and shops. The parish church has a Gothic tower built in 1685 and a baroque interior. The castle has a small courtyard and chapel and a museum with fossils, copies of rock drawings and local history items. At **Torren**, on the opposite bank of the Salzach, the chapel of St Nikolaus is unusual in having an outside pulpit. It also has a gallery with a lovely stone balustrade. Just outside the village, some 45 minutes' walk from Golling or Kuchl, are the Gollinger Waterfalls.

Four miles beyond Golling the road reaches **Kuchl** (population 5,200), another town with attractive old houses. The parish church is late Gothic with a Romanesque portal in the tower and remnants of paintings from 1200. The Georgenberg church (1682) stands on the site of a fifth-century basilica, and has a baroque high altar by Johann George Mohr (1716). Nearby, at the foot of the Hohen Göll (2,522m, 8,270ft) there is a nature park.

As Route 159 runs down the broad valley there are more and more houses on either side and factories appear to the left. Nevertheless, it is a pleasant road, often tree-lined, with rugged mountains never out of sight. Eight miles from Golling, on the outskirts of Hallein, a set of lights control traffic through the middle of a paper works where a chubby little red steam engine puffs and clanks across the road. **Hallein** (population 15,000) today is a busy working town with old buildings and narrow alleyways. Its name is derived from *hallen*, the Celtic word for salt. In the former offices of the salt company there are a large number of representations of scenes from the salt workings. These offices also house a Celtic museum with a collection of rare items from 500 to 15BC which were found at Dürrnberg, and it contains the archives of Franz Xaver Gruber who composed the music of *Silent Night* and other works. The parish church has a Gothic choir from the fourteenth century, neoclassical marble altars, and the chapel of St Peter dates from 1384.

The area around **Bad Dürrnberg**, a mile south-west of Hallein, has been settled since prehistoric times, and it has been extensively excavated. At **Keltendorf** there is an open-air exhibition of finds, and reconstructions of a Celtic farm and a 2,000-year-old grave. The pilgrimage church is seventeenth century and on the magnificent high altar there is a miracle picture from 1612. Nearby there is a marble

The steep path up to the Eisreisenwelt ice caves

※ wellhead from 1530. A cablecar goes up to the Dürrnberg (800m, 2,624ft) where there is an old salt mine, 450m (1,476ft) deep, with a salt

Mozartplatz, Salzburg

lake and slides, which is open to visitors.

From Hallein Route 159 continues into the city of Salzburg which is about 20 miles from Golling, 25 miles from Bischofshofen, and 56 miles from Zell-am-See.

SALZBURG

Salzburg has been a site of settlement since Neolithic times. Its attraction for those early peoples must have derived from its location on the northern edge of the Alps, poised between the south German plain to the west and the Danube basin to the east, on the banks of the river Salzach, and, especially, from its proximity to the salt mines to the south. It stood on an important Celtic east-west trade route and later on a road south to Rome, just as today the E11 and E14 motorways intersect on the south-west side of the city. Inevitably it enjoyed a varied history and suffered successive occupations by German and French forces. Its role as an ecclesiastical centre, for the propagation of Christianity in the surrounding region, was assured by the foundation of the abbey of St Peter and the Nonnberg convent by St Rupert in 690. The prince-archbishops of the Holy Roman Empire were powerful politicians with determined enemies and the steep slopes of the Mönchsberg were ideal for the construction of an impregnable fortress. Over the years the city's political importance waxed and waned but the progressive development — especially under the influence of the famous architects Fischer von Erlach and Johann Lukas von Hildebrandt — of its magnificent architectural heritage continued despite the damage caused by several fires which engulfed many fine buildings.

Today Salzburg is one of the most beautiful cities in Europe. The new town, on the right-hand bank of the river Salzach, is overlooked by the Capuchin monastery, and the old town, tucked into the foot of the shear escarpment of the Mönchsberg, is dominated by the Hochensalzburg fortress. The visitor can find a wealth of interest in the churches, the cathedral, the palaces and museums, and may delight in the period houses which line the spacious squares, and the elegant shops and cafés along the narrow alleyways. Salzburg is a centre of cultural excellence and offers an abundance of music, drama and the arts of the highest international standard.

The provincial capital, with a population of 145,000, is easily reached by road, rail, or air (the airport is only 2 miles from the city centre). Accommodation ranges from first class hotels to small inns, as well as guest houses, three youth hostels, and nine camp sites. Coffee houses and restaurants offer international dishes from hamburgers to *haute cuisine*. Evening entertainment includes dancing, beer cellars and wine bars, gambling at the casino, cinema and theatre.

The city also provides sporting activities including golf at Kleisheim, fishing in rivers and lakes, indoor and outdoor swimming, tennis, shooting, bowling, flying and gliding, riding, cycling, football, athletics, skiing, mountaineering and walking. There are 30 miles of walks within the city boundary, and, east and south-east of the city, on the Heuberg (900m, 2,952ft), in the Guggental, on the Nockstein (1040m, 3,411ft), to the Glasenbachklamm, on the Erentrudisalm (905m, 2,968ft), and to St Jakob am Thurn.

A walking tour of the old town of Salzburg may conveniently begin at the information office in the Mozartplatz for there the visitor will find all of the leaflets, maps, programmes, postcards etc he or she is likely to need. However, since the tour is circular, it can be joined at any location along the route.

The Mozartplatz is a pleasant square, busy in summertime when budding violinists may burst into a sonata, or a pianist, complete with piano, may appear from nowhere to entertain the passing throng beneath Schwanthaler's bronze statue of Wolfgang Amadeus Mozart. It was unveiled in 1842 in the presence of the composer's sons, his widow Constance having died earlier that year (see the memorial tablet on house No 8). The features of the monument are not considered to be a good resemblance of Mozart.

From the Mozartplatz bear west and to the right, leaving the Glockenspiel Café on the left, passing through the Waagplatz, the city's oldest market square, into the Judengasse, site of the ghetto until 1404 when the Jewish community was expelled from the city. The medieval lanes off this street have retained much of their character. Note that

Franz Schubert, the composer, resided at No 8 in August, 1825.

The old market (Alter Markt), on the left, is worth a diversion. This picturesque square is formed by period houses, mostly eighteenth century, which include Café Tomaselli (1703), the oldest coffee house in the city; '**The Smallest House in Salzburg**', now occupied by an optician (note the dragon rainspout); the baroque **Hofapotheke** (court apothecary, 1591); and the remarkable doorway of the Salzburger Sparkasse bank which, in 1774, was the entrance to the loan office. St Florian's fountain statue dates from 1734 (railings 1583). No longer the principal venue for the market, nevertheless, a few stalls find their way into this elegant square.

Continue along the Judengasse into Getreidegasse to the **old town hall** (Alte Rathaus), with its rococo façade, on the right-hand side. Built in 1407, a marble figure of Justice and the arms of the city stand over the door. The phases of the moon can be read from a blue and gold sphere above an oval window in the clock tower. Most of the hall is not open to the public but visitors are allowed to see the panoramic painting of Salzburg by Franz Kulstruck (1916) on the second floor.

The Getreidegasse is a narrow, pedestrianised street of shops displaying their enchanting gilt and wrought-iron trade signs, their graphic representations derived from times when few citizens were able to read. They include perhaps the world's most modest 'M for McDonald' sign. The houses are mostly *Burgher*'s homes of the fifteenth to eighteenth centuries and there are many side alleys and courtyards — notably at Nos 3, 5, and 9 — where there are coffee houses and shops.

The most frequented house in Getreidegasse is No 9 (**Mozart Geburtshaus**) where, on 27 January 1756, Mozart was born. He lived here, with his parents and sister Nannerl, until 1763. Three floors now accommodate the Mozart museum, a collection of letters, portraits, manuscripts, the prodigy's violin, and various string and keyboard instruments used by him, as well as model presentations of his operas.

At the end of the Getreidegasse, opposite and to the right, stands the **church of St Blasius** (1327), a Gothic edifice with three aisles but without an apse, by an unknown architect. It adjoins the **Bürgerspital almshouses** (1570), two superimposed rows of pensioners' cells cut into the rock face of the Mönchsberg and opening onto a delightful arcade which was rebuilt after World War II.

[Note that the tour may be shortened by turning left rather than right at the end of the Getreidegasse.]

Proceed to the right beneath the Schleifertor into Anton-Neumayr Platz where the statue of the Virgin, with fountain and railings, dates from 1691. On the left is the Mönchsberg lift (daily in summer from 7am to 2am; in winter from 7am to 10.30pm) rises inside the rock to a terrace which affords an excellent view over the city, and which provides access to the Café Winkler and its casino.

The busy pedestrianised Getreidegasse, Salzburg

 Continue north into Museumplatz where the **Carolinum August-eum museum** houses an extensive collection of historic Salzburgian

A Fiaker passes the Horsepond, Salzburg

items from early to modern times. On the opposite side the **natural history museum** (Haus der Natur) is world famous with eighty rooms of collections and displays. Around the corner, to the left, at the end of the Ursuline convent, is **St Mark's church** (1699) by Fischer von Erlach. Return via Gstättengasse, noting, at No 4, the oldest bakery (1429) in Salzburg; retrace steps through the Schleifertor, pass the Getreidegasse on the left, and enter Sigmundsplatz.

At the corner, next to the traffic lights, is the splendid **Horsepond** (Pferdeschwemme). Thought to be the design of Fischer von Erlach, it was constructed in 1695 and watered the horses of the archbishop's stables. The *Horse Tamer* was sculpted by Michael Mandl. Behind the frescoes of the rear wall is a disused quarry. Adjacent is the Neutor Tunnel (1767), 123m (403ft) long, which leads to the district of Riedenburg. A marble relief of Prince-Archbishop Sigmund bears the inscription '*Te saxa loquuntor*' ('Stones will tell of thee').

From the Sigmundsplatz bear left alongside the **old university** (founded 1623, closed 1810, re-opened 1964) into Universitätsplatz where a fruit and vegetable (and bread and cheese) market is held daily except Sundays. On the right is the **collegiate church of the Immaculata** (1707) which is one of the most beautiful baroque churches in the city, and, again, attributed to Fischer von Erlach. Its high, white columns carry many lovely reliefs. The gilded high altar is small but there are two very large side altars as well as two smaller ones. They are dedicated to the faculties of the university: St Thomas, patron of theology; St

Benedict, law; St Luke, medicine; and St Katharine, philosophy. Its treasures include altar paintings by Johann Rottmayr; sculptures by Guggenbichler, Pfaffinger, and Mandl; and, behind the altar, a magnificent representation of the Virgin Mary in a sunburst, surrounded by stucco clouds and angels, by Carlone and del' Allio (1707).

Continue around the east side of the collegiate church through the open-air meat and poultry market into Max Reinhardt Platz. On the right, in the Hofstallgasse, is the **playhouse** (Festspielhaus). The new (or large) playhouse contains a 2,340-seat auditorium with a 130m-high (426ft) stage cut into the Mönchsberg rock. In the foyer a steel relief, *Homage to Anton von Webern*, is by Rudolf Hoflehner, and the tapestry, *Amor and Psyche*, is by Oskar Kokoshka. The old (or small) playhouse can seat 1,300 people and was converted from the archbishop's stables. On the ceiling is a large painting by Rottmayr of *Tilt the Turk*, an equestrian sport. Adjacent is the **Felsenreitschule**, the open-air, galleried theatre where tournaments and animal-baitings were held. Conducted tours of the playhouse are available.

Salzburg is especially a city of music. It celebrates its favourite son — Wolfgang Amadeus Mozart — in the most appropriate way with a programme which begins with 'Mozart Week' in late January, followed by a festival at Easter, the month-long August festival, as well as individual concerts and opera performances and the 'Salzburger Kulturtage' in October. Orchestras and soloists of repute come to Salzburg to perform Mozart's glorious compositions in the setting in which so many of them were conceived and written.

Proceed eastward into Franciskanergasse to the **Franciscan church**, first consecrated in 1223, on the site of St Mary's church which was destroyed by fire in 1167. This is a church of contrasting styles, the dark Romanesque nave leading to the elevated, well lit, twelve-sided Gothic choir. The present high altar by von Erlach (1709), in pink and grey marble, dates from 1710 but includes the Madonna from the original altar by Michael Pacher. The Mother and Child sculpture is by Simeon Fries (1709). To the rear is a marble winged altar from the old cathedral (1561). The semi-circle of nine chapels, by Hans Stethaimer (1432), are notable, as is the pulpit. Just above the plinth of the Romanesque west door (1200) is the remnant of an upraised hand symbolising the ancient right of sanctuary.

Leave the Franciscan church by the south door (1220) and pass under the arch into the courtyard of **St Peter's abbey**, founded about 690 by St Rupert, and, until 1110, the residence of the archbishops. **St Peter's fountain** (1673) is by Bartholomew Opstal. Adjoining the church, on the left, is the old **Well House**, with its wrought-iron, spiral cage and baroque canopy; on the right is St Peter's wine cellar (1529).

The **abbey church of St Peter** (1130) is Salzburg's only Romanesque church. Above the rococo doors the Latin inscription reads: 'I am the door; by me if any man enter in, he shall be saved'. The original interior frescoes were whitewashed in the late sixteenth century but some fragments remain. Many further alterations were made over the years. In 1622 the eight-sided dome was built over the crossing, and the fifteenth-century crypt was filled in. In the eighteenth century the church was redecorated in rococo style in white and green plasterwork. The high altar painting is by J.M. Schmidt of Krems who painted all but two of the sixteen altarpieces in the side chapels. The abbot's chair and choirstalls are by Jakob Adelhardt of Hallein (1926). The bronze sanctus lights on the balustrade of the rococo pulpit are French, were commissioned by Archbishop Wolf Dietrich in 1609, and bear his coat of arms. St Peter's is a very beautiful church with superb ceiling decoration and a dozen magnificent side altars.

In the south transept, to the left of the high altar, is the tomb of St Vitalis with a remarkable marble relief (1497) which is attributed to 'Master Hans'. A door on the right leads to the Maria Zell chapel (formerly St Katharine's) founded in 1215 by Duke Leopold VI of Austria. At the rear of the altar, in the south aisle, is St Rupert's fifth-century tomb containing his sarcophagus. St Rupert predicted that the town would be destroyed when his light was extinguished, and so the sanctuary light has been kept burning continuously for over 800 years. Opposite the tomb a monument to Michael Haydn (1806), composer Joseph's brother, carries an urn said to contain his skull. Also in the south aisle is a memorial (1829) to Marianne, Baroness Berchtold von Sonnenberg, who was Mozart's sister Nannerl.

A passageway from the west courtyard leads to **St Peter's church-** ☀ **yard**, the oldest cemetery still in use in the city, and a place of beauty and tranquillity. The arcades along three sides contain family vaults, including: No 16, Lorenz Hagenauer, landlord to the Mozart family; No 31, Santino Solari, architect of the cathedral who also built the Hell-brunn palace; No 39, Sigmund Haffner von Imbachhausen, to whom Mozart dedicated his *Haffner Symphony*; No 51, Wolfgang Hagenauer, designer of the Neutor Tunnel and the statue of the Virgin Mary in the Domplatz. On the right of the entrance to the catacombs is the **chapel of the Cross** (1170). In 1614 it was converted into a mausoleum for Prior Anton, Graf von Lodron, and is now used as a mortuary chapel. **St Rupert's prayer cell** is located behind the Romanesque altar, and on the left-hand side a flight of steps rises to **St Ägidius chapel** which is thought to have been St Rupert's first dwelling place in Salzburg.

Also near the entrance to the catacombs is a vault where notables, including Marianne Mozart and Michael Haydn, are buried. Guided tours of the third-century catacombs are available. In **St Gertrude's chapel** (1178) a fifteenth-century fresco depicts the martyrdom of St Thomas à Becket. At a higher level is **St Maximus chapel**, previously held to be the site of the martyrdom of St Maximus and fifty companions.

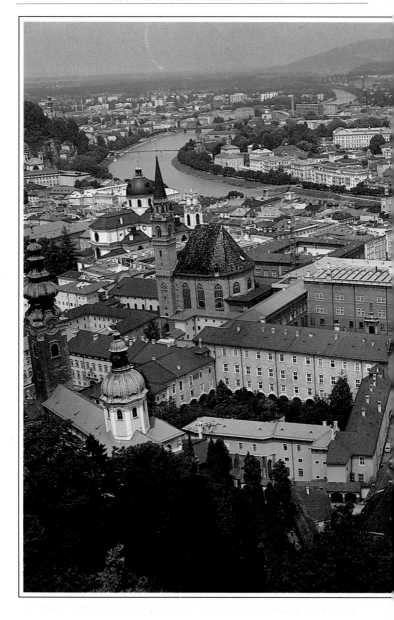

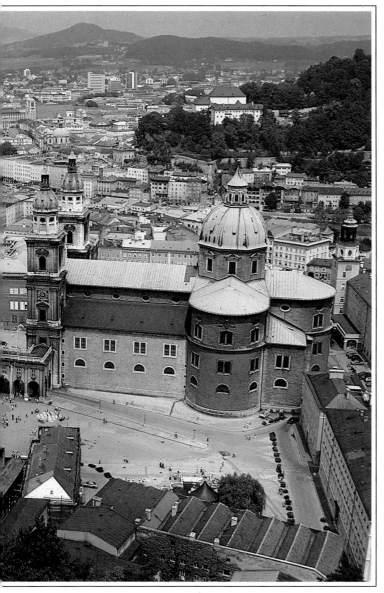

View from the Hochensalzburg fortress, with the cathedral in the foreground

St Margaret's chapel (1491), at the centre of the churchyard, is late Gothic. It is now open only when in use as a mortuary chapel but two peep-holes in the door allow a glimpse of the elegant rib-vaulting and Renaissance frescoes of the interior. Around the chapel the graves are immaculately trimmed, hedged, and flowered, the oldest marked with delicate wrought-iron crosses bearing pictures of the deceased. St Peter's and its churchyard create lasting memories for the visitor. Leave by the gate on the east side, into the Festungsgasse, and turn right.

At the first bend in the Festungsgasse is the lower station of the funicular railway which takes passengers up to the **Hochensalzburg fortress** (1077). Its terraces and the watch-tower afford splendid panoramas of the city, with the river Salzach curving northward along the German border to keep its rendezvous with the Danube, and of the surrounding area, especially of the Tennengebirge and Salzburg Alps to the south. Guided tours are available. Visitors are conducted through the keep; the state apartments (which are the best example in Europe of Gothic interior design), including the golden chamber which contains a magnificent majolica stove of 1501; the cells and torture chamber; and both the fortress and the Rainer museums. St George's chapel has twelve reliefs of the apostles and a painting of St George above the altar. The courtyard contains a red marble relief (1515) of Leonhard von Keutschach, who, in about 1500, constructed the fortress in its present form, and whose insignia — a turnip — is much in evidence. Beneath the 350-year-old lime tree in the middle of the courtyard there is a water cistern and hand pump from 1539.

Also to be seen from the fortress are the slopes of the Mönchsberg which provide easy woodland walks and many good viewpoints, from the 'Friends of Nature' house, on the north-eastern side, to the old fortifications on the southern side.

The Kapitelplatz may be reached either by the return trip on the funicular railway or on foot down the pathway from the courtyard, turning left down the steps to the Festungsgasse. In the Kapitelplatz the **Neptune fountain** dates from 1732 and once provided water for the horses of the cathedral chapter. In summer the west side of the square is lined with market stalls, and people can be seen playing street chess with 3ft-high pieces on a tarmac chessboard. An archway leads into the Domplatz where the **Mariensäule column** dates from 1771. During the August festival the Domplatz is filled with tiers of wooden benches for performances of Hofmannsthal's play *Everyman* (*Jedermann*).

The first **cathedral** was built on the present site by Bishop Virgil, an Irishman, in 767. Over the centuries successive rebuilt and enlarged edifices were burned down until, in 1598, Wolf Dietrich had the courage to demolish the ruins and make a fresh start. In 1611 he fell from grace and was condemned to the fortress where, 5 years later, he died. Marcus Sitticus succeeded him as archbishop and brought Santino Solari from Italy to design the cathedral in its present form — in late Renaissance style with baroque overtones. It was consecrated in 1628 under Archbishop Paris Lodron. In 1944 the dome was destroyed and the interior badly damaged during an air-raid. Restoration was completed, and re-consecration took place, in 1959. The cathedral is of generous proportions and can seat 10,000 worshippers. Its seven bells, consecrated in 1961, weigh a total of 32 tons, and are the largest in Europe.

The façade, of Untersberg marble, carries seventeenth-century statuary by Opstal, Mandl, and Garona, and the coats of arms of Marcus Sitticus and Paris Lodron. The bronze doors are modern (1958), that on the left representing *Faith*, by Toni Schneider-Manzell; in the centre, *Charity*, by Giacomo Manzu; and on the right, *Hope*, by Edward Mataré which was donated by the Krupps family.

Along the left-hand aisle the first side chapel is the baptistry in which the altar is by Frans de Neve. The bronze font (1321), in which Mozart was baptised, is carried on twelfth-century lions from the Romanesque cathedral. The modern cover is by Schneider-Manzell. The following three chapels are dedicated respectively to St Anna, by J. Sandrart; the Transfiguration, by Francesco di Siena; and the Crucifixion, by Karl Skreta. The indirect lighting of the nave serves to accentuate the flood of light from the dome into the crossing. Together they provide a clear perspective of the ample dimensions of the interior, of the beautiful stucco (1630) by J. Bassaimo, and of the frescoes on the nave vaulting, and on the dome, executed by Donato Mascagni with Ignazio Solari and Francesco di Siena.

To the left of the high altar is *The Entombment* by Solari, and St Rupert's oratory. The high altar has sculptures by Hans Parnegger and a representation of *The Resurrection* painted by Mascagni, as was *Christ in Limbo* on the right-hand side, adjacent to St Virgil's oratory.

On the right-hand side of the crossing are the steps down to the crypt which houses the tombs of the archbishops of Salzburg, a central chapel with a crucifix of 1220 from Seekirchen, and the recently discovered crypt of the Romanesque cathedral. A floor mosaic describes the ground plans of the three cathedrals which have stood on this site.

Proceeding along the right-hand aisle, the bronze pulpit supported by a marble column is by Schneider-Manzell (1959). The organ was originally built in 1703 by J. Christopher Egedacher and was refurbished and enlarged in 1959 to 120 registers and 10,000 pipes from 3cm (1in) to 10m (33ft) long. Half-hour recitals are given at 11.15am daily during July and August.

The side chapels along the right-hand aisle are dedicated to the Holy Ghost, by Karl Skreta; Hieronymus, by J.H. Schönfeld; St Charles Borromeo, by various artists; and St Sebastian, by Schönfeld. In the portico is the entrance to the **museum**, inaugurated on the 1,200th anniversary of the cathedral. It displays a fascinating collection of *objets*

A gatehouse at the Hochensalzburg fortress

d'art of religious and historical significance, including St Rupert's crosier and travelling flask; an eleventh-century, jewelled, double

The Residenzplatz fountain, Salzburg

cross; a communion cup in the form of a pigeon made in Limoges in the twelfth century; a sepulchre cup and a legate's cross made in Salzburg in 1499; seventeenth-century tapestries, vestments, and other ecclesiastical charivaria. One section of the museum — the 'Chamber of Art and Wonders' — is furnished in the style of the seventeenth century.

Passing through the north archway from the Domplatz into the Residenzplatz note the entrance to the **excavations museum** which exhibits foundations, mosaics, etc from Roman times to the Middle Ages found on the site of the cathedral.

The Residenzplatz is the starting point for the Fiakers — horse-drawn taxi-cabs — which carry their passengers around the streets of the old city. It is the largest of the city's squares and contains the world's largest baroque fountain which was constructed of Untersberg marble by Tommaso di Garona in 1661. The **Residence**, on the west side, was completed in 1619 on the site of an earlier palace, and was the seat of the prince-archbishops until 1803. Conducted tours of the state apartments take visitors through the guard room (Karabinieresaal); the conference room where Mozart once performed; the audience room; the private apartments; the throne room; the blue room; the chapel; the gallery (Schöne Gallerie); the white room (Weissersaal); and the imperial room (Kaisersaal). Wall and ceiling paintings are by J.M. Rottmayr and M. Altomonte and tell the story of Alexander the Great. Tapestries from Brussels and portraits of the Habsburg emperors are also on view. The gallery, on the third floor, presents paintings by European artists of the sixteenth to nineteenth centuries including works by Rembrandt, Rubens, Brueghel, and Goya.

On the opposite side of the Residenzplatz stands the **New Residence** (Neugebäude) erected by Wolf Dietrich in 1602. Here too there are conducted tours of the state apartments which include the guild room (Ständsaal) on the second floor, with its unique stucco ceiling by Elia Castello, and a portrait gallery of Salzburg's archbishops. Overlooking the New Residence is the Glockenspiel Tower. The carillon of thirty-five bells, cast in Antwerp in 1689, was not put into working order until 1704. Even then the hammers were not properly matched to the bells so that they are sometimes noticeably out of tune. They play compositions by Mozart daily at 7am, 11am and 6pm, and conducted tours start about 15 minutes before each of these performances.

The rococo **St Michael's church**, on the north side, dates from 800, having been rebuilt in 1139 and 1776, and is the oldest parish church in the city. At the north-east corner the Residenzplatz adjoins the Mozartplatz and the tour is completed.

An additional short walk may be made into the Pfeifergasse, just south of the Mozartplatz. In 1525 the famous Doctor Paracelsus lived at No 11. He died 16 years later, aged 48, and bequeathed his fortune to the poor people of Salzburg. At No 18 lived the composer and organist Paul Hofhaymer (1459-1537), and the artist Sebastian Stief died at No 4. In the Kaigasse is the **Chiemseehof** which, during the fourteenth to nineteenth centuries, was the seat of the Bishops of Bavaria and is now the administrative headquarters of the Land Salzburg government. Toward the end of the street a flight of steps leads up to the **Nonnberg convent**.

The Benedictine convent of Nonnberg has been in continuous existence since AD700 when it was founded by St Rupert who installed his niece St Erentrudis as the first abbess. The present edifice dates from 1471, the original having been destroyed by fire in 1423. It contains a Gothic choir, twelfth-century frescoes, the tombs of St Erentrudis, and of St Regintrudis, as well as St John's chapel with its magnificent Gothic altar by Viet Stoss. The convent is only open to art history groups which should apply at the convent door from 9 to 10.30am and 2 to 4pm weekdays, May to October.

Along the banks of the river Salzach there are pleasant, tree-lined walks with kiosks, cafés and seats. The Salzach, a fast flowing, canalised river, is spanned by a railway bridge, three road bridges and four foot bridges. The Staatsbrücke and the Makartsteg provide the most convenient routes from the older to the newer section of the city, on the right-hand bank.

The beautiful **Mirabell gardens** (main entrance from the Makart- platz) were designed by Fischer von Erlach in 1690 and revised by Anton Danreiter in 1730. The formal layout includes a large fountain with sculptures by Ottavio Mosto (1690) which employ mythical figures to represent air, earth, fire and water. At the north end of the gardens stands the remains of **Schloß Mirabell** which was built (as Schloß Altenau) by Archbishop Wolf Dietrich for his mistress Salome Alt in 1606. The superb baroque staircase was designed by J.L. von Hildebrandt in his conversion of 1727 and survived the fire of 1818 which destroyed most of the palace. The stairs lead to the Marmorsaal where weddings and concerts are now held. Just north of the *Schloß* is the Kurpark with its medicinal and modern conference facilities. On the west side the **Bastions garden**, a terrace which formed part of the city fortifications, has a collection of grotesque, marble dwarfs. The nearby small garden house (the **Zauberflötenhäuschen**) was transported from Vienna in 1874 and is reputed to be where Mozart, in September 1791, composed his opera *The Magic Flute*. Also on the west side is the open- air **Heckentheater** of 1718. The **aviary** (Vogelhaus) (about 1700) is now used for exhibitions, and the orangery now houses the **Salzburger Barockmuseum** (1973) which contains Italian and other European architectural sketches from the seventeenth and eighteenth centuries.

In the Makartplatz, named after the artist Hans Makart (1840-84), is the **Landestheater** which stands on the site of the birthplace of Christian Doppler (1803-53), discoverer of the 'Doppler effect'. Next door is the world famous **Salzburg marionette theatre**, established in 1913 by Anton Aicher, which presents ballet and opera from Easter to September. Adjacent is the international music academy, the **Mozarteum**. In its library there are about 200 original manuscripts of Mozart's works. Guided tours and organ concerts in the Great Hall are available during July and August. On the other side of the square, at No 8, are the remains of the house occupied by the Mozart family from 1773 to 1787. Most of the house was destroyed in World War II but the ballroom and music room have survived. The Makartplatz is dominated by the **church of the Holy Trinity** and its priest house, on the east side, which was commissioned by Archbishop Johann Ernst, Count Thun and designed by Fischer von Erlach in 1694. The four sculptures on the façade are by Michael Bernhard Mandl (1699) and the frescoes in the dome are by Johann Michael Rottmayr (1700). In Theatergasse, off the southern corner of the square, is the Café Bazar, a favourite haunt for artists.

St Sebastian's church, in the Linzergasse, is early sixteenth century, refurbished in baroque style in 1749. The sculptures at the door are the work of Josef Anton Pfaffinger and Franz Anton Danreiter (1754), and the wrought-iron is by Philip Hinterseer (1752). St Sebastian's is best known, however, for its graveyard. Half-way down the steps from the church itself are the tombs of Dr Paracelsus (Theophrastus Bombastus von Hohenheim) (1541) and of Elia Castello, the sculptor (1602). In the middle is the Gabriel chapel (1603) which is the mausoleum of Wolf Dietrich, and is lined inside with porcelain tiles by Hans Kapp. Here also is the tomb of the Mozart family: Mozart's wife Constance who, after his death, married Nikolaus von Nissen, and his father, Leopold. Behind the cemetery, in Paris-Lodron Strasse, is the **Loreto church** (1648) with three old chapels, and the *Salzburger Kindl*, an elegant, ivory figure of a child dating from 1620, which is on the right-hand side of the altar.

The city is overlooked by the **Capuchin monastery**, which was built by Wolf Dietrich in 1602, and may be reached from No 14 Linzergasse. The Capuchin church has notable Gothic doors (1450). A superb view of the city and its environs may be obtained from the bastion (Hettwär-Bastei) below the monastery. Near the highest point of the Kapuziner Berg is the café-restaurant Franzisci-Schlössl.

AROUND SALZBURG

Schloß Hellbrunn, an early baroque palace in a country park on the south side of Salzburg, was built in 1615 for Marcus Sitticus by Santino Solari. The paintings by Arsenio Mascagni, in the Festsaal and the Oktagon are especially notable, and there is a Chinese room with eighteenth-century tapestries. In the pleasure gardens there are waterworks and a mechanical theatre (1750) with 150 figures as well as statues and fountains. The Monatschlössl (1615), a hunting lodge, was used for only one month of the year. Since 1924 it has housed the **Salzburg folk museum**. A wooded walk leads to the 'Watzmannblick' lookout point and to the open-air **Stone Theatre** (Steinerne Theater). The first performance of an Italian opera (Monteverdi's *Orfeo*) in a German-speaking country took place here in 1617. There are also **zoological gardens** (Tiergarten) in the park.

Also on the south side of the city is **Schloß Leopoldskron**, a beautiful baroque palace built in 1736 by Archbishop L.A. Firmian to a design by Bernhard Stuart. It has a lovely park with a lake and an open-

Schloss Leopoldskron and the Hochensalzburg fortress

air theatre. The orangery was the location for a scene in the film *The Sound of Music*. Nearby is the moated **Schloß Freisaal** which dates from 1549, and several other castles in private ownership — Aigen, Anif, Emsberg (1618), Emslieb (1618), Frohnburg (1670; now a student hostel), Glanegg, and Goldenstein. On the western edge of the city is **Schloß Kleisheim** which was built by Fischer von Erlach in 1709.

The **pilgrimage church of Maria Plain** is on the Plainberg, about 2 miles north of the city centre. Built by Giovanni Antonio Dario in 1674, in commemoration of a miraculous image of the Madonna and Child, it features paintings by Kremser Schmidt (1765) and Frans de Neve (1679); sculptures by Thomas Schwanthaler, Simeon Fries, and Wolf Weissenkirchner; and a *pietà* by Franz Schwanthaler. The approach to the church is lined with fifteen roadside shrines dating from 1705. In 1779 Mozart's *Coronation Mass* had its first performance here.

Also north-west of Salzburg, some 14 miles along Route B156, is the town of **Oberndorf-bei-Salzburg** (population 3,800) where a delightful little chapel commemorates the first performance, in 1818, of the carol *Silent Night* by Franz Xaver Gruber.

There are two excellent viewing points within easy reach of the city by car or by bus. The Untersberg (1,806m, 5,924ft), 7 miles to the south, is reached by a cable car and affords a superb view of the city and mountains. The Gaisberg (1,286m, 4,218ft) is 10 miles to the east and the Chiemsee and the Dachstein group can be seen from it. These hills are convenient ski-slopes for the citizens of Salzburg.

PART 2   THE SALZKAMMERGUT AND BAD ISCHL

In 1829 a learned traveller wrote in his diary: 'if any other small country boasted even a hundredth of the wonderful sights with which Nature has adorned this tiny corner of land ... then it would long ago have been as much famed as the Salzkammergut is unknown'. Today the region is very well known to the large number of visitors who enjoy its scenery, facilities, and hospitality. It is an area extending some 40 miles to the west of Salzburg, overlapping the borders of Land Salzburg, Upper Austria, and Styria. It is bounded to the south by the mighty Dachstein group which rises to the Hoher Dachstein at 2,995m (9,824ft). On the west side are the Tennengebirge range which peak at 2,412m (7,911ft), and the lovely, rolling hills south-east of Salzburg which inspired *The Sound of Music*. On the east side are the Totes Gebirge, up to 2,515m (8,249ft) which contain many little lakes at high levels, and to the north there are the forests and farmland of the Danube basin. It is a region which enjoys high rainfall, and drizzle — called *Schnürlregen* — may persist for several days so that the countryside acquires a shrouded beauty reminiscent of other Celtic lands. On summer evenings cloud around the peaks of the mountains is said to herald good weather the following day.

When the prehistoric seas receded from this region they left behind large deposits of salt. Man soon discovered this treasure and salt has been mined here since earliest times. Salt was the principal source of prosperity during the Middle Ages and is an important product today. High rainfall produces good pasture so that, with Salzburg providing a good market for dairy products, farming is also a major industry. Since the nineteenth century tourism has been strongly promoted and has developed as another important source of income.

Bad Ischl, in Upper Austria, is the 'capital' of the Salzkammergut. Unlike St Wolfgang, St Gilgen, and Mondsee it does not stand beside a lake but a choice of watersports facilities is not far away. Bad Ischl has long been a favourite with those who enjoy the elegance of an imperial spa, and it is a very convenient centre for touring the Salzkammergut and for visiting Salzburg. In describing tours of the area Bad Ischl will be taken as the starting point.

BAD ISCHL

Bad Ischl (population 14,000) is surrounded on three sides by the waters of the river Traun, its tributary the Ischl, and the lovely wooded hills beyond. It is a town of villas and one-way streets which have changed little since its imperial heyday in the late nineteenth century. The **Kurhaus**, in Wirerstrasse, stands in a delightful little park with horse chestnut trees lining the footpaths between flower beds and well kept lawns. A bronze bust commemorates the work of Dr Wirer who, in 1838 discovered the healing powers of the waters and laid the basis for Bad Ischl's prosperity as a health resort. Today the treatment includes brine and mud baths, salt- and sulphur-fountains, gymnastics, pressure chambers, and electrotherapy. A new treatment house is located in Bahnhofstrasse, and the Kurhaus is now used for plays and operettas.

Bad Ischl achieved international fame as a health resort after the Austrian royal family discovered its benefits. Emperor Franz Josef became acquainted at an early age with the healing waters and, in 1853, his mother converted an old mansion on the north side of the town, across the river Ischl, into the **Kaiservilla** as a wedding present. This was convenient not only for the social life and the treatment rooms in the town, but also for the hunting in the adjacent woods and hillsides, and Bad Ischl became the summer residence of the imperial court. Today the parkland around the Kaiservilla provides lovely walks throughout the year and the house itself is well worth a visit. It contains an extensive collection of the furnishings, paintings, and utensils of Franz Josef and his family, and its walls are adorned by many hundreds of pairs of delicate little horns which were the trophies of the Emperor's hunting parties. But the pathos and tragedy of the slaughter is brought home most vividly by the mounted body of the 2,000th chamois to be killed. It is beautiful even in death but how much more spectacular it would be running free on the hillsides. Alas, in Europe as elsewhere, nineteenth-century morality considered such lovely animals to be fair sport.

Kaiser Franz Josef himself knew deep tragedy toward the end of his long reign. His beloved wife Sissi died in Geneva at the hand of an assassin; his only son, the Archduke Rudolf, died at Mayerling in a suicide pact with his lover, Maria Vatsera; and the Crown Prince, Franz Ferdinand, was shot at Sarajevo, an act which initiated World War I. That war lead to the collapse of the Habsburg monarchy, after a continuous rule of 645 years, and to the dissolution of the Austro-Hungarian Empire. In the Emperor's study there is a small side table with a glass top which covers a collection of four-leaved clover leaves. Not so lucky clover!

Many of the citizens of Bad Ischl recall those imperial days with nostalgia. On Sunday mornings national costumes are much evident amongst the congregation which overflows the doors of the **parish church of St Nikolaus** (1780; fourteenth-century tower). The men wear smart suits of grey *loden* material trimmed with green velvet and swept-back hats which sport what appear to be feathers but are in fact the hairs of the chamois. The ladies wear prettily decorated skirts and blouses and elegant *loden* cloaks. The Café Zauner, in Pfarrgasse — now over a hundred years old — is crowded from early morning with churchgoers enjoying their choice of a vast array of delicious cakes and pastries accompanied by strong Austrian coffee. A visit to Bad Ischl is incomplete without an indulgence in the famous Café Zauner.

The high social life of Bad Ischl attracted many famous writers, artists, and composers and some — including Lehar, Brahms, Johann Strauss, and Bruckner — had villas in the town. Anton Bruckner became the organist and choirmaster at the parish church, and Franz Lehar's operettas — especially *The Merry Widow* — were great favourites. Today his villa, on the south bank of the river Traun, which was his home from 1912 until his death in 1948, is the **Lehar museum** where his household effects are exhibited, and a festival of operettas is held from July to September of each year. Adjacent to the Lehar museum is the **local history museum**, and another interesting museum is in Concordiastrasse, in the former home of the Haenel-Pancera family. Gabriele Pancera (1870-1932) was a celebrated concert pianist. The museum has items she collected on her tours of the Far East, and autographs of great musicians such as Johannes Brahms, Franz Liszt, Johann Strauss, Edward Grieg, and Richard Strauss. In the Marmor-Schlössl, a small marble, neo-Gothic palace built for the Empress Elizabeth in 1861 in the Kaiserpark, there is a **photographic museum** which contains a rare collection of early equipment illustrating the historic development of photography.

There are many interesting and pleasant walks in the vicinity of the town, many of them along marked footpaths, all of them easy. For example, cross the Traun from Schröpferplatz to Grazer Strasse, on the south bank, turn right, then left along Siriuskogelgasse, and finally turn right again to reach the bottom of the double chairlift up to the Siriuskogel (599m, 1,965ft) from which there is a café and a view across the town. There are various pathways through the surrounding woodland; No 11 provides a circular route along the Traunkai beside the river to return to the town centre in about an hour. Another walk from the Schröpferplatz follows path No 6 along the esplanade, on the north bank of the Traun, into Kaltenbachstrasse, then along Lindaustrasse to the peaceful Nussensee where there is bathing and a guest house. This walk should take about 2 hours. Alternatively, instead of turning into the Lindaustrasse continue leftwards along the Kaltenbachstrasse, then go ahead up Dumbastrasse to reach the bottom of the cableway up to the Katrin (1,450m, 4,756ft). There are also many delightful walks on the north side of the town, notably in the Kaiserpark.

Some 2$\frac{1}{2}$ miles south-east of Bad Ischl, at **Perneck**, there are salt mines dating from 1563 which are open to the public for guided tours.

From Bad Ischl there are two principal tours around the Salzkammergut. The larger lakes — the Wolfgangsee, Mondsee, Attersee, Traunsee — all lie to the north, while to the south there are several smaller but very beautiful lakes — Hallstätter See, Altausseersee, and

Grundlsee. This chapter is extended to include descriptions of the Gosausee lakes.

Route 6b   The Southern Lakes of the Salzkammergut

Leave Bad Ischl southwards on Route 145 toward Bad Aussee. At **Anzenau**, near Lauffen, there is an open-air museum comprising an old farmhouse with bakery and mill. Turn right onto Route 166 into **Bad Goisern** (population 6,500) which is renowned for its superb hand-made walking boots. Amongst the sixteenth- and seventeenth-century houses there is a mill dating from 1600, a local history museum and an old smithy which is now an open-air museum. There are many good walks on the nearby Wurmstein (1,002m, 3,287ft) and the Predigtstuhl (1,278m, 4,192ft).

After Bad Goisern bear right through Au and turn right over the bridge to cross the river Traun and enter Steeg. The road then runs alongside the Hallstättersee, on the left, to reach a 'T' junction after 7 miles. The road to the right goes to Gosau. Turn left toward Hallstatt. The corniche road then winds along the lakeside with good views across the water to Hohe Sarstein (1,975m, 6,478ft). Traffic lights control vehicles through a single-track, rock tunnel into Hallstatt. The road rises quite steeply in the first half of the tunnel, emerges briefly to cross a small river before entering a second tunnel in which it descends to reach a car park after 10 miles. Access to the centre of the village can only be made on foot.

The Hallstättersee is about 5 miles long, just over a mile wide, and up to 135m (443ft) deep. The steep, heavily wooded mountains which surround it have encouraged comparison with a Norwegian fiord. **Hallstatt** (population 1,300) is one of the prettiest villages in Austria and owes much of its attraction to the fact that it is located on a mere toe-hold on the side of the lake, hard up against the steep slope of the Salzberg (1,030m, 3,378ft) on the west side. All of the available land on this small shelf has long since been built upon so that there is no room for expansion. This is especially true of the graveyard of the parish church. Therefore, a limited amount of fresh burial has been made possible by digging up some of the older graves and removing the skulls and thigh bones to the charnel house where they may be viewed by relatives and visitors. Amongst the collection of skulls there are some which have been painted to indicate the cause of death — such as snake poisoning! The church has a notable double-panelled altar from 1515, and in the chapel there are beautiful stained glass windows from 1440. The Corpus Christi procession (Frönlicht), takes place on the lake

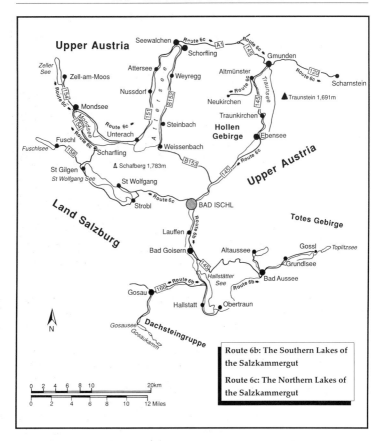

Route 6b: The Southern Lakes of the Salzkammergut

Route 6c: The Northern Lakes of the Salzkammergut

in two 'Muzen' — boats once used for carrying salt. One boat carries the salt-miners brass band, and the other, called the 'Boat of Heaven', bears the Holy of Holies.

  The Salzberg is a mountain of salt and there are conducted tours (1 hour) of the mine. The latter may be reached either via the cableway from Lahn, which is immediately south of Hallstatt, followed by a walk of some 20 minutes, or by walking all the way up the Salzbergweg. Salt has been mined here since prehistoric times and was traded throughout Europe. There have been many finds of tombs, vases, spears, and burial treasures from the ninth to fourth centuries BC, some originated from the Mediterranean and from northern Europe. That was the first stage of the Iron Age in Europe, and it is referred to as the Hallstatt period. Some of these finds can be seen at the mine, and in the Hallstatt

Hallstatt in a beautiful lakeside setting

Celtic museum in Seestrasse, but the more important discoveries are now in the Carolinum Augusteum in Salzburg, and in the natural history museum in Vienna. In Hallstatt the fourteenth-century market hall houses a local history museum.

The road continues around the southern end of the lake for some 2 $^1/_2$ miles to reach **Obertraun** (population 750), starting point for the cableway up into the caves of the Dachstein group. The first stage rises to the Schönbergalm at 1,350m (4,428ft). From there is a walk of at least 15 minutes up a steep, narrow, zig-zag pathway to reach the entrance to the Dachstein caves (Dachsteinhöhlen). Reaching a depth of 1,174m (3,851ft), these rank amongst the most impressive ice caves in the eastern Alps. The highlight of the 1-hour conducted tour is the Giant ice cave (Reiseneishöhle) which has several beautiful frozen rivers and waterfalls and a summer temperature of -1˚C (30˚F). Conducted tours of the Mammoth cave (Mammuthöhle) take about 1 $^1/_2$ hours. This is not an ice cave but consists of a labyrinth of caves and columns washed out by an ancient underground river. Tours are also available through the Roaring cave (the Koppenbrüllerhöhle) which contains a waterfall and stalactites, on the east side of Obertraun.

The Dachstein caves are remarkable natural wonders and are well worth seeing. However, visitors should be aware that the footpath up to the caves is very steep, and that tours inevitably involve a succession of rising and falling stairways which are physically demanding. Also note that the caves are both damp and cold so that suitable clothing is required even on the hottest day outside the caves. Many thousands of tourists visit the caves every year and, with just a little forethought, enjoy an unforgettable experience.

From the Schönbergalm the cableway continues to the Berghaus Krippenstein (2,079m, 6,819ft) on the side of the Hoher Krippenstein (2,109m, 6,918ft). After some further 20 minutes' walk there is a chapel which commemorates the deaths while climbing in the Dachstein group, in 1954, of a group of thirteen students and teachers from Heilbronn, in West Germany. From the Krippenstein another cableway descends to the Gjaidalm (1,795m, 5,888ft). In winter this is a very popular area for skiing. Beyond Obertraun the road rises very steeply (gradients up to 24 per cent, 1 in 4) eastward 6 miles to Bad Aussee. This road is not recommended. To visit Gosau return via Hallstatt and along the lake to reach the junction with Route 166 after 18 miles from Bad Ischl. Go ahead up the hill to join Route 166 signposted Gosau.

The beautiful road follows the ravine of the Gosaubach river through narrow passes between high mountains with magnificent stands of tall trees on both sides. After 22 miles the road emerges into a wide basin filled with pastures and cows, the sound of their bells ringing across the valley. Twenty-five miles from Bad Ischl the road reaches the pictur-esque village of **Gosau** (population 1,800), winter and summer resort, and centre for touring, walking, and climbing in the Dachstein mountains. Here there is an unusual exhibition of stones and fossils, and stone polishing is a local speciality. In the centre of the village, where the main road turns sharply to the right, go left toward the jagged peaks at the head of the valley. The small road rises past flower-decked *Gasthöfe*, winds between wooden farmhouses, along the banks of the river, then climbs up through woodland to reach a series of five large car parks catering for the many people who visit the Gosausee in the high summer season and at holiday weekends. At 30 miles the road reaches the upper car park.

There are three lakes at the feet of the towering Gosaukamm ridge which runs from the Grossen Donnerkogel (2,055m, 6,740ft) at the north-west end, to the Grossen Bischofsmutze (2,459m, 8,066ft) at the south-east end. The first lake is the Vorderer Gosausee where there is a *Gasthof* as well as a cableway up to the Zwieselalm (1,480m, 4,854ft). On the north side of the lake there is a road (closed to vehicles) which leads up about 4 miles, past the small lake into which the Launigg Waterfall pours, to the Hinterer Gosausee (1,154m, 3,785ft), beneath the Hoher Dachstein (2,995m, 9,824ft). The beauty of these lakes and mountains is breathtaking and should not be missed.

Return to Gosau along the Gosaubach. At the junction with Route 166 (at 34 miles) either go ahead to return along 166 and 145 to Bad Ischl (a total distance of 48 miles), or turn left, westward onto Route 166 which rises rapidly (gradients up to 17 per cent; 1 in 6) to the Gschütt

Pass. There it crosses into Land Salzburg, and descends through lovely hill country past the little village of Rußbach. After 10 miles it reaches the Salzburger Dolomitenstrasse about 2 miles east of Abtenau.

Bad Aussee (population 5,500) is best reached from Bad Ischl via Route 145. The town has many interesting old houses dating from the prosperous period of salt mining in the fourteenth century and after. There are three churches: the parish church of St Paul, which is thirteenth and fifteenth century, contains many sculptures and a baroque altar; the Spitalkirche (1395) has a Gothic winged altar from   1449; and the early fifteenth-century chapel of St Leonhard which has a lovely eighteenth-century altar. The old courthouse is now a local history museum which has a section on caves (spelaeology). The environs of the town attract much attention in June when the wild narcissi bloom and a spring festival is held.

Some 3 miles north of Bad Aussee is the little spa town of **Altaussee** (population 2,000) on the shore of the Altaussee lake. The lake is 2 miles long and a mile wide, and it is set in a picturesque location beneath the steep slopes of the Totes Gebirge Mountains. The Aussee salt mine is 2 miles to the north-west and is open to visitors from May to October. In a similar setting 3 miles north-east of Bad Aussee is Grundlsee (population 1,300) and the lake of the same name which is 4 miles long and just over half a mile wide, and surrounded by low hills. A road runs along the north bank to the eastern end of the lake and the hamlet of Gössl. It is but a short walk through the woods to the Toplitzsee, a smaller lake set amongst the trees which run down the steep mountain slopes to its edge. The third lake in this beautiful chain is the Kammersee which is a 10-minute climb beyond the Toplitzsee, at the foot of the Totes Gebirge range. A footpath from Gössl leads northward to the lower and upper Lahngangsee lakes (about 2 hours of steady walking), and on up the steeper inclines to the little Elmsee and the Phürlinger Hütte (another 2 hours of moderately difficult climbing).

From Bad Aussee return along Route 145 to Bad Ischl.

Route 6c The Northern Lakes of the Salzkammergut (see map page 200)

For a round tour of the major lakes of the Salzkammergut leave Bad Ischl by following the Route 158 Salzburg signs. After 2 miles a small road on the right goes through the hamlets of Haiden, Radau, and Rußbach and alongside the Wolfgangsee (6 miles by 1^1/$_2$ miles; 114m, 374ft deep) to reach St Wolfgang after 9 miles.

St Wolfgang (population 2,500), at the foot of the Schafberg (1,783m, 5,848ft), was founded in the tenth century by Bishop Wolfgang

The pilgrimage church and the village of St Wolfgang from the Wolfgangsee

and drew large numbers of pilgrims after he was canonized in the eleventh century. Today it is a pretty holiday resort in a beautiful setting beside the Wolfgangsee with many delightful hotel, *Gasthöfe*, restaurants and shops, and excellent facilities for watersports. It is connected to St Gilgen, Strobl, and several other points around the lake by a regular ferry service, and there is a footpath around the north bank to St Gilgen (easy to Falkenstein then a difficult climb over the bluff; allow 2 hours to St Gilgen). The road from Bad Ischl goes on about 2 miles to a dead end. Motorists would be wise to use the car parks at the entrance to the village as parking in the centre is limited.

The parish church of St Wolfgang is of special interest. It was built in 1414 on the site of an earlier twelfth-century church of St John the Baptist. Inside there are two large altars. The winged altar by Michael Pacher dates from 1481 and is regarded as one of the most important Gothic treasures in Austria. Normally the closed altar shows four paintings which illustrate the life of St Wolfgang; on Sundays eight paintings represent scenes from the life of Jesus Christ; and on 'red letter days' the shrine is opened as well as the altar. About 1675 the Abbot of Mondsee commissioned Thomas Schwanthaler to replace Pacher's altar which he regarded as outdated. Fortunately, the artist appreciated the great merit of the earlier work and defied the Abbot by locating his new altar so that the masterpiece could be preserved. Schwanthaler's baroque double-altar is itself magnificent and is considered his greatest work. The pulpit and altars (1706) on the north side by

*The White Horse Inn
at St Wolfgang*

Meinrad Guggenbichler are also notable. The altars (1745) on the south side are by Anton Koch, and those in the choir (1731) are by Jakob Zanussi. The ceiling is decorated by more than fifty magnificent panels. The adjacent chapel is on the site of St Wolfgang's hermitage. The fountain beside the church — manufactured from bell metal — is late Gothic (1515). The bishop's palace is partly connected to the church and is late Gothic, rebuilt in 1696. At Falkenstein there is a chapel (1626) to commemorate St Wolfgang's first hermitage on that site.

St Wolfgang has two 'town squares', one before the church and the Old Post Hotel, where evening entertainments are presented throughout the summer, and the other beside the Weisses Rossl Hotel which was the locale for the famous operetta *The White Horse Inn* by Ralph Benatzky. In the Villa Bachler-Rix there is an interesting puppet museum. The ascent of the Schafberg can easily be made on the rack-railway which was built in 1893 and still uses the original steam engines. This service is open from May to October and trains run when they are full. The journey up via the Schafberg (1,363m, 4,471ft) to the Schafberg Station (1,783m, 5,848ft), where there is a hotel, takes about 45 minutes whereas the climb up on foot takes about 4 hours. The view

Mozart memorial at St Gilgen

from the top is one of the best in the eastern Alps — but watch the weather!

From St Wolfgang return to the Strobl junction and turn right to bypass **Strobl** (population 2,700) at 12 miles. This is a popular summer resort with good access to watersports. There is a local history museum in the old 'Lipp House'. At 13 miles turn right onto Route 158 toward Salzburg. From this road there are very pleasant views across the Wolfgangsee to the Schafberg. At 20 miles turn right onto a service road which leads down beside the lake about a mile to the centre of St Gilgen.

St Gilgen (population 3,100) is a delightful resort on the Wolfgangsee which attracts many holidaymakers. It too has all of the advantages of the lake itself — including the ferry service, excellent accommodation and eating out facilities, and evening entertainments during the season. The parish church of St Ägidius is a relatively modest Gothic edifice from about 1375 with a baroque interior. At No 15 Ischlerstrasse, in 1720, Maria Pertl was born, later to become the mother of Wolfgang Amadeus Mozart. His sister Nannerl was also born here and returned to St Gilgen with her husband, Baron Berchtold zu Sonnenberg. A small bronze statue of a violinist — presumed to be Mozart himself — stands in the centre of the village where there are many houses with painted façades, and a local history museum is housed in Pichlerplatz.

South of St Gilgen, about $2^1/_2$ miles, is the Zwölfer Horn (1,522m, 4,992ft) which may be reached by a gondola lift beside the main road. The views are spectacular and there is good walking in the nearby hills. In winter this is a popular skiing area.

Leave St Gilgen through the village centre — bearing left — and turn right at the junction with Route 158. As the road rises bear right at the fork onto Route 154 Mondsee. Note, however, that 158 goes on to reach **Fuschl** (population 1,000), on the Fuschlsee ($2^1/_2$ miles long, 1 mile wide), after a further $4^1/_2$ miles. This is a small, picturesque resort on a small lake and very attractive for those who want a quieter holiday. It is a good centre for walking and touring as well as watersports. At the other end of the lake is Schloß Fuschl, a sixteenth-century hunting lodge of the Archbishops of Salzburg, now a hotel.

From St Gilgen Route 154 passes the battlemented, privately owned Schloß Pucha and the little Krotensee to reach Scharfling, on the south bank of the Mondsee (7 miles by $1^1/_2$ miles; 86m, 282ft deep) which is the warmest lake in the area with summer temperatures up to 25°C (77°F). The road runs alongside the lake beneath the steep slopes of the Drachenwand hills which rise to 1,329m (4,359ft) on the left, and after 29 miles from Bad Ischl it reaches Mondsee.

Mondsee (population 2,200) stands at the north-western end of the lake on a low plateau. To the west there are gently rolling hills and Salzburg is 18 miles away. To the east the ground rises more rapidly to the Mondseeberg (1,029m, 3,375ft), and the lake at the southern end is dominated by the Schafberg (1,783m, 5,848ft).

Mondsee owes its existence to the founding by Odilo, Duke of Bavaria, in 748, of a Benedictine abbey. Consequently Mondsee became an important cultural centre and the surrounding settlements — which dated back to Neolithic times — developed and flourished. The abbey was dissolved in 1784 but the market town continues to prosper as a result of tourism and is the social centre for the farming community. The heart of the village is very attractive with painted façades on the sixteenth- to eighteenth-century *Gasthöfe* and shops.

The parish church — formerly the collegiate church — of St Michael was built in the fifteenth century and stands on the site of a twelfth-century Romanesque edifice. Its two tall towers and concave façade above the west doors are impressive. There are four Roman stones in the porchway. Inside, the hall of the church is of grand proportions, reflecting its former eminence. The choir is fourteen steps above the level of the nave. The high altar (1626), by Hans Waldburger, with its larger-than-life figures is dominant. Five of the side altars (1679-84) are by Meinrad Guggenbichler, as is the altar in St Peter's chapel. There are also four altars (1742) by Anton Koch, and one (1776) by Leopold

Schindlauer. The wrought-iron doors to the sacristy — north of the choir — date from 1487 and are notable.

The former library of the abbey now houses a local history museum which has interesting items of pottery from 2,500 to 1,800BC, the period of the Mondsee culture, and a collection of works by Meinrad Guggenbichler. There is also an open-air museum (the 'Rauchhaus') comprising an original fifteenth-century farmholding with outhouses, furniture and utensils, as well as the Austrian lake dwelling museum which has several early dugout canoes. Also of interest are the pilgrimage church, which dates from 1450 and has internal decorations by Meinrad Guggenbichler, and the seventeenth-century lake chapel. The village is actually set back about half a mile from the lakeshore where there is a very pleasant promenade and the station for the Mondsee ferry boat.

About 3 miles north of Mondsee on Route 154 is **Zell-am-Moos** beside the peaceful Zeller See (or Irrsee). This is a wholly unspoiled little village which is a favourite with the more discerning weekenders of Salzburg — especially the fishing fraternity. Accommodation is limited. Further north-west the Wallersee, Obertrumersee, Mattsee, and Grabensee are also relatively uncrowded and the nearby villages — Seekirchen, Obertrum, Mattsee, Seeham — offer off-the-beaten-track holidays. This is not part of the Salzkammergut but it is an area well worth exploring

From Mondsee follow the lake around the eastern shore on Route 151. The road is narrow between Lolbichl and Unterach then it improves. It runs pleasantly close to the Attersee (13 miles by 2 miles; 170m, 558ft deep) which is the largest lake in the Salzkammergut. Along its shores — for example at **Unterach** — evidence of Stone Age and Bronze Age settlements has been discovered. In the nineteenth century Unterach was a favourite summer resort for writers and musicians such as Hugo Wolf and Johannes Brahms. Also at Unterach is the southern terminus of the Attersee ferry boat service.

The tree-lined road winds through small lakeside hamlets as it heads north through Nußdorf to reach **Attersee** (population 1,300) after about 17 miles from Mondsee, 46 miles from Bad Ischl. In this small summer resort there is the notable parish and pilgrimage church of Maria Himmelfahrt with a magnificent late baroque high altar in stucco marble. There is also a local history museum. At **Abtsdorf**, $1^1/_2$ miles

west, the late Gothic parish church of St Lawrence has a superb baroque interior by Meinrad Guggenbichler. After a further 5 miles the road enters **Seewalchen** (population 4,000) where the first steam boat was launched on the Attersee in 1869. It is a popular holiday centre with easy access off the A1 motorway. The parish church is late Gothic (1439), has interesting figures and a crucifix from 1515. There is a very enjoyable lakeside promenade, and nearby on a small island is the

Litzlberg palace. Some 2 miles north, at **Gampern**, the parish church

of St Remigius has a famous winged altar by Lienhart Astl from about 1500, and a remarkable carved figure of Mary with Child (the *Piesdorfer Madonna*) from 1510.

As an alternative to the round tour the eastern shore of the Attersee may be reached by turning right off Route 151 onto B152 which bypasses Schörfling and goes to Weyregg, to **Steinbach** — where there is an open-air museum and a cottage which was once the home of Gustav Mahler — and to Weißenbach. There either go ahead to return to Unterach, or turn left onto B153 to return to Bad Ischl. The latter is 24 miles from Seewalchen by this route. To continue the tour to include the Traunsee join the A1 eastbound motorway (signposted Wien) at Seewalchen then exit at the next junction — after 7 miles — to join Route 145 to reach Gmunden after 58 miles.

Gmunden (population 12,700) is a city at the northern end of the Traunsee where the river Traun flows out of the lake on its journey to the Danube. In the Middle Ages salt mined in the Salzkammergut was transported by boat across the lake and down the river so that Gmunden was a convenient and effective centre for controlling production and collecting taxes. Friedrich III, and his son Maximilian I, fully appreciated the importance of Gmunden to the balances of their exchequers and often visited the city, which therefore became a fashionable spa with the usual health cure facilities as well as a theatre. Today the city is a busy resort which is famous for its hand-painted pottery. The old salt office (Kammerhof) now houses a local history museum with collections of pottery, and of salt-mining equipment. The Gmundner Keramik and Keramik Pesendorfer works are open to visitors.

There are many old houses in the town with colourful façades, including the Cumberland palace, built in Tudor style by Duke Ernst August of Cumberland in 1875. Once the residence in exile of King George of Hannover, it is now a hospital. Seeschloß Ort is built in the lake and connected to the Landschloß on the bank by a 130m-long (426ft) footbridge. It has an arcaded courtyard and a late Gothic chapel. The town hall, in the old market square, is sixteenth century with Italianate loggias, a baroque façade, and ceramic bells in the tower. The parish church is a Gothic basilica dating from the fourteenth century. The beautiful altar of the Three Kings (1678) is by Thomas Schwanthaler of Ried, and in the wall to the left of St Katharine's altar there is a notable stonework relief of *The Last Supper* (1600). At Weyer, on the south-eastern side of the city, there is a cable car up to the Grünberg (986m, 3,234ft) where there are fine panoramic views. A track on the eastern shore of the lake leads about 3$\frac{1}{2}$ miles to the district of Traunstein where there are opportunities for walking on the slopes of the Traunstein (1,691m, 5,546ft) and up to the Laudachsee.

Note that at Grünau, 13 miles east of Gmunden, off Route 120, in the Almtal, there is a nature reserve and wildlife park, as well as an amusement park for children. At **Scharnstein**, 11 miles east along Route 120 there is an unusual museum of criminology.

Leave Gmunden south-westward along the lakeshore to pass Schloß Ort on the left, and on the right Route 145 to the motorway followed by Schloß Traunstein, standing on a high mound, which is now a boarding school. Go ahead onto Route 145 southbound. About 3$^1/_2$ miles from the centre of Gmunden is the old monastery town of **Altmünster** (population 8,500). Alas the tenth- and thirteenth-century monasteries have long disappeared. Altmünster today is a summer health resort with a lovely lakeside park and promenade. The parish church dates from the fifteenth century and stands on the site of the tenth-century abbey. It has a richly decorated interior with notable sculptures (1690) and paintings (1636) on the high altar, and the figures on the side-altar are from the school of Thomas Schwanthaler. The seventeenth-century Schloß Ebenzweier stands in lovely parkland, and a small road goes up to the Gmundner Berg (830m, 2,722ft) where there are walks and views. At **Neukirchen**, 5 miles west of Altmünster, there is a local history museum in a typical farmhouse ('Einhaus' — home and stables under one roof), and a mile beyond the village there is a wildlife park (Wildpark Hochkreut).

Continue on Route 145 alongside the lake. The Traunsee is 8 miles long and up to 2 miles wide and 190m (623ft) deep. There is no road on the eastern bank which is formed by the magnificent luminescent white cliffs of the Traunstein (1,691m, 5,546ft) which dominates the view from the west bank. The road passes through scattered small hamlets as it progresses southward then sweeps to the left around a bay and onto a small peninsula where a sharp right-hand bend takes it into the middle of **Traunkirchen** (population 1,600) at 66 miles. This is a picturesque summer resort with a pleasant little harbour for the ferry boat service and a footpath around the headland to the remarkable parish church of Mary's Coronation (Maria Krönung).

This one-time abbey church dates from 1652 and has three naves and a lovely high altar. It is famous for the gilded 'fisherman's pulpit' (1753) which celebrates the 'Miracle of the Fishes'. It takes the form of a boat with two oars containing the apostles James and John hauling in a net which is heavy with fish. On the rear panel Peter kneels before Jesus Christ, and on top of the gilded canopy is the figure of St Francis Xavier. Sadly the artist who created this magnificent work is unknown. The high altar is also magnificent. It dates from 1754 when it was built by Franz Preisl. The painting illustrates the Coronation of Mary and is flanked by statues of Sts Paul and Francis Regis on the right, and Sts Peter and Francis Borgias on the left. Above are the evangelists Matthew, Mark, Luke and John, and at the top are the archangels Michael, Gabriel and Raphael. On each side there is a large and a small altar. The small altar on the left is the 'Happy Death Altar' by Arthur

Rauch of Altmünster. A beautiful painting of *Christ on the Cross* is framed by cherubs and a statue of St Josef stands on the altar table. The crypt chapel dates from 1697, has an image of St Francis Xavier and a statue of the Madonna. In the churchyard the graves are marked by wrought-iron crosses. An unusual church in a superb setting, and well worth visiting.

The old monastery beside the church has two courtyards, one of them arcaded. St John's chapel, on a hill overlooking the town, dates from 1356, contains the 'Knorpelwerk' altar (1622), and has a seven-teenth-century Dutch painting. Since 1632 the Corpus Christi proces-sion has taken place on the lake — a tradition shared only with Hallstatt. Traunkirchen has long been favoured by artists as a place of tranquillity and wonderful scenery. Today it is an increasingly popular haven for the discerning holidaymaker.

South of Traunkirchen the road stays close to the water's edge. This section is narrow — it reduces briefly to single track to pass through a rock archway — and carries occasional large vehicles. When travelled with due care it affords splendid views of the mountains across the lake and it passes through welcoming little villages along the lakeside.

Ebensee (population 9,000), at the southern end of the lake and the mouth of the river Traun, is reached after 69 miles. The old market town's prosperity dates from the seventeenth century when the short-age of wood for the evaporation plants at Hallstatt and Bad Ischl resulted in their transfer to Ebensee. Brine was then piped overland from the mines, and salt was transported by boat across the lake to Gmunden. Today it is a busy working town with the largest salt works in Austria producing half a million tons of salt each year. Tourism has been promoted since the end of World War II and the town is now an all-year-round health resort. The Gaßl-Tropfsteinhöhle stalactite cave is open to visitors, there are conducted tours of two lead-crystal works, and there is a local history museum. A cable car on the west side takes visitors up to the Feuerkogel (1,594m, 5,228ft) for winter skiing and summer rambling. About 5 miles to the west are the Langenbathsee lakes, and 10 miles south-east is the Offensee.

From Ebensee Route 145 runs swiftly up the Traun valley where fishermen may be seen waist-deep in the river casting flies to tempt the trout. After 77 miles Route B153 is passed on the right and at 80 miles the road reaches Bad Ischl. The circular tour is complete.

7 THE DANUBE, KREMS AND STEYR VALLEYS

The alpine chain runs up from Italy through Switzerland and ends abruptly on the border with West Germany and along a near-straight line from Salzburg almost to Vienna. North of that line is the relatively flat, gently rolling farmland of the Danube basin and its tributaries. The river Danube rises in the Black Forest, near Donaueschingen, and flows north-eastward around the Bavarian plateau, collecting the waters of the Iller, the Lech and the Inn before entering Austria at Passau. By then it is already a mighty river and its flow is further enhanced by the addition of the Krems, Steyr and Enns catchment. Just beyond Vienna it becomes the border between Hungary and Czechoslovakia then it meanders idly across the 'puszta' (a grassy plain) southward to Budapest. On into Yugoslavia to Belgrade, then eastward again, avoiding the Carpathian Mountains, and along the border with Bulgaria before turning north into Rumania and finally east into the Black Sea. Of its total length of 1,754 miles, only 224 miles are inside Austria, across the provinces of Upper Austria and Lower Austria and through Vienna.

The Danube has long been an important route for transportation, being navigable by sea-going ships as far as Budapest, and by barges of up to about 1,000 tons as far as Regensberg in West Germany. Before the advent of steamships crude wooden barges were floated downstream from Ulm to Vienna where, after discharging their cargo, being unable to make the return journey, they were broken up for firewood. Steamships first appeared in 1829 and commercial and passenger traffic expanded rapidly. The Danube became an international waterway and much engineering work was done to improve navigation. In the Austrian section there are barrages at Jochenstein, at Aschach, Altenworth, Ottensheim-Wilhering, at Ybbs, and at Wallsee and further projects are planned. Passenger trade fell off with the competition of the railways and later the motor car and coach, but steam boat journeys are readily available today and offer a comfortable, unhurried and enjoyable mode of travel.

The Danube too has been of strategic military importance, forming an easily defensible, natural barrier against an enemy trying to invade from the north. It was effectively the northern boundary of the Roman Empire and in the first to the fourth centuries the Romans built fortifications along the right-hand bank. Those who followed them — notably the Babenbergs — built castles so that today the valley is well supplied with Roman museums and picturesque castles overlooking the river. It is an area also of significance in ecclesiastical history, and from the eighth to eleventh centuries many great abbeys were built on the high ground of the river bank and beyond it — for example those at Melk, Wilhering, St Florian, Kremsmünster, Schlierbach, Göttweig, Krems, and Klosterneuberg.

Although livestock farming is the most evident industry in this area — despite the rare appearance of animals due to the use of intensive farming methods — there is also a considerable concentration of chemical, and iron and steel, works between Salzburg and Linz, as well as textile and timber, cement, oil, gas, and hydro-electric plant. In the Wachau district — along the Danube between Melk and Krems — the primary products are wine and fruit.

It is not an area that is as frequented as the Salzkammergut or the Tyrol, lacking the spectacular scenery of lakes and high mountains. Nevertheless, many visitors enjoy the beauty of the rivers and valleys, the relaxation of quiet towns and villages, the links with the past, and the warmth of the very friendly and helpful people. A good area for the visitor to taste the delights of a farm holiday amongst the pigs and the poultry and the prolific wildlife of the countryside.

LINZ

Linz (population 200,000), on the banks of the river Danube, is the third largest city in Austria and capital of the province of Upper Austria (Oberösterreich). The city grew out of the second century Roman settlement of *Lentia*. By the ninth century it was an important market town, and from 1489 to 1493 it was the residence of Emperor Frederick III. In 1832 Austria's first railway opened between Linz and Budweis in Czechoslovakia. Today Linz is a busy industrial city with steel and chemical works and surrounded by gently rolling farmland. It has many interesting features to attract the visitor and is a convenient centre for exploring the Mühlviertel to the north, and the Danube valley.

The spacious — 220m-long (722ft) and 60m-wide (197ft) — Hauptplatz is at the heart of the old town. It is lined with beautiful Renaissance and baroque façades. On the east side is the seventeenth-century **Rathaus** which has an eight-sided tower from 1515. Around the corner, Johannes Kepler resided at No 5 Rathausgasse from 1612 to 1626. Opposite the Rathaus there is a **Trinity column** of white Untersberg marble from 1723, and on the west side is the **Feichtingerhaus** which has a lovely arcaded courtyard. At the north end is the **New Gallery** and **Wolfgang Gurlitt museum**, with nineteenth- and twentieth-century paintings by Kokoschka, Egger-Lienz and other artists, and the **College of Art and Industrial Design** is sliced in half by the roadway to the

Nibelungen bridge which leads to the district of Urfahr.

On the west side the Hofgasse leads steeply up to the **Linzer Schloß** which now houses the Upper Austria provincial museum. The castle was first mentioned in 799 but Friedrich III rebuilt it in 1477. At the west gate Friedrich's Tower was part of the original castle and bears a stone coat of arms with the letters AEIOU (*Alles Erdreich is Österreich untertan* — Austria rules the world). The museum has a large collection of items from prehistoric to modern times, viticulture and railway sections, and an old pharmacy. Beyond the first courtyard there is a small garden and the ramparts of the castle with views across the Danube. Steps and a pathway leads to the delightful little **St Martin's church**, the oldest church in Austria to be preserved in its original state. Roman walls were used as the foundations and the church was first mentioned in 788. It is a rare example of Carolingian architecture and has fifteenth-century frescoes.

Return along Römerstrasse and cross Lessingstrasse into the Promenade. On the right is the **Landestheater** built by Carlo Antonio Carlone in 1696. Follow the Promenade around to the left to the **provincial government building** which has a pretty façade and onion-domed tower. Opposite is the entrance to Herrenstrasse which leads to the **bishop's palace**, and to the **new cathedral** (1862-1924) which can seat a congregation of 20,000 people. Also in Herrenstrasse is the birthplace of the writer Herman Bahr (1863-1934).

At the south-west corner of the Hauptplatz, on the right-hand side of Klostergasse, is a three-storeyed, arcaded, Renaissance house where, in 1783, Mozart stayed as the guest of the Count of Thun and composed his *Linz Symphony*. The Linz tourist office now occupies the ground floor.

On the south-east corner of the Hauptplatz is the Domgasse and around the corner is the **old cathedral**, originally the Jesuit church of St Ignatius, built in 1669-78 by Pietro Francesco Carlone. The west door is flanked by twin-domed towers. The beautiful interior is baroque with a great deal of stucco. The pews, which date from 1633, are remarkable, the ends being ornately carved with animals and dwarfs.

Anton Bruckner was the cathedral organist from 1855 to 1868. He was also the organist at the **parish church**, around the corner in Pfarrplatz, which was built on the site of a basilica from 1286. On the pillars of the nave there are carved figures of the apostles. The Johann-Nepomuk chapel (1736) is an example of the work of Johann Michael Prunner, and the external Mount Olives chapel dates from 1695.

At the south end of the Hauptplatz is the Landestrasse which is traffic free — but look out for the trams! This is the hub of city life with shops, restaurants and coffee houses. The city's response to Vienna's *Sacher Torte* is the *Linzer Torte* which goes well with a cup of coffee.

Half-way along Landestrasse is the **Ursuline church** (1740) which

The fountain and old houses in the Hauptplatz, Linz

has a late baroque façade and twin towers. The high altar dates from 1741 and has a painting of St Michael by M. Altomonte. The wrought-iron screen to the tower chapel dates from 1748. The church is now used as the provincial culture centre. A little further down Landestrasse is the **Carmelite church** (1716) which has stucco decoration by Diego Francesco Carlone and Paolo d'Allio (1715) and notable confession boxes.

In addition to the Landesmuseum there is the **Francisco Caro-** **linum museum**, in Museumstrasse, and the **Nordico municipal** **museum** in Bethlehem Strasse. On the south-west side of the city (just over half a mile from Landestrasse via Bischofstrasse, Baumbach- strasse, and Kapuzinerstrasse) there are **botanical gardens** with tropical and orchid houses and a cactus collection.

From Jägerstrasse, in Urfahr, a quaint funicular railway winds steeply up between villas and gardens to the Pöstlingberg (537m, 1,761ft). From the terrace there is a panoramic view of the city and beyond to the distant Alps. One of the old towers has been converted into a **grotto railway** which carries its passengers through a fairy-tale world, and there is a scale-model of the Hauptplatz. Also at the top of the hill there is a charming baroque pilgrimage church (1748) with an eighteenth-century miraculous *pietà*.

Linz is a good centre for railway buffs. At **St Florian** there is a railway museum which runs regular steam train excursions during the summer months. Likewise, steam trains run from Steyr to Grünburg, a distance of 10 miles, from June to September. Up-to-date information should be obtained from the tourist office in the Hauptplatz.

Linz has excellent sporting facilities which include an 18-hole golf course at St Florian-Tillysburg, an ice rink, sports stadium, swimming lakes and pools, fishing, cycling, tennis and horse-riding. There are ample opportunities for excursions. At **Altenfelden** (23 miles north-west of Linz) there is a wildlife park. At **Wels**, 16 miles south-west, the Volksgarten has lovely old trees and a zoo, and 8 miles north-west of Wels, at **Krenglbach**, the bird park has examples from five continents. At **Walding**, 10 miles north-east, the zoo has elephants, tigers, leopards, black panthers, monkeys, camels, zebras, flamingos, and other animals, and children's rides. At Schloß Hohenbrunn, a mile from St Florian, there is a hunting museum. At Wels there is a cultural centre in the castle, which also houses the Austrian bakery museum and agricultural museum, and a town museum.

The city has an extensive programme of seasonal entertainments including concerts and plays in the modern Brucknerhaus and in Schloß Tillysburg, and games of chance in the casino.

The wide range of accommodation includes two youth hostels, and a camp site at Pichlinger See (5 miles south-east), and there are excellent road and rail connections as well as Linz Airport which has regular flights to Vienna and Frankfurt.

Route 7a   The Krems and Steyr Valleys

Leave Linz southward on Route 1 passing the Pichlinger See on the left and after 9 miles turn right to **Markt St Florian**.

St Florian is a market town with old houses and a well dating from 1604 in the market place. At the east end of the town there is an open-air museum (Freilichtmuseum Sumerauerhof) which has a collection of 400-year-old furniture, artefacts and craftwork associated with country life. There is also a railway museum (see Linz), and a firefighting museum at the abbey.

The abbey of St Florian commemorates the life and death of St Florian, an officer in the service of the governor of the Roman town of *Lauriacum*, who, in AD304, refused to give up his Christian beliefs and was put to death by drowning. In the eleventh century an Augustinian abbey was built around his tomb, and in the late seventeenth/early eighteenth centuries Carlo Antonio Carlone, Jakob Prandtauer and Gotthard Hayberger rebuilt it in the baroque style. It is famed as one of the best examples of baroque architecture as well as the last resting place of Anton Bruckner (1824-96) who was organist here in1845-55.

The abbey church is the masterpiece of C.A. Carlone who started to build it in 1686. The delicious stucco work is that of B. Carlone and

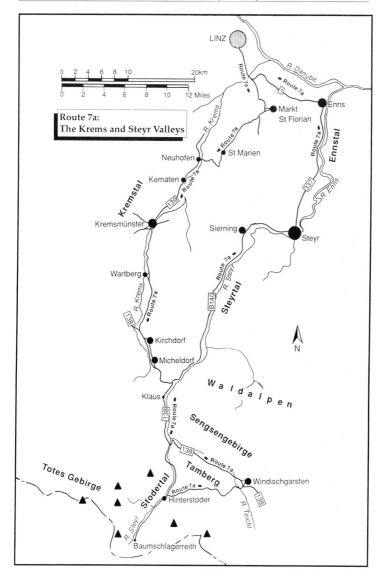

**Route 7a:
The Krems and Steyr Valleys**

the frescoes are by J.A.Gumpp and M.Steidl. The choir stalls (1691), by Adam Franz, are beautifully carved and gilded. The high altar is by G.B. Colomba (1690) and the four side altars are early eighteenth century. The pulpit is constructed of black marble and the Bruckner organ was built by Franz Xaver Krismann in 1774 and Bruckner's coffin is in the crypt beneath it. Guided tours of the abbey include the imperial apartments — reached by a magnificent staircase, the Altdorfer Gallery — which contains a collection of paintings by Albrecht Altdorfer (1480-1538) and the library, which is reached across the eagle fountain courtyard, and which has a lovely ceiling painted by B. Altomonte.

Since St Florian is the patron saint of flood and fire it is not surprising that the firefighting museum is housed at the abbey. The boys choir school is world famous and the abbey carries on the great tradition of sacred music established by Bruckner.

From St Florian turn south on the road to Steyr then almost immediately turn right onto the small road and cross the rolling farm country to St Marien. In the village go right then left and at the T-junction turn right to Neuhofen. Turn left onto Route 139 and, 28 miles from Linz, enter Kremsmünster alongside the abbey.

Kremsmünster (population 6,000) is cradled in a narrow valley with the beautiful abbey on the steep western slope, Schloß Kremsegg opposite, and a blue bottle factory on the bank of the river Krems which flows quietly through the little town. There are two pleasant market squares, several picturesque old houses and *Gasthöfe*, and neat farmland all around.

According to legend, in 777 the Bavarian Duke Tassilio III, kneeling over his son Gunther who had been killed fighting a wild boar, saw a stag with a bright cross between its antlers. He chased the animal in vain and at the place where he lost sight of it he founded the Benedictine abbey of Kremsmünster. It became an important outpost of the Holy Roman Empire and a religious and cultural centre. That tradition is maintained today in the abbey college and in the concerts which are held in the baroque emperor's hall.

The abbey was redesigned in the baroque style in the seventeenth and eighteenth centuries by Carlo Antonio Carlone and Jakob Prandtauer and is one of the largest foundations in Europe. There is limited car parking in the outer courtyard where there is an excellent restaurant. The inner courtyard is reached via a short bridge (1349) and through an archway surmounted by a marble portal by J.P. Spaz (1667) with statues of Duke Tassilio III, Emperor Karl the Great, and Emperor Heinrich III. A tour should include the charming fish pond (*Fishbehälter*) built between 1690 and 1717 by Carlone and Prandtauer in Italian Renaissance style. The emperor's hall contains portraits of emperors from Rudolf of Habsburg to Karl VI painted by Martin Altomonte in 1721, and a magnificent ceiling painted by M. Steidl in 1696. The treasury

Portal to the abbey of St Florian near Linz

contains a gilded chalice and candlesticks donated by Tassilio as well as other valuable and rare items. The library dates from 1675 and is superbly decorated with stucco and a superb ceiling painted by several artists. There are some 100,000 books, 400 manuscripts, and the *Codices Millenarii* — eighth-century illuminated manuscripts of the Gospels which were also donated by the Duke Tassilio.

The present abbey church was built in the thirteenth century and converted to baroque in 1712. It has a very beautiful interior with much stucco work, beautiful painted ceiling panels, and white pillars clothed at the bottom with tapestries. The pulpit has a delightful canopy and balustrade, and there are eighteen wonderful small marble angels which were carved by J.M. Zurn the Younger, of Gmunden, between 1682 and 1685.The church contains the tomb of Tassilio's unfortunate son Gunther who lies with his dog and a black boar alongside him. The Marien chapel, redesigned by Carlone in 1677, is very beautiful.

Also of interest is the 60m-high (197ft) observatory or mathematical tower which dates from 1759 and is now a museum of natural science with a varied collection displayed on eight floors.

Kremsmünster also has a lovely Gothic parish church and Schloß Kremsegg which dates from 1707 and now houses a motor car museum with models from the earliest days of motoring.

From Kremsmünster follow the unnumbered road alongside the small river Krems up a verdant valley to **Wartberg**, overlooked by the Gothic church of St Killian which has a winged altar from 1470. Then bear right to **Schlierbach** where the fourteenth-century Cistercian abbey is prominent, high on the left-hand side of the village. The abbey church, rebuilt between 1660 and 1679 by the Carlone family, is one of the finest examples of the heavy baroque form. The divided ceiling is decorated with frescoes and stucco figures are plentiful. There are four delightful side altars, one with a painting of St Catherine by J.M. Rottmayr. In the cloister there is a Marienkapelle with the Schlierbach Madonna from 1320. The library has magnificent ceiling paintings, columns, and gilded balustrades on the galleries.

About a mile after Schlierbach the road joins Route 138 and, after 14 miles from Kremsmünster, the small town of **Kirchdorf** (population 3,500) lies to the left. There are several pretty old houses and the parish church has a crucifix from 1520. Two miles further, and again to the left of the road, is **Micheldorf**, known for its old smithies which were renowned for the quality of their scythes. The parish church has a lovely altar from the abbey church of Schlierbach.

Beyond Micheldorf the valley narrows and the river Krems is left behind as the road runs upstream along the right bank of the river Steyr. The scenery is superb, the forested slopes and screes being reminiscent of the Rocky Mountains. About 12 miles from Kirchdorf turn right up the pretty Stodertal to **Hinterstoder** (population 1,100). This is a secluded village with good skiing facilities and walking. The road goes further up the Stodertal past scattered houses and through small orchards to Hinterberg and a single-lane track goes through the woods for the last 1$\frac{1}{2}$ miles to **Baumschlagerreith** where there is a *Jusenstation* — a small café serving a limited menu. The scenery here is dominated by the spectacular peaks of the Totes Gebirge which rise to

The peaks of the Totes Gebirge at the head of the Stodertal

the Hebenkar (2,285m, 7,495ft) on the west side of the valley. The river Steyr rises nearby.

Return to Hinterstoder then bear right toward Windischgarsten. The road rises through woodland and several bends to Vorderstoder then descends past the old village of Roßleithen to cross the A9 motorway and Route 138 to reach **Windischgarsten** (population 2,000) after 80 miles. A pleasant and spacious resort with many old decorated buildings, Windischgarsten is a good centre for walking in the lovely hills which surround it. The parish church of St Jakob has a fine baroque interior with many gilded figures and an unusual representation of the hearts of Jesus and Mary — the former bearing a crown of thorns and the latter a crown of roses — on the Marienaltar. In the churchyard there is a beautiful wrought-iron, partly gilded cross surmounted by five small figures which is known as the *Schoiswohlkreuz*.

Return to Route 138 and turn northward toward Steyr. The road runs swiftly down the valley alongside the river Teichl with the Sensengebirge mountains on the north side. After a left-hand hairpin bend pass the Hinterstoder road on the left and, at Frauenstein, bear right onto B140. The scenery of the Steyr valley is enjoyable and, after joining Route 122 at Sierning, the road reaches Steyr, 40 miles from Windischgarsten. After the hospital (on the left) turn right into Wiesenberg, cross the Steyr river, pass through a short tunnel then turn left into Handel-

Mazzetti Promenade where there are five car parks.

Steyr (population 41,000), at the confluence of the rivers Steyr and Enns, grew around the thirteenth-century Styraburg castle as a centre for the iron trade. After a disastrous fire in 1727 economic depression came to the town and it wasn't until the nineteenth century that Josef Werndl modernised the industry and led it to recovery. Steyr became famous for its iron and steel products — armaments, knives, scythes, nails, etc — and the works continue to flourish today. However, Steyr manages to combine modern industry with the beauty of a well preserved Gothic/baroque town. The long central Stadtplatz is lined with superb façades around the elegant tower of the town hall (1778). Opposite, at No 32, is the 'Bummerlhaus' (1497) — the 'Dog House' — so named after the sign of a lion which once hung over the door when it was a guesthouse. This is one of the best examples of late Gothic architecture in Austria. It has a notable staircase up to the attic and an early Gothic stone staircase at the rear. At No 12 the 'Sternhaus' ('House of Stars') is very picturesque, as are the 'Apothekerhaus' at No 7, and the 'Schönthanhaus' at No 9 which has an arcaded courtyard.

At the south end the Stadtplatz narrows and divides. In the Grünmarkt stands the Dominican church, formerly part of a convent, which was restored in the baroque style in the seventeenth century. At the far end of the Grünmarkt (No 26) is the double-gabled 'Innerberger Stadel' which was built in 1612. Formerly used as a granary, it is richly decorated in Renaissance style with much graffito. On the façade is a fresco depicting Joseph's brothers buying corn in Egypt, a double eagle bearing the coat of arms of the Innerberger Iron Trades Association, which had its headquarters here in the nineteenth century, and wrought-iron gargoyles. Since 1909 it has been owned by the town and is now used as a municipal museum. The collection of about 500 knives from all over the world is well known. There are also numerous items of furniture, weapons, artwork, and an iron museum which has an old drop hammer used to make scythes, and a nail forge. The museum also houses the 'Steyrer Kripperl', a mechanical puppet show. An industrial museum was opened on the north bank of the Steyr in 1987.

The parish church, in Brucknerplatz, towers over the old town. It is a late Gothic building from 1443 by Hans Puchsbaum, architect of St Stephan's cathedral in Vienna. The north entrance is notable with statues from 1410 and relief from 1526. On the high altar there is a painting of *The Adoration of the Three Kings* by Carl von Reslfeld from 1688. St Michael's church (1677), on the north bank of the Steyr, has a remarkable gable fresco of *The Descent of the Fallen Angels* which dates from 1770. Nearby is the Tabor, once a watch tower, now a restaurant with a splendid view of the town. At the north end of Gleinker Gasse stands the last remaining town gate, the Schnallentor, from 1613, which has graffito decoration.

Schloß Lamberg, formerly the Styraburg, built in 980, was badly damaged by the fire of 1727 and restored as a baroque castle by Domenico d'Angeli and Johann Michael Prunner of Linz. It is entered by an arcaded bridge across the moat and through an archway with a fresco of two knights. In the courtyard there is a figure of a dog which was the heraldic symbol of the Counts of Lamberg who owned the castle from 1666. There is a clock tower from 1730, a chapel and a library. The large castle park with its lake is delightful in every season and nearby is a memorial statue of Joseph Werndl and four of his workers sculpted by Viktor Tilgner in 1894.

Steyr offers a wide range of accommodation and a full programme of cultural (it has two theatres) and sporting activities for the visitor. It is a good centre for walking and touring.

One of the most popular excursions is to the pilgrimage church of the Divine Christchild, popularly known as Christkindl. In 1695 Ferdinand Sertl of Steyr, organist and bell-ringer, was given a wax figure of the child Jesus by the convent nuns. He took it into the forest and placed it in a spruce tree. Every Sunday he prayed to the Christchild and in due course he was cured of epilepsy from which he had suffered all of his life. Pilgrims soon flocked to the figure in the tree. A wooden chapel was built around it and in 1708 Carlo Antonio Carlone began the construction of the present church which was completed by Jakob Prandtauer in 1725. At the centre of the beautiful high altar is the original spruce tree with the figure of the Christchild. In 1950 the Christmas post office was opened at Christkindl and over 1 million letters and parcels are mailed there each Christmas. Christkindl is 1 mile south-west of Steyr.

The parish church of Garsten, formerly the collegiate church of a Benedictine abbey now used as a prison, is also worth visiting. It dates from 1082 and was rebuilt in the baroque style by Carlone and Prandtauer. The interior has many beautiful statues and paintings by the Carlone family, Kremser Schmidt, Carl von Reslfeld and others. The Losensteiner chapel is especially notable.

From Steyr take Route 337 northward via Kronstorf to Enns. For the last 4 miles the road runs along the left bank of the river Enns.

Strategically situated at the junction of the rivers Enns and Danube, **Enns** (population 10,000) is built on the site of the Roman town of *Lauriacum*, capital of the Roman province of *Noricum*. St Florian was martyred here in the fourth century. In the centre of the town square is a watch tower which doubles as a clock tower, erected in 1568 by Emperor Maximilian II, surrounded by the splendid façades of old, arcaded houses. A museum on the first floor of the town hall has collections of prehistoric items from the Hallstatt period and of Roman finds. The parish church is of unusual planform with a double nave, and has a fourteenth-century Wallseer chapel with notable stone statues from the fourteenth to eighteenth century. On the west side of the town stands the basilica of St Laurentius. Excavation revealed that the church was built on the sites of a temple, an early Christian basilica, and a Carolingian pilgrimage church. Roman consecration stones were also found. In view of the importance of the site in the early ecclesiastical history of the region the former parish church was designated a papal basilica and in 1968 became the seat of an archbishop. Inside there are bronze reliefs depicting the life of St Florian, a *pietà* from 1420, and remains of a winged altar.

From Enns follow Route 1 (or take the A1 motorway) to return to Linz after a circular tour of some 145 miles.

Route 7b   The Danube Valley:
Linz to Vienna (see maps pages 225 and 229)

The swiftest route from Linz to Vienna is along the 115 miles of the A1 motorway which comes up from Salzburg and traverses the rolling farmlands of the Danube valley affording occasional glimpses of the river. A more leisurely journey follows the river itself through the country of the Nibelungen and the picturesque vine and fruit growing area of the Wachau.

From Linz take either the A1 motorway or Route 1 to Amstetten, a distance of about 35 miles, then turn left onto Route 119 and cross the long, slender bridge at Tiefenbach to reach the left bank and the small town of **Grein** (population 3,000). In the central square there is a fountain and attractive old houses. The parish church is Gothic and has an eighteenth-century altarpiece by B. Altomonte. Schloß Greinburg is built on a high bluff overlooking the ravine. It has a delightful three-storeyed arcaded courtyard in which drama and music is presented during the Austrian Danube Festival. The town theatre claims to be the oldest in Austria.

After Grein go ahead onto Route 3 which hugs the meandering stream. Here the river is about 250m (820ft) wide and large barges and boats are a frequent sight. The forested sides of the valley rise steeply leaving only a little room for the river, the road, and the railway.

About 44 miles from Linz the road reaches **Persenbeug-Gottsdorf** (population 2,000) which has an ornate baroque house — the 'Schiffmeisterhaus', and Schloß Persenbeug, perched on a rock overlooking the river, where Austria's last emperor, Karl I, was born. A bridge and a ferry connect the village to **Ybbs** (population 6,000) on the south bank. The town has a delightful square with a Renaissance fountain surrounded by fifteenth- and sixteenth-century houses. The parish church of St Lorenz is fifteenth-century Gothic and has a notable painting of *The Mount of Olives* from 1500. There is a local history

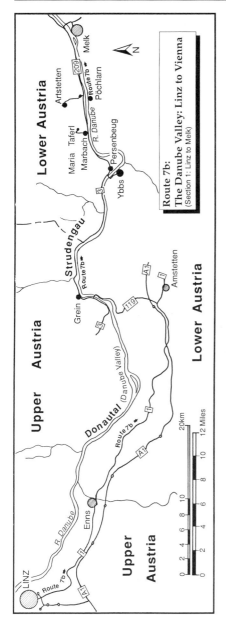

Route 7b:
The Danube Valley: Linz to Vienna
(Section 1: Linz to Melk)

museum in Kirchengasse.

Ybbs is the start of the country of the Nibelungen, a legendary race of dwarfs whose name was applied to the heroes of the German epic stories. The famous *Song of the Nibelungen*, by an unknown twelfth-century composer, relates the overthrow of the kingdom of Burgundy by the Huns in the fifth century, and praises the patriotic spirits of the heroic Burgundian warriors. This saga inspired Richard Wagner to write *The Ring of the Nibelungen* (1869), considered to be one of the greatest manifestations of European culture, but he located the action in the Rhine valley.

Returning to the left bank Route 3/209 now continues down the valley, cutting a corner then returning to the riverside to reach **Marbach** (population 1,600). Here the parish church of St Martin is Gothic. In the central square the town hall is sixteenth century and opposite it is the residence of Count Starhemberg and Löwenstein from 1575. Above the village and set back from it on a granite ridge is the famous pilgrimage church of Maria Taferl. Built in 1660, the dome was added by Jakob Prandtauer in 1711. In the nave and the dome there are frescoes depicting scenes from the lives of St Joseph and of the Virgin Mary. The magnificent high altar is by J.M. Götz (1736), and the side altars have altarpieces by J.G. Schmidt, of Vienna and by Kremser Schmidt. There are splendid views from the terrace across the Danube and as far as the Alps.

Artstetten-Pobring, a picturesque resort on a hill above the Danube, is 2 miles north of Kleinpöchlarn. It has a twelfth-century castle with five onion-domed towers set in parkland. Here the tomb of the Archduke Franz Ferdinand and his wife Sophie, whose assassination in 1914 led to World War I, is the basis of an exhibition which illustrates the Archduke's life and explains the events of 1914.

From Kleinpöchlarn there is a ferry boat across the river to **Pöchlarn** (population 3,500), a town of pretty old houses, an old town well, a statue of St Wolfgang, and two towers — one with a local history museum. Schloß Pöchlarn, set in a lovely park, was the seat of the Bishop of Regensburg for almost a thousand years from 832 to 1803. The Gothic parish church has three altar pictures by Kremser Schmidt. Oscar Kokoschka was born in No 29 Regensburgerstrasse which is now a museum with photographs and other memorabilia of the artist's life.

Soon the magnificent building of Melk abbey comes into sight on a rock set back from the river. Continue to Emmersdorf then cross the bridge to **Melk** (population 5,000), 60 miles from Linz. When the Babenbergs moved to Tulln Leopold III gave his castle to the Benedictine monks who in 1089 converted it into an abbey. After a disastrous fire, construction of the present baroque edifice was started by Jakob Prandtauer in 1702. It is a treasure house of ecclesiastical artwork such as the Melk Cross from 1360. Conducted tours take just over an hour and include the prelate's court, the imperial galleries, the marble hall with its wonderful ceiling paintings by Paul Troger (1732), and the library with its collection of manuscripts, some as old as twelfth century. The abbey church has twin towers and a large dome. It is richly decorated with gold marble, and frescoes, with numerous figures mounted on the altar, nave and dome, and an ornate pulpit. The paintings are by Paul Troger, Johann Michael Rottmayr, and Gaetano Fanti. On the high altar Sts Peter and Paul are depicted saying farewell before their martyrdom. It is one of the finest baroque churches in Austria.

The town of Melk has a picturesque square with the Nuremberg Gingerbread House (Lebzelterhaus) from 1657, an old town hall, and old houses in Sterngasse. The parish church is fifteenth-century Gothic and has a notable Calvary group. The Melk International Summer festival is held in the garden of the abbey. About 5 miles south of Melk, sixteenth-century Schloß Schallaburg has an especially attractive two-storeyed arcaded courtyard, a Renaissance museum, and an unusual garden laid out in the mannerist style.

Return again to the left bank and follow Route 3 to enter the Wachau. Across the river the twelfth-century Schloß Schönbuhel stands on a high rock. At **Aggsbach-Markt** there is a late Romanesque, thirteenth-century parish church. Four miles west is the pilgrimage church of Maria Laach which has a lovely winged altar, a wooden figure of the Madonna and Child dating from 1440, and a remarkable tomb of Baron George von Kuefstein from 1603.

On the south bank the remains of Schloß Aggstein stand on a sheer rock high above the valley. It was built in the twelfth century by the robber barons, the Kuenringer, who barred the river with chains to plunder the shipping and were said to throw their prisoners from the castle. The dungeons, kitchen, and chapel have survived its turbulent history, and in summer the castle is used as a youth hostel.

The road bypasses **Willendorf** where a 30,000-year-old, Stone Age limestone statue, the 'Venus of Willendorf' (now in the natural history museum in Vienna), was discovered during excavations of a Palaeolithic camp used by Ice Age mammoth hunters. The village of **Schwallenbach** also lies to the left of the main road. It has many Renaissance houses, a late Gothic parish church with an altarpiece by Kremser Schmidt, and a castle with open arcades and an outside flight of stairs. A short distance downstream a sheer rock formation is called the 'Tafelsmauer' ('Devil's Wall').

Half a mile before Spitz the ruined Kuenringer castle, Schloß Hinterhaus, dates from the thirteenth century. **Spitz** (population 2,000) stands around the 'Tausendeimerberg' ('Thousand Buckets Mountain') whose vineyards produce a thousand buckets of wine in a good year. The town hall is Gothic and Schloß Spitz is seventeenth century. The Erlahof, a former church foundation, now houses the Danube shipping museum — a beautiful collection of models and artefacts which are superbly displayed. The fifteenth-century parish church has an altar painting by Kremser Schmidt. The only remaining town gate — called the Red Gate — dates back to the Swedish Wars of the Reformation. **Wösendorf** has a late baroque parish church (1791) with three baroque altars bearing paintings by Kremser Schmidt, and ceiling paintings by his pupil Anton Mayer.

Picturesque **Weißenkirchen** (population 1,600) is the largest wine-making centre in the Wachau. The Wachau museum — which has a collection of paintings by the Wachau artists, including Kremser Schmidt — is housed in the Teisenhoferhof which dates from 1542 and has an unusual arcaded courtyard surrounded by battlements. The fifteenth-century parish church was originally fortified with round towers. Here there is a lovely riverside promenade.

At **Dürnstein** (population 1,100) the romantic ruins of the Kuenringer castle stand high on a rocky outcrop above the village. In 1193 the

English king, Richard the Lionheart, was held prisoner in this castle and was found by Blondel when he responded to the minstrel's song. The following year Richard was released in exchange for a ransom of 150,000 marks in silver but the Pope excommunicated the Babenburg duke for molesting a Crusader. An Augustinian priory was founded here in 1410 and was dissolved in 1788. It has elegant doorways into a lovely courtyard. The church was converted to baroque by artists including J. Prandtauer and M. Steinl and has a magnificent interior with paintings by Kremser Schmidt on the side altars. The superbly ornamented tower is by M. Steinl and J. Munggenast. The town has pretty houses and alleyways and a town hall with extensive archives.

Just before Krems a bridge spans the river to **Mautern** (population 3,000) where there is a museum with Celtic items and finds from the Roman military camp of *Favianis* which was established here in the first century. Roman relics include a wall, a tower, and a road. There are notable old houses in the town and the parish church has paintings by Kremser Schmidt.

Four miles south-west of Mautern the large Benedictine monastery of Göttweig stands high on a hill and has been called the 'Austrian Monte Casino'. Founded in 1083 by the Bishop of Passau, it was rebuilt in baroque style by Lukas von Hildebrandt. It has a magnificent staircase beneath a breathtaking ceiling painting by Paul Troger (1739). The church has beautiful heavily carved choir stalls and paintings by Kremser Schmidt. The library has notable collections of manuscripts and of artwork by Dutch and German masters. There is a splendid view from the garden terrace over the village of Furth which stands surrounded by vineyards on the edge of the Dunkelstein Forest.

Krems (population 23,000), 83 miles from Linz, was first mentioned in 955. An old commercial centre trading mainly in wine, and in salt, wheat, and iron, it has also long been a cultural centre. Toward the end of the Gothic period it was known as the centre of the 'Donau school' of artists, and during the baroque period as the home of Martin Johann Schmidt (Kremser Schmidt) whose beautiful work is much in evidence in the Danube valley as well as further afield. At the centre of the town is the traffic-free shopping street, the Landestrasse, which is entered from the west end through the Steiner Tower of 1480 which connects Krems to the twin town of Stein. In Krems three churches are now in use. The superb parish church of St Veit is early baroque and dates from 1630; the late Gothic piarist church has an altarpiece by Kremser Schmidt; and the Spitalskirche is in the late Gothic style. The former Dominican monastery, with its very attractive early Gothic cloister, has been converted into a museum. In Krems — as in Stein — there are many old houses with fine façades and archways. On the south side of the Hohen Markt the Gozzoburg dates from 1270 and is Italian in style with a delightful loggia.

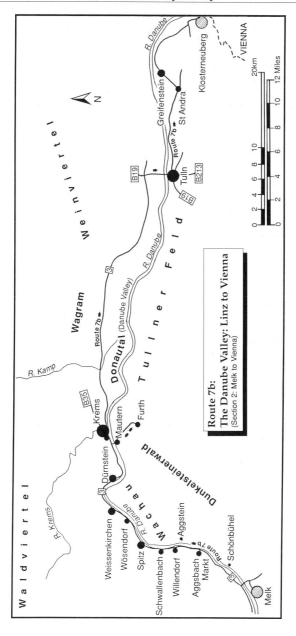

Route 7b:
The Danube Valley: Linz to Vienna
(Section 2: Melk to Vienna)

Stein has two town gates — Linzer Tor and Kremser Tor. The former home of Kremser Schmidt has a baroque façade, and the parish church of St Nikolaus is Gothic. Art exhibitions are held in the former minorite church. The former Frauenkirche stands on a rock and is now a war memorial. East of Krems and high above the river there is a large round powder magazine from 1477. Krems-And-Stein (And is the name of the district between the two towns, hence the joke: Krems-And-Stein are three towns!) is a very convenient centre for exploring the Forest Quarter (Waldviertel) to the north-west and the Wine Quarter (Weinviertel) to the north-east. A festival is held annually on 21 June, the Austrian Wine Fair is held here each spring, and in alternate Septembers Krems hosts the Lower Austria Exhibition which ends with a colourful parade of national costumes.

From Krems continue on Route 3 which now becomes a fast and busy highway offset from the river. After 25 miles from Krems turn right to cross the gigantic river to **Tulln** (population 11,000). Now one of the most important commercial centres in Lower Austria and the venue for national trade fairs, Tulln developed from the Roman fortress *Comagena* to become a cultural and economic centre in the Middle Ages. From 1042 to 1113 it was the imperial residence of the Babenbergs. In 1683 it was the assembly point for the army led by the Duke of Lorraine which finally drove out the Turkish invaders and relieved besieged Vienna. Roman remains include a third-century tower and a milestone. The parish church of St Stephan, is a twelfth-century pilaster basilica with an apostle gate, and a charnel house from 1240. The baroque minorite church (1739) has remarkable acoustics. There are lovely old houses in the town as well as part of the old town wall and moat, and a local history museum.

Leave Tulln on the eastward road signposted Klosterneuberg. After 7 miles, at St Andra, turn left to **Greifenstein**. Schloß Greifenstein was built in the eleventh century by the Bishop of Passau and was restored after damage by the Turks in 1670. Today collections of weapons, furniture and sixteenth- and seventeenth-century glass are on view.

After a journey of about 126 miles from Linz the road reaches Klosterneuberg and shortly crosses the northern boundary of the City of Vienna.

8 VIENNA

If there are many Austrias, there is only one Vienna. It is a city of colour and romance at the historic crossroads of Europe. Most people fall in love with Vienna on their first visit. It is a city built on a timeless scale, almost wholly free of those transient fads of modern architecture which elsewhere have failed to survive the test of time. It is a city which reaches the ultimate heights of cultural achievement and, at the same time, panders to the most lurid excesses of human weakness. Vienna has everything. Vienna is one of the great cities of the world.

The history of Vienna is largely the history of Austria. The city is located on the site of the Roman outpost of *Vindobona* where Emperor Marcus Aurelius spent his last days. In 1155, during the 270-year reign of the Babenberg family, the court took up residence in the Am Hof and Vienna became the capital. At that time it was protected by high walls with six gateways and nineteen towers. The Vienna of today is a Habsburg city which enjoys the ongoing benefits of the benevolence of Maria Theresa in the eighteenth century and of Franz Josef a hundred years later. Maria Theresa, through her sponsorship of the arts and music, laid the foundations for the cultural pre-eminence of the city. Despite the threats of disastrous foreign excursions and revolution at home Franz Josef found the time to re-design Vienna. The old defensive walls were pulled down and the best architects came to the city to compete for the honour of designing the splendid buildings which now line the sweeping boulevards of the Ring.

Vienna offers the visitor a menu of cultural events and exhibitions unequalled in any other city of the world. It is the international capital of opera; the home of the European classical music tradition; renowned for its modern drama productions and is a leading centre for new German literature. The city's numerous palaces, museums, and galleries house the finest collections of historical items from prehistoric, Roman, medieval, and modern times as well as examples of the works of the world's greatest artists.

Vienna is a baroque city. The best example of high baroque architecture is the Karlskirche, but baroque is everywhere — in the façades of the gentlemen's residences along the streets, in the palaces and churches, and around every corner.

The many worthwhile places to visit in Vienna are scattered over a wide area. Sightseeing bus tours afford an easy way to see the more popular of them and sometimes also offer entertainment and meals. These tours must, of course, operate to a time schedule so that individuals may not be able to linger at ports of call which are of special interest to them. Nevertheless, they are convenient means of sampling the city's sights.

Public transport facilities in Vienna are excellent. The U-Bahn (underground railway) is cheap, safe, clean and speedy. There are three lines (U1, U2 and U4) which cross at the Karlsplatz (access outside the opera house) and connect UNO City, the Prater, the Belvedere palace, the Rathaus, Heiligenstadt, the fleamarket, and the Schönbrunn palace. One price is charged for all journeys and books of five tickets can be purchased at U-Bahn stations and in tobacco shops. There are also first class bus and trolley, and rail services to all parts of the city. Details and advice are available from tourist information offices.

A leisurely way to see some of the sights of the old part of the city is by horse-drawn carriage — the Fiaker. As the tour progresses the driver — also called Fiaker — will narrate a commentary composed of stories, some of which date back to the seventeenth century.

Visitors who wish to browse amongst the life, history, and cultural heritage of this unique city must, as elsewhere, spend some time on foot. Fortunately the Viennese terrain is relatively flat so that the walking is mostly easy. In the city centre guided walking tours are available daily at various times and venues (ask at the tourist information centre for the *Wiener Spaziergänge* leaflet). Some are in English; they take approximately $1^1/_2$ hours, and cost (1987) AS85 per person inclusive of gratuities but excluding entrance fees.

An important factor in creating an unhurried, tranquil atmosphere in the city is the fact that the principal shopping streets are truly free of traffic. In the Kärntnerstrasse (between the opera house and the cathedral), and the Graben (from Stephansplatz to the Kohlmarkt), and in the adjacent side streets — notably the Neuer Markt — there are elegant stores which display the very best in design from all over Europe. Clothes, footwear, porcelain, ceramics and glass, gold- and silver-ware, furniture, books and maps, antiques, etc of the highest quality are on offer. Such treasures are not cheap but visitors should bear in mind that they can claim a refund of tax (up to 20 per cent in 1987) on items costing more than AS1,000 if they are taken out of Austria without being used. Shopping here is a leisurely and enjoyable activity with many sidewalk cafés and restaurants for refreshment.

Adolf Hitler made his triumphant entry into Vienna in 1938 along the Mariahilfer Strasse. Now tram No 58 runs along this street which meanders all the way from the Messeplatz to the Schönbrunn palace, and which has many departmental stores to attract the keen shopper. Here also, at No 2, is the tobacco museum, at No 88, is the state collection of period furniture, and, at No 212 the museum of technology. Currently the street is unfortunately disrupted by work on the 'missing' U3 underground railway line. When this work has been completed then the delights of the Mariahilfer Strasse will be more readily accessible.

THE INNER CITY

Where better to begin a description of Vienna than its most significant building — the **opera house** — which also serves as a convenient starting point for tours of the city, for shopping, and for communications to the suburbs. The opera house, being most important in the hearts of the Viennese, was the first building to be reconstructed after World War II. Its re-opening in 1955 was heralded as the rebirth of the city. It was rebuilt in its original Renaissance style but enlarged. From the magnificence of the grand staircase in the entrance vestibule to the glittering chandeliers and 'wedding cake' tiers of boxes it is a memorable spectacle. The backstage area is larger than the auditorium and the sight of the rotating stage — one of three stages — folded and lifted into the roof for storage, is remarkable. A tour guided by one of the 1,000 full-time employees is well worthwhile.

The opera house opened in 1869 with a performance of Mozart's *Don Juan*. Under the direction of many famous musicians — including Gustav Mahler (1897-1907) and Richard Strauss (1918-24) — it became the foremost opera house in the world and remains so today. Demand for tickets far exceeds its 1,500 seats and 500 box-seats and prices are high. Season tickets are only available by inheritance! There are, however, a limited number of standing places. For the annual opera ball prices are astronomical but there is no shortage of buyers. The season runs from October to July. In August/September the stage is taken over by the Folk Opera Company, which presents less ambitious works, when tickets may be available through the ticket bureaux though even then they are not cheap.

Visitors who wish to see the old city for themselves may take the route described below. Allow at least 3 hours either side of lunch for the whole tour which is comfortably level and easy to follow. The description is necessarily brief but the observant will see many interesting houses and former palaces along the way.

From the opera house walk along Kärntnerstrasse to Stephansplatz and **St Stephan's cathedral**. The original parish church of St Stephan in the diocese of Passau, founded in 1147, was a Romanesque basilica. In the fourteenth and fifteenth centuries it was converted to the Gothic style, alterations continuing into the middle of the nineteenth century. During the prolonged bombardment of the city at the end of World War II the cathedral was severely damaged. 'Die Pummerin' ('The Boomer'), the great bell in the north tower which had been cast in 1711 from cannons captured from the Turkish army in 1683, fell into the nave; the east end was almost completely destroyed, including the Gothic choirstalls from 1486 in which the young Joseph Haydn sang as a choirboy, and the stained glass windows and the organ were also lost. The south tower survived as it had done through the Turkish sieges of the sixteenth and seventeenth centuries and the French incursion of 1809. Known affectionately as 'Alte Steffl' this tower has come to symbolise the indestructibility of Vienna.

From the Graben the colourful roof is striking and the scene is dominated by the south tower and the spire that seems to grow out of it to a height of 137m (449ft). The top of the tower (72m, 236ft) can be reached by means of 345 steps but the spire is not normally accessible. After the withdrawal of the Turks in 1529 a war trophy — a large gold star and crescent — was hung from the point of the spire, and when the Turks returned in 1683 Count Rüdiger von Starhemberg used it as an observation point from which to direct the defence of the city.

At the base of the Heathen's Tower (Heidentürme) the west door dates from 1259 and is called the 'Giants' Doorway' (Riesentor). This name derives from the huge bone which hung above it for many centuries and was said to be from the leg of a giant drowned in the Flood but which was more likely to be the tibia of a mammoth. Above it now are the figures of Christ with two angels and apostles and evangelists. Below them there is a 'menagerie' of wild and weird animals symbolising the perils and dangers of life. On the left is a figure of St Stephan dated 1500, and there are several small Romanesque figures on the rather sombre façade. On the north side, the bishop's door, which has an Epiphany sculpture of 1430 above it, is not now in use. A lift in the north tower (access in north transept) takes visitors to a height of 60m (197ft) where the 'Neue Pummerin' bell can be seen. It was cast in St Florian, weighs 22 tons, and was consecrated in 1952. At the north-east corner is the open-air pulpit from which Capistran preached in support of the Crusade in 1450. Nearby is the portico used for funerals of paupers where, in December, 1791, Mozart's body was consecrated.

On the east end there are numerous badly weathered figures including a Crucifixion known, irreverently but for obvious reasons, as 'Christ with toothache'. On the south side the most westerly of the four gables at roof level dates from 1455, the others from the nineteenth century. The south-west door is surmounted by scenes from the life of St Paul, and by figures of the male saints, a reminder that this entrance was once reserved for men only. On the lower right-hand side is the statue, from about 1370, of Duke Rudolph IV carrying a model of the cathedral which he founded. Further to the right, also from 1370, is the Gothic figure of *Christ in Agony* (Schmerzensmann).

The interior of the cathedral is of majestic proportions, the Gothic vaulting soaring to a height of 28m (92ft) above the broad nave. The Gothic choir and pulpit combined with baroque altars, many statues and

St Stephan's cathedral,
Vienna, from the Graben

tombs, and the subdued lighting create an overwhelming impression of reverence and mystery. The cathedral's treasures are best described in detail by one of the cathedral guidebooks. The principal items of interest are briefly described below.

In the south aisle, adjacent to the Elegius chapel, is the miraculous painting of Maria Pötsch which came from Hungary in 1676. The beautiful font with its carved wooden cover (1481) was the work of Ulrich Auer, of Salzburg. Inside the south tower is St Catherine's chapel, where the saint with her sword and wheel are depicted at roof level. In the south choir is the magnificent tomb of Emperor Friedrich III, father of Maximilian I whose remarkable memorial is in the Hofkirche at Innsbruck. Friedrich died in 1513. His tomb, built by Nikolaus Gerhart, of Leyden, over a period of 45 years, has a marble top in which a superb relief depicts the Emperor in his coronation robes and regalia. The tomb bears the Emperor's famous motto 'AEIOU' ('Austria rules the world'). Friedrich invented the *Semmel* — the bread roll which visitors will meet every morning at breakfast

The high altar is early baroque and was completed in 1647. The altar in the north choir carries the lovely 'Wiener Neustadt' panelled altarpiece from 1447. On the wall of this choir are early Gothic figures removed from the cathedral yard when it was de-consecrated in 1735.

Above the baroque 'Peter and Paul' altar in the north aisle, at the bottom of an organ base, is the figure of Anton Pilgram. He also designed the notable Gothic pulpit (1515), on which, framed by delicate carvings, are the figures of Sts Augustine, Gregory, Hieronymous, and Ambrosius, and, at the bottom, another likeness of Pilgram himself. The balustrade leading up to the pulpit bears a succession of frogs, lizards and other animals depicting evil and, at the top, a dog, symbol of fidelity, to prevent them entering the pulpit. Next to the pulpit is the *Servants' Madonna* (1330), a very fine piece of early Gothic sculpture, said to have been donated by a countess who was unable to look the Madonna in the eye after unjustly accusing one of her servants of theft.

At the end of the north aisle are the delightful wrought-iron gates (1736) to the 'Tirna' chapel, named after a mayor of Vienna, which contains the tomb of Prince Eugene of Savoy who died in 1736. Beside this chapel there is an unusual wall plaque dedicated to Cuspinian, the humanitarian, who appears with his two wives and their eight children. Finally, the tall pipes of the organ stand above the lovely balustrade of the west gallery and the sensitive curve of the archway to the west door.

 The cathedral and diocesan museum is housed at No 6 Stephansplatz and contains a number of notable items including a portrait of Rudolf IV of Habsburg, and the fourteenth-century Gothic Erlacher Madonna and Child.

Leave the cathedral by the west door, turn left and cross Stephansplatz — where all manner of spontaneous display is likely to be found from day to day — toward Kärntnerstrasse, then turn left into Singerstrasse. A short way down, on the left, is the **Deutschordernkirche** which was built in 1326 for the Order of the Teutonic Knights. On the high altar there is notable gilded and painted Dutch panelling which dates from 1520.

 Toward the end of Singerstrasse, on the right, is Franziskannerplatz and the **Franciscan church** which dates from about 1607. The baroque interior includes a high altar by Andrea Pozzo (1707) with a carved wooden figure of the Madonna and Child from 1500. The side altars have notable oil paintings, and there is a beautiful baroque organ. The adjoining decorated cloisters are early seventeenth century.

Retrace the route into Singerstrasse but almost immediately turn right into Blutgasse (Blood Lane), aptly named as the home of the city's surgeons and still bearing the brass plates of many medical practices.

 Opposite the end of Blutgasse, at No 5 Domgasse, is the **Figaro House**, the home during 1784-7 of Wolfgang Amadeus Mozart and his family, and now a museum. Here he wrote twenty-six of his celebrated instrumental works as well as his delightful opera *The Marriage of Figaro*. Here too he was visited by Joseph Haydn and Ludwig von Beethoven; a remarkable gathering of the world's greatest musical genius. Mozart died in 1791 in a house in Rauensteingasse — some 300m (328yd) south of the cathedral — and, to the eternal shame of

The decorative roof tiles on St Stephan's cathedral

Vienna, was buried without ceremony in an unmarked pauper's grave.

On leaving the Figaro House turn right and right again along Strobelgasse, right on Wollzeile, then left into Essiggasse, and at the end turn right into Bäckerstrasse. At the end of this street is Dr-Ignaz-Seipel-Platz and the **Jesuit church**. Built in 1631 and restyled in baroque it is richly decorated with a notable high altar, pulpit, and dome frescoes by Andrea Pozzo. Also located here are the **old university** — founded by Rudolf IV in 1365 — and the **Academy of Sciences**, formerly the university auditorium. The latter has notable rococo decoration.

Return briefly along Bäckerstrasse then go right through Windhaaggasse, and across Sonnenfelsgasse into Schönlaterngasse. On the left is the **Heiligenkreuzerhof**, a thirteenth-century town house of the abbey of Heiligenkreuz. It has a lovely, restful seventeenth-century courtyard and a small eighteenth-century St Bernhard's chapel with a high altar by Martin Altomonte. At No 9 Schönlaterngasse an old forge has been preserved.

Proceed along Schönlaterngasse — lined with sixteenth-century houses — which swings left past the post office, then turn left into Fleischmarktgasse, past the Greek church with its unusual Byzantine façade, to reach, on the right, the **Reichenburger Greichenbeisl**, probably the oldest inn in Vienna. First mentioned in the city records in 1447, the building incorporates a remnant of the city wall — a tower with a saddle roof — which dates from about 1200 and is said to have Roman foundations. Turkish cannonballs embedded in the old walls have been preserved, and the figure of Augustin, a seventeenth-century folk singer, staring up through a grating, adds colour to a characterful house which was frequented by Beethoven, Schubert, Wagner, Strauss, Brahms, and by Mark Twain. Visitors can today enjoy good food and drink as well as the historic atmosphere, and the Greichenbeisl is an excellent place to enjoy lunch, and to rest before continuing the tour.

From the Greichenbeisl follow the Fleischmarkt then turn left into Rotenturmstrasse. To divide or shorten the tour go ahead to return to the Stephansplatz. Otherwise take the next turning on the right through the Lichtensteg into the Hoher Markt, the oldest square in Vienna.

Here stood the praetorium of the Roman town of *Vindobona*. At No 3 there is an entrance to the ruins of two Roman houses beneath the square. The Romans set up their outpost in the first century AD, about 400 years after it had been settled by the Celts. This garrison came under attack by the barbarians and Emperor Marcus Aurelius came from Rome to take command of the eastern frontier of the empire. He died in AD180 in a palace in the Hoher Markt. The Emperor Probus also came to *Vindobona* and is said to have brought with him the vines which were the rootstock of the vineyards of the Vienna Woods.

In the centre of the square is the **Vermählungsbrunnen** (Wedding Fountain) designed by J.E. Fischer von Erlach and erected in 1732. In the south-east corner is the **Ankeruhr**, a mechanical clock. It was designed in 1913 by Franz von Matsch and daily at 12 noon its chimes are accompanied by a musical parade of twelve figures which include Prince Eugene of Savoy, Empress Maria Theresa and her husband the Duke of Lorraine, and Joseph Haydn.

Note the streets of the craftsmen around the square: Bognergasse (bowyers), Goldschmiedgasse (goldsmiths), Färbergasse (dyers), and Naglergasse (nailmakers).

From the Hoher Markt turn right into Judengasse — centre of the rag trade — and walk to **Ruprechtskirche**. The present thirteenth-century church is said to be on the site of a Carolingian church of 740 and of one of the gates of *Vindobona*. It contains a thirteenth-century stained glass window above the choir, and a beautiful Romanesque high altar. A side altar has a sixteenth-century carved wooden figure.

Leaving Ruprechtskirche turn right into Sterngasse, then left into Fischersteige (Fisherman's Steps, a reminder that this was the fishing quarter), and right into Salvatorgasse where the late thirteenth-century **chapel of the Saviour** is immediately on the left. The notable Renaissance portal dates from 1520. The interior is Gothic with classical altars and statues from the fourteenth century.

At the end of Salvatorgasse is the **church of Maria am Gestade** (church of Our Lady of the Riverside) which is currently (1987) being restored. First mentioned in 1158, the present Romanesque edifice dates from 1262. The tower is 56m (184ft) high and has a pierced spire. In the Gothic west façade the portal is surmounted by an unusual stone canopy. The choir and nave are thirteenth- and fourteenth-century Gothic. On the right-hand side St Clement's chapel has an altarpiece from 1460 comprising two panels depicting the Annunciation and the Coronation of the Virgin. The beauty of the serene faces is emphasised by the Dutch style of painting with very bright colours.

Bear left along Schwertgasse, turn left onto Wipplingerstrasse, where there are notable baroque buildings, then right into the Juden-platz. This was the centre of the Jewish ghetto until the Jews were expelled from the city in 1421. Open-air summer concerts are now held here. Go ahead into Parisergasse to reach the spacious Platz Am Hof.

The bronze **Mariensäule** dates from 1667 and commemorates victory against the Protestant Swedish army in the Thirty Years' War. The lovely baroque houses on the west side of the square include the **Märkleinschen Houses** (1730) designed by Lukas von Hildebrandt, the headquarters of the Vienna fire brigade, and the firefighting mu-seum. In the south-west corner a plaque records the founding of the Red Cross by Henry Dunant, of Switzerland, after the bloody battle of Solferino in 1859. Here, during the uprising of 1848, which sought poli-tical reform and removed Chancellor Metternich from power, the un-fortunate Theodore Latour, Minister for War, was hanged from a lamp post by an angry mob. On the east side, at No 13, on the corner of Schul-hof Platz, stands the **Collalto palace** where the 6-year-old Mozart made his first public appearance. At No 2 Schulhof is the **clock mu-seum. Am Hof church** has an early baroque façade and ceiling paint- ings by F.A Maulpertsch from 1752. The paintings in the side chapels are notable, as is *Maria with the Nine Choirs of Angels* (1798) on the high altar.

After the demise of the Roman Empire Vienna suffered from some 500 years of incursions by Huns, Goths, and Slavs until the Babenberg family drove out the Magyars. In 1156 the Holy Roman Emperor gave them the Duchy of Austria and the first duke, Heinrich II Jasomirgott, brought his court to the Platz Am Hof, so establishing Vienna as the capital city. On 6 August, 1806 Emperor Franz II came to the Platz Am Hof to renounce the German imperial crown so ending the Holy Roman Empire and changing the course of history.

From the Platz Am Hof turn right into the triangular Freyung and to the **Scottish church**. The adjacent abbey was founded in the twelfth century by Scottish and Irish Benedictine monks. Alas, the monks earned a sad reputation from their boisterous behaviour and were

The plague column and the Graben

eventually ejected. The original church was a Romanesque pillared basilica, and was converted to the Gothic style in the fifteenth century. Some two centuries later it was rebuilt by the architects Carlo Antonio Carlone, Andrea d'Allio and Silvester Carlone. The baroque interior has beautiful stucco decoration and ceiling paintings.

Return along the Freyung and turn right into the narrow Naglergasse (Nailmaker's Lane). At the end turn right into the Kohlmarkt to reach **Demel's Coffee House**, one of the most famous coffee houses in Vienna, a 'must' for every visitor, and a good place to enjoy a delicious *torte* and a cup of exquisite coffee. But note that Viennese coffee is very strong, and, although invariably served with a glass of water to dilute it, is often too much for many tastes. Nevertheless, a visit to a Viennese coffee house is an experience not to be missed.

From Demel's return along the Kohlmarkt and turn right into the elegant Graben. This traffic-free, broad street is lined with fashionable shops and restaurants around the remarkable **plague column**. During the plague of 1679 Emperor Leopold I fled to Mariazell. At the height of the fever he pledged that when it ended then he would commission a special work of art as a symbol of gratitude for deliverance. The epidemic claimed 75-100,000 lives. The Pestsäule was designed by Matthias Rauchmiller, J.B. Fischer von Erlach, Paul Strudel, and others, and erected in 1693. Faith looks upward, cross in her left hand, her right hand pointing to a 'loathsome harpy', representing the plague, which is falling headfirst. Leopold kneels on a cushion looking smug.

On the left-hand side of the Graben is **St Peter's church**, which dates from 1703. Its four towers are placed diagonally around an elliptical dome. Inside there are numerous art treasures including the splendid dome frescoes by J.M. Rottmayr (1713), and a delightful pulpit by Matthias Steinl (1714). The Nepomuk altar has a notable sculpture depicting the fall of the saint into the river Moldau.

At the end of the Graben, squeezed between Stephansplatz and Kärntnerstrasse, is Stock-im-Eisen-Platz ('Stick-set-in-iron-plaza'). It is named after the old tree trunk, first mentioned in 1533, which is said to be the last tree from the time when this part of the city was a woodland. In the Middle Ages travelling locksmiths thought it lucky to drive a nail into the wood and their nails can be seen today.

And so into the Stephansplatz and the circular tour is complete.

A TOUR OF IMPERIAL VIENNA

A tour of the imperial palaces of Vienna requires the use of transport but starts on foot from the opera house. Immediately north-west of the opera house is the triangular complex of buildings which includes the Hofburg palace. The most pleasant approach is along the tree-lined sidewalk of the Opernring to Goethegasse then through the shady Burggarten which contains, on the south side, statues of Franz I, Goethe, and Mozart. On the east side there is a café and a large glasshouse, and at No 3 Hanuschgasse, the Austrian theatre museum.

Continue along the Opernring past the end of the ethnological (Völkerkunde) museum and turn right into the Helden Platz. Here there are fine equestrian statues of Archduke Karl and of Prince Eugene, the latter standing before the new Hofburg palace which houses the **Ephesus museum**, and the collections of weapons, and ancient musical instruments of the museum of fine arts.

Pass through the archway (which has an informative plan of the buildings) into the inner courtyard (In der Burg) of the **Hofburg palace** with its monument to Franz II by Pompeo Marchesi. Former imperial residence, some of it dating from about 1220, the palace today houses the offices of the president of Austria, the world's finest collections of state and ecclesiastical treasures, and the Spanish riding school. Directly across the courtyard an archway contains the entrance to the fabulous state apartments with their sumptuous furnishings — especially the Aubusson and Flemish tapestries and magnificent chandeliers — which recall the splendour of a lost age.

In Michaelerplatz are entrances to the porcelain and silver collections, and to the **Esperanto museum. St Michael's church** dates from the fourteenth century, the inside being mainly Gothic. The high altar (1781), by Jean Baptiste d'Avrange, and the baroque side altars are

The Schönbrunn palace and gardens, Vienna

notable. The wooden crucifix behind the altar dates from 1510. In the choir there is a beautiful painting of *The Adoration of the Children* by F.A. Maulpertsch. In the chapel there are fragments of Roman frescoes.

Alternatively, from the In der Burg courtyard, turn right through another archway into the much smaller Swiss Court. In the right-hand corner is the stairway up to the **imperial chapel** (Burgkapelle) (1449) where every Sunday (and religious holiday) morning from September to June the Vienna Boys' Choir sings mass. Tickets are scarce and expensive and applications should be made at least 2 — and preferably 5 — months ahead; standing places are free, must be applied for in person on the Friday afternoon preceding the performance, and are also in heavy demand; but the angelic sounds may be worth the effort.

The entrance to the **imperial treasury** (Schatzkammer) is in the northern corner of the courtyard. This unique and sparkling collection of artwork in gold and silver, enamels, pearls and precious stones, includes the crown and sceptre of the Holy Roman Empire from 962, and the ninth-century Holy Lance, once believed to be the sword which was thrust through Jesus Christ's side. The Habsburgs were avid collectors of symbols of power. The crown of Rudolf II — topped by an enormous sapphire — was made in Prague in 1602, is a masterpiece of Renaissance art, and was used as the Austrian imperial crown from 1804 to 1918. Here too is the Turkish crown from 1605, a 2.43m-long (8ft) 'unicorn's' horn, and the rich treasures of the Duchy of Burgundy, acquired by the Habsburgs by marriage in 1477. The collection also includes the dazzling costumes, crosses and other valuables of the

Fiakers in the In der Burg courtyard of the Hofburg palace, Vienna

Order of the Golden Fleece.

At present the treasury is being renovated and a temporary exhibition has been mounted beneath the Burgkapelle. The entrance is under the external staircase.

Through yet another archway enter Josefsplatz. In the centre is an equestrian statue of Josef II, eldest son of Maria Theresa, who came to the throne in 1765 and continued his mother's liberal policies. On the right is the **Grand Hall** (Prunksaal) which now houses the principal collection of the national library. Near the opposite corner is the entrance to the Spanish Riding School.

The **Spanish Riding School** presents one of the best known ☀ displays of horsemanship in the world. The all-white Lipizzaner horses, a Spanish breed, came originally from Lipizza, in Yugoslavia, where Archduke Karl, the son of Ferdinand I, established a stud, but since 1920 they have been bred in the Austrian national stud at Piber, near Köflach, in Styria. Using methods developed in the seventeenth century these magnificent animals are trained to dance to the rhythms of the quadrille, the polka, the gavotte, and the waltz carrying their riders around the riding hall. The latter, designed by Josef Fischer von Erlach, is lined with two galleries supported on columns and is itself a superb example of eighteenth-century baroque art. The programme of morning and evening performances extends from September to June and they last about 80 minutes. Applications for tickets must be made in writing and well in advance. For morning training sessions, from September to mid-December, tickets are sold at the entrance.

Around the corner from the Spanish Riding School is the **Stallburg**, a Renaissance building dating from 1565 with an arcaded courtyard which now houses the new gallery collection of the works of nineteenth- and early twentieth-century artists including Van Gogh and Cézanne. On the north-east side of the Josefsplatz are the sixteenth-century **Pallavicini** and **Palffy palaces** which are now used for concerts.

Leave the Josefsplatz at the eastern corner into Augustiner Strasse. On the left is the **Lobkowitz palace** (1687). On the right is the entrance to **St Augustin's church**, a fourteenth-century Gothic edifice noted for the pyramidal tomb in Carrara marble of Archduchess Maria Christine, daughter of Maria Theresa, designed in 1805 by Antonio Canova, and for the Heart Vault (Herzgruft) which contains fifty-four silver urns, each containing the heart of a member of the Habsburg family. On Sunday mornings visitors to St Augustin's can join the packed congregations to hear the best choirs and soloists sing great oratorio as it was intended to be sung — in the churches of Vienna — against the simple, high, white vaulting which is in serene unity with the magnificent gilded altar.

A little further along on the right is the entrance to the **Albertina**, founded by Duke Albert in 1781, which now accommodates a famous, and the world's largest, collection of graphic artwork. Amongst the 40,000 items are works by Rubens, Raphael, Brueghel, Van Dyke, Holbein, and Dürer. Here also are the collections of papyrus, and of music, of the national library, as well as the Goethe museum, and the Austrian film museum. At the apex of this triangular building steps lead up to the statue of Duke Albrecht which overlooks Albertina Platz. Around the corner to the right is the Burggarten.

To the left, across Fürichgasse is the Neuer Markt and, on the corner, the **Capuchin church**, and the imperial burial vault of the Habsburgs (Kaisergruft). Between 1633 and 1920 some 137 members of the imperial family, including twelve emperors and sixteen empresses, were buried there. The only outsider granted the privilege of lying alongside the family was the Countess Fuchs, beloved governess of Maria Theresa. The tomb of Maria Theresa, by Jean Jadot, is considered to be one of the most beautiful examples of rococo art.

Return to Albertina Platz past the Fiakers waiting for their fares and turn left into Philharmoniker Strasse. Stop at the Hotel Sacher for a coffee and a slice of *Sacher Torte* before returning to the opera house.

A visit to the **Schönbrunn palace** is highly recommended. Take the U4 underground line, or the No 52 tram, either to Schloß Schönbrunn, for the main gate, or to Hietzing, the next station, for the north gate. The beautiful palace, started in about 1700 by J.B. Fischer von Erlach and finished by Nicholas Pacassi in 1749, was the favoured residence of Maria Theresa. Her only daughter Marie Antoinette, later to become the consort of Louis XVI, King of France, spent her childhood here. It was here too that the 6-year-old Mozart displayed his prodigious talents for the Empress and is said to have proposed marriage to her daughter. In

1805, and again in 1809, it was Napoleon's headquarters.

When, in 1814, Napoleon's empire was finally defeated the victorious crown heads, with their noblemen and diplomats, came to the Congress of Vienna to divide the spoils. During a year of negotiation they enjoyed the glittering life of the city and banquets and balls were the order of the day. Prince Metternich, Austria's Foreign Minister, emerged as the key mediator of the Congress, and, by arranging the marriage of Archduchess Marie-Louise to Napoleon, made Austria the predominant influence in Europe. Napoleon's son ('The Young Eagle') was brought up at Schönbrunn by his grandfather Emperor Franz and it was here that he died at the age of 21.

Emperor Franz Josef was born at Schönbrunn in 1830 and died here in 1916 after 68 years on the throne. On 11 November,1918, in the Blue Room, Emperor Karl I signed the abdication, so bringing to an end 636 years of reign of the House of Habsburg, and the next day the Austrian Republic was proclaimed so bringing to an end another great empire.

The palace comprises several buildings linked together along the south bank of the river Wien and unified by green window frames and ochre masonry — said to be Maria Theresa's favourite colour and frequently used on buildings all over Austria. The *Schloß* itself — the Ehrenhof — is built around a large central courtyard. Visitors may enjoy guided tours of some forty-five of the 1,200 rooms of the palace which start at the spectacular 'blue staircase' and include the apartments formerly used by Maria Theresa, by Marie Antoinette, and by Franz Josef and his lovely wife Elizabeth, as well as Napoleon's study. The stucco embellishments in red, white and gold complement the beautiful tapestries, chandeliers, the fine furniture, and the Chinese rosewood panelling and combine to make a memorable tour.

Also on view are the palace chapel (1700) which has an altar painting by Paul Troger, the coach house (Wagenburg) with its very interesting collection of seventeenth- to nineteenth-century carriages, and the Bergl room which contains exotic murals dating from 1777 by Johann Bergls, a student of Paul Troger. Also worth seeing is the Schloß theatre (1747) — decorated in baroque and rococo style — in which Haydn and Mozart once conducted, now used to present small-scale operas during the summer.

The palace stands in the most delightful park with colourful formal gardens containing thirty-two sculptures of mythological figures, an obelisk, and 'Roman ruins' (1778), and the spectacular Neptune fountain. Zigzagging footpaths then go up the short but steep little hill to the Gloriette — a triumphal arcade from which there is a superb view to the north of the park, of the palace, and of the city beyond, and of the Vienna Woods to the south. West of the Gloriette is the Tirolergarten, with two Tyrolean houses and a collection of alpine plants, and adjacent to it there are zoological gardens (1752), a palm house (1882), and botanical gardens (1848).

Schloß Schönbrunn and its lovely parkland is a wonderful memorial to the best-loved Empress Maria Theresa, and affords the visitor a most enjoyable day-long outing.

Prince Eugene of Savoy came from Paris, an unsuccessful soldier, and a former monk. In 1683, at the age of 20, he came to Vienna to seek fame and fortune and found both in good measure. The city, barely recovered from the plague of 1679, was under siege by an army of 250,000 soldiers under the command of the Grand Vizier. The imperial court had fled and the city was defended by only 25,000 men under Count Rudiger von Starhemberg. The prince quickly demonstrated his brilliant understanding of military tactics and became a general in the Austrian army. In September the beleaguered garrison was relieved by the Duke of Lorraine's troops who had crossed the Danube at Krems, and on 12 September, at Kahlenberg, the intruders were routed. The Turkish threat had been finally defeated and the Emperor (Leopold I) was recognised by all of Europe as the saviour of Christianity and western civilization. Prince Eugene became commander-in-chief and went on to greater victories. In 1704 he stood with the Duke of Marlborough at the Battle of Blenheim to defeat the French army and save Vienna yet again. The Emperor's gratitude to his most famous general was boundless and in 1716-23 the **Belvedere palace** was built by Johann Lukas von Hildebrandt as Prince Eugene's residence.

The palace comprises upper and lower belvederes, linked by beautiful formal gardens and an orangery. Prince Eugene was a short man, not renowned for his good looks. It was said, unkindly, that his female companions were of strange physique, and the bizarre statues around the upper belvedere were intended as a joke. He died in 1736 unmarried and without heir, and the Emperor (Karl VI) acquired the property. Today the upper belvedere, reached from Prinz Eugen Strasse and the Gürtel, houses the Austrian gallery of nineteenth- and twentieth-century art, with works by Kokoschka, Makart, and others. On the south side of the building there is a lovely alpine garden and pools and fountains. From the north terrace there is a spectacular view across the formal gardens to the city. The lower belvedere, off the Rennweg, houses the Austrian baroque museum, and the museum of medieval art is in the orangery.

AROUND THE RING
Emperor Josef II's plans to remove the city walls had to wait until the disruptions of the Napoleonic Wars were over. In 1857 Franz Josef ordered the creation of the Ring, a broad, tree-lined boulevard bordered by impressive buildings specially designed by great architects, and verdant parks, to surround the inner city. Today the Ring is as spacious and impressive as ever it was despite the busy city traffic.

The route from the opera house via the Burggarten to the Hofburg palace has already been described. Opposite the Goethe memorial, on the south side of the Opernring, behind the Robert-Stolz-Platz is the Schillerplatz and the **Academy of Fine Arts**. Dutch paintings include works by Rubens and Rembrandt. There is a notable collection of copper-plate engravings, and about 30,000 drawings and water colours, and 70,000 prints.

Opposite the New Hofburg, across the Burgring, is the Maria Theresien Platz with a memorial to the greatly loved empress which was erected in 1888. Maria Theresa, daughter of Karl VI, came to the throne in 1740 at the age of 23. Married to François, Duke of Lorraine, who became Holy Roman Emperor in 1745, she had sixteen children. She proved to be a ruler of great character, a good judge of people, and a skilled diplomat who introduced many popular administrative and social reforms. She arranged the marriages of her daughters to serve Austria's interests. Maria-Antoinette became Queen of France, Maria Carolina became Queen of Naples, Maria Amalia became Duchess of Parma, and Maria Christina became Regent of the Netherlands. She was also a keen promoter of the arts and encouraged the city's musical eminences: Gluck, Haydn, and Mozart. She won the hearts of her people and even today is remembered with affection.

Maria Theresien Platz is flanked on the south side by the **museum** **of fine arts** — which has a magnificent collection of works by great artists, including Rubens, Franz Hals, Dürer, Brueghel, Vermeer, Tintoretto, Titian, Raphael, Canaletto and Velasquez. On the north side is the **museum of natural history**. Amongst its vast collection occupy- ing forty rooms are the most significant finds from Hallstatt, and the famous 'Venus of Willendorf' which is 20-30,000 years old. The fourth side of the square is the Messeplatz and the **Messepalast.** This imposing building was begun by J.B. Fischer von Erlach, in 1723, and completed by his son Today it is used for international and specialist trade fairs. At the north end of the Messeplatz is the **Volkstheater** which dates from 1889.

On the north side of the Helden Platz is the **Volksgarten**, Vienna's oldest park, with rose gardens, delightful walkways, and a Theseus temple (1823) by Peter Nobile. Across the Dr-K.-Renner Ring is the **Austrian parliament building** (1883) with its fine group of statuary and staircase. At the north end of the Volksgarten is the **national theatre** (Burgtheater) (1888) where guided tours of the baroque interior are available. Across the Dr-K.-Lueger Ring is the **city hall** (1883) — which has a magnificent arcaded courtyard used for summer concerts — and in front of it is a pretty little park full of statues. At the north end of this park is the **university**, and around the corner, to the left, across Sigmund Freud Park, is the **votive church** with its three doors and twin, 99m-high (325ft) towers. Amongst its rich treasures are the high altar, the fifteenth-century Antwerp altar, the bishop's chapel, and the tomb of Nicholas, Count of Salm, which dates from 1546.

The Schottenring runs north-west past the stock exchange (the Börse) to the Ringturm and the northern end of the Franz-Josefs-Kai. The latter extends about 1.3km (three-quarters of a mile) southward along the bank of the Danube canal to Julius Raab Platz.

Starting again from the opera house, the Kärntner Ring may be crossed via the *Opern-passage* which leads into the Karlsplatz. Despite the intersection of several very busy city streets nearby, this is a delightful little park with several very interesting features. The scene is dominated, by the **church of St Charles Borromeo** (Karlskirche), Vienna's most beautiful baroque church. Dating from 1737, it was commissioned by Emperor Karl VI in 1713 after a long succession of plague epidemics, and dedicated to the plague saint. Construction was begun by J.B. Fischer von Erlach and completed by his son J.E. in 1737. It comprises a very large rotunda with an oval dome, a façade reminiscent of a Greek temple flanked by twin towers with Turkish-style belfries, and two unusual triumphal columns, with spiral reliefs which tell the life-story of Charles Borromeo, and which are decorated with eagles and crowns. Inside there are notable frescoes by J.M. Rottmayr (1730) on the high dome. The high altar, the work of the elder von Erlach has very lovely stucco relief. The overwhelming impression is of the architectural harmony of light, colour and form typical of the baroque style.

On the north side of the Karlsplatz, on the corner of Akademiestrasse, is the **Old Handel Academy** of 1862, and on the opposite corner is the **Künstlerhaus** (1868) which has works by Rubens, Leonardo da Vinci, and Michelangelo. Next door is the **Musikverein** (1869), home of the world-famous Vienna Philharmonic Orchestra. On the southern side of the *Platz* is the classical façade of the **Technical University**, and the Ressel Park with a statue of Josef Madersperger, of Hall-in-Tirol, who invented the sewing machine. Between the Karlskirche and the Musikverein is the **City of Vienna historical museum** which has a fascinating chronological series of collections of items dating from the earliest times to the end of World War II.

Also in the Karlsplatz there are statues of Brahms, Donner, and Girardi, and a modern sculpture by Henry Moore. In front of the Künstlerhaus is the **municipal railway pavilion** (Stadtbahnpavillion) designed by Otto Wagner and used for summer concerts. Across the Wiedner-Hauptstrasse, on the corner of Friedrichstrasse, is the whitewalled and golden-domed little temple known as the **Secession** (1898) which commemorates the 'Jugendstil' movement of Viennese architects who, led by Otto Wagner, broke away from traditionalism to develop the functional modern style.

East of the Karlsplatz is the Schwarzenbergplatz which, on the south side, connects the Ring to Prinz Eugen Strasse and the Rennweg, and so to the Belvedere palace. An equestrian statue commemorates the commander-in-chief of the allied armies at the battle of Leipzig in 1867, and there is a fountain, by Anton Gabrielli (1873). To commemorate the liberation of the city the Russian Army erected, in 1945, a 12m-high (39ft) statue of a Soviet soldier holding a banner on top of a 20m-high (66ft) pillar. When the Red Army departed in 1955 the people of Vienna 'liberated' the statue! Also on this south side is the **Schwarzenberg palace** which was designed by J.L. von Hildebrandt in cooperation with J.B. Fischer von Erlach in 1723 and has a very graceful façade. It is now partly a hotel and is also used for concerts. Across the *Platz*, along Lothringerstrasse, are the **concert house** (which has recital rooms seating 2,000, 900 and 400 people) and the **Little Theatre**, the **School of Music**, and the **Academy Theatre**. In the Beethovenplatz there is a statue of the great composer by Caspar Zumbusch (1880). Beyond the Johannesgasse is the city park (Stadtpark).

Of the many statues in this lovely public park — opened in 1862 — the most famous is the Johann Strauss group which depicts the popular composer playing his favourite violin. Nearby is the Kursalon where on summer evenings visitors can listen and dance to the pleasant strains of Viennese waltzes while enjoying café hospitality.

Alongside the Stubenring stand the high school and the **museum** **of applied arts** in a building which was erected in 1871 in the Italian Renaissance style. The façade is decorated with majolica medallions and between the school and the museum there is a Minerva spring with a mosaic picture of the palace of Athene. The museum has collections of gold- and silver-work, oriental works, textiles and carpets, glass, porcelain, ceramics and furniture. At the end of the Stubenring, on the right, are government offices, and opposite is an equestrian statue to General Radetzky — to whom Strauss dedicated his *Radetzky March*. In Julius Raab Platz is the **Urania building**, the oldest 'People's culture house' in the city with lecture rooms, cinema, and observatory.

ACROSS THE DANUBE CANAL

On the east side of the Danube canal the major attraction is the Prater which may be reached by taking subway line U1 from Karlsplatz to Praterstern.

The **Prater**, formerly a hunting park, was opened to the public in 1766 by Emperor Josef II. It became fashionable to visit the park on warm summer evenings and on Sunday afternoons, and it was here about 1820 that Josef Lanner and Johann Strauss first played their waltz melodies — developed from a Tyrolean dance called the 'Ländler' — which were to find favour all over the world. The waltz reached the peak of its popularity in the middle of the nineteenth century when Johann Strauss junior employed over 250 musicians.

Centrepiece of the Prater is the 64³/₄m-high (212ft) giant Ferris wheel (*Riesenrad*), built by an Englishman, Walter B. Basset, in 1896-7, and repaired after 1945. The wheel has 120 spokes, is of 61m (200ft) diameter, and weighs about 245 tons. Its fourteen cabins — rather like commodious garden sheds — move slowly around its periphery affording splendid views across the city and the Danube, and of the funfair and the park below.

Near the giant Ferris wheel, in the Hauptalle, is the planetarium, which presents popular special performances for children, and the Prater museum.

Also east of the canal is the **Augarten palace** surrounded by delightful parkland with walkways and children's playgrounds. The original hunting lodge was destroyed by the Turks in 1683, and the present palace was built by J.B. Fischer von Erlach at the end of the seventeenth century. For the past 200 years it has been used for concerts and Mozart, Beethoven and Liszt performed here.

The palace is the home of the Vienna Boys' Choir (Wiener Sängerknaben), and of the Vienna Augarten porcelain factory. The famous beehive trade-mark originated in 1717 and Maria Theresa brought the factory to Augarten.

At No 9 Karmelitergasse, off the Taborstrasse, which joins the Franz Josefs Kai at the Swedish Bridge (Schwedenbrucke), there is an amusing **circus and clown museum**.

Beyond the river Danube itself is the Donaupark which was laid out in 1964 as a flower garden with a pretty lake. One of its attractions is the 252m-high (827ft) **Danube Tower** (Donauturm), which was erected in 1962 for television transmission. At 169m (554ft) it has a rotating restaurant and a terrace which affords a panoramic view of the city and beyond. At the other end of the park is the **Vienna International Centre** and the modern buildings of UNO city.

OTHER PLACES TO VISIT IN THE CITY

Another interesting art collection is that of the **museum of modern art** which is in the Liechtenstein palace, in Liechtenstein Park, at the north end of Liechtensteinstrasse. The latter runs off the Schottenring, almost opposite the Börse. The exhibition includes works by Picasso and Kokoschka. The Berggasse crosses Liechtensteinstrasse and No 19 is the former home of Sigmund Freud which is open to the public.

Tram No 46, from the Burgring, goes along Lerchenfelderstrasse and Thaliastrasse to the Ottakring where, in the tram depot, there is a **streetcar museum**. From May to October tours on vintage trams start at the Karlsplatz. Tram No 44, from the Schottenring, runs along Universitätstrasse and Alser Strasse, then crosses the Gürtel into Ottakringer Strasse. The first intersection is Veronikagasse where there is a **Fiaker museum** which is open in the morning of the first

Wednesday in every month.

As well as the Figarohaus, Mozart's home, the former residences of Beethoven, Haydn, Schubert and Strauss can be visited and contain various items of furnishings, musical instruments, and personal belongings, including original scores. In the central cemetery (Zentralfriedhof), some 4¹/₂ miles south-east of the opera house, there is a section devoted to memorials for the great composers — Beethoven, Brahms, Mozart, Schubert, Strauss, Schönberg and others. It can be reached by tram No 71 from Schwarzenbergplatz.

The **museum of Lower Austria** (Niederösterreichischer Lan- desmuseum) is at No 9 Herrengasse. Its collection extends from pre-Roman times and traces the development of ecclesiastical and secular art and culture in this province. Works by Rottmayr, Troger, Kremser Schmidt and Kokoschka, and Joseph Haydn's piano are on display. The Herrengasse runs from Michaelerplatz (before the Hofburg) to the Freyung. Amongst the one-time eighteenth-century gentlemen's residences with their balconied façades No 13, the **Niederösterreich-** **ischer Landhaus**, is very attractive.

The city's **aquarium** is located in the charming little Esterházy Park which is on Gumpendorfer Strasse and can be reached by tram No 57A from the Opernring.

For visitors with an eye for a bargain the fleamarket is held every Saturday from 8am to 6pm at the southern end of the Naschmarkt and very close to the Kettenbrückengasse station on the U4 (first west-bound stop from the Karlsplatz).

One of the prettiest parks in the city is the **Türkenschanzpark**, which is about 3 miles north-west of the opera house and can be reached by taking the U4 to Hütteldorf then the Schnellbahn to Gersthof, or by car along the Währinger Strasse, across the Gürtel, and along Gersthofer Strasse. Nearby are Schloß Pötzleinsdorf and Schloß Geymüller. Also near Hütteldorf is the **church of St Leopold am** **Steinhof** (1907) which was designed by Otto Wagner in the Jugendstil style. It has notable altar mosaics by Rudolph Jettmar, and stained glass by Kolo Moser.

At the western edge of the city, beyond Schloß Schönbrunn, is the **Lainzer Tiergarten nature reserve**, a large forest inhabited by wild boar. There the Hermes villa, former residence of the beautiful Empress Elizabeth, wife of Franz Josef, is used for special exhibitions from the city of Vienna historical museum. Take the U4 to Hietzing then either bus No 60 or 60A.

Finally, at No 19 Goldeggasse, quite close to the upper Belvedere palace, there is an **undertaker's museum** (Bestattungsmuseum).

9 AROUND VIENNA

This book ends with a description of areas which are not part of Vienna but which are within easy reach of the city. They may be regarded either as excursions from the city, or as convenient bases from which to explore the outlying areas and the city itself. To the north there are Grinzing, Kahlenberg and Klosterneuberg; to the east, Gänserndorf and Petronell; to the west, Baden and the Vienna Woods; and to the south, Eisenstadt and the Neusiedler See.

GRINZING, KAHLENBERG, AND KLOSTERNEUBERG

The tract of forested high ground immediately north of Vienna is very popular for afternoon and evening excursions to enjoy the views across the city and the fresh wine in the village taverns.

The ground rises gently through the popular village of Grinzing to the Kahlenberg heights. To reach Grinzing by road take the Gürtel northbound then the Heiligenstrasse to **Heiligenstadt**. Turn left onto Grinzingerstrasse to reach the middle of Heiligenstadt. For a short while in 1817 Beethoven lived at No 2 Pfarrplatz, which is now a *heurigen* . In Probusgasse, at No 6, inspired by the despair of his growing deafness, he wrote his *Testament of Heiligenstadt*. Continue on Grinzingerstrasse and bear left into the village of Grinzing. Alternatively, take tram No 38 from Sigmund Freud Park, next to the university, direct to Grinzing.

Grinzing is a country village with probably the best known *heurigen* — vineyards which are allowed to sell their fresh wine and which offer simple fare. The rustic tables in their vine-covered courtyards are crowded with visitors enjoying evening meals to the strains of violins and accordions playing 'Schrammelmusik'. Garlands of pine branches hung from their signs indicate that wine is available for sale.

At the top of the village turn right onto Grinzinger Allee then left onto Cobenzlgasse. The road rises through four wooded hairpin bends to the Höhenstrasse. Turn right and rise through two further hairpins to reach **Kahlenberg** (or take bus No 38A from Grinzing). There is a delightful view from the restaurant terrace across the vines to the city.

Returning to the Höchstrasse turn right then right again to **Leopoldsberg**. Here too there is a splendid view from the restaurant eastward to the border with Hungary — just 30 miles away — and to the

Leithagebirge to the south-west. St Leopold's church has a relief map of Vienna in 1683 — a reminder that it was in that year that the Turks were finally defeated here on the Kahlenberg heights. Continue along the Höhenstrasse to Klosterneuberg.

The picturesque Babenberg town of **Klosterneuberg** (population 23,000) stands between the river Danube and the low northern hills (Hermannskogel 542m, 1,778ft) of the Vienna Woods. There were Celtic and Roman settlements here and the Augustinian abbey was founded in 1106. According to legend the twin-towered collegiate church was founded in 1136 to commemorate the recovery from an elderberry bush of a veil which the wind had torn from the face of Agnes, wife of Count Leopold the Holy. Originally a Romanesque basilica, the inside was converted to baroque between 1634 and 1730. It has a notable high altar by M. Steinl (1723), and an impressive organ — on which Bruckner played — built in 1642. In the former chapterhouse, now Leopold's chapel, in the twelfth- to fourteenth-century cloisters there are magnificent gilded and enamelled altar panels (1181) by Nikolaus von Verdun and lovely frescoes.

The extensive libraries and museum of the monastery are important resource centres for research. Amongst the treasures is the Kloster-neuburg Madonna of 1310, and collections of altar pictures, and of bronzes, and a statue by Donner (1735). Conducted tours take visitors through the imperial and archducal apartments which house notable collections. It is customary on St Leopold's Day (15 November) to slide down the side of the Thousand Keg Cask in the cooper's workshop.

At the north end of the town is the parish church of St Martin which has an archaeological museum with 1,000-year-old relics. In the town square there is a Mariensäule from 1784 and the town hall has a late   eighteenth-century façade. West of the town, the lower slopes are covered with vines and many *heurigen* offer their hospitality. At **Gug-ging**, 5 miles to the west along the road to Tulln, there is a youth hostel. Klosterneuberg is a pleasant and popular holiday centre, convenient by road or rail for Vienna, and a good base for walking in the Vienna Woods and along the Danube. Return to Vienna along Heiligenstädter Strasse.

GÄNSERNDORF AND PETRONELL-CARNUNTUM

North-east of Vienna, at **Gänserndorf**, 20 miles along Route 8 via Deutsch Wagram (where there is a local history museum), there is a wildlife park with elephants, tigers, lions, rhinoceros, giraffes, a child-ren's corner, and occasional stunt performances. There is also an oil museum in the town hall.

The river Danube flows east from Vienna to enter Czechoslovakia at Bratislava. This section of the valley is relatively uninteresting except for the Roman town of *Carnuntum* at **Petronell** (20 miles on Route 9). The fortress was established in the first century AD to protect the 'amber' road and the adjacent township which at one time housed up to 100,000 people. Three Roman emperors resided here at various times. Excavations of the fort (just west of Petronell) and of the town (to the east) can be visited. There are two amphitheatres, and ruins of the 'Heathen's Gate' (Heidentor). Most of the finds are now in the Carnuntum museum at Bad Deutsch Altenburg, 2¹/₂ miles beyond Petronell.

Note also the twelfth-century round chapel in Petronell and the interesting *Schloß* which now houses the Danube (Donau) museum. Also at **Bad Deutsch Altenburg**, in Schloß Ludwigstorff, there is an African museum. At **Rohrau**, 3 miles south of Petronell on Route B211, Haydn's birthplace is now a museum and there is a collection of pictures in Schloß Harrach where Haydn's mother was in service.

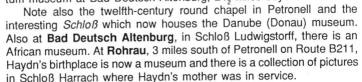

Route 9a   Baden and the Vienna Woods

The Vienna Woods extend around Vienna from the north to the southwest. They are very beautiful tracts of woodland with several interesting features. They provide for the citizens of Vienna an easy escape from their urban environment, to enjoy the sights, sounds, and smells of the countryside on their doorstep.

BADEN
The thermal springs of Baden (population 24,000) were known to the Celts and the Romans, and in 1813-34 the town was the fashionable summer residence of the imperial court. Such an illustrious history has left its mark on the town which has elegant buildings along its leafy avenues and many large and small hotels. Baden is a good centre for exploring the Vienna Woods. It is also very convenient for Vienna, 15 miles away along the A2 motorway, with frequent and fast services by train (to Vienna's south station), and by tram, and bus (to the opera house), which operate into the early hours of the morning, and take as little as 30 minutes. The hotels of Baden are worth considering as an alternative to the more expensive city hotels. Baden also has an excellent camp site.

The central town square and the adjacent streets are traffic free. In front of the town hall there is a magnificent baroque **Pestsäule** from 1718. Kaiser Franz I used No 17 as his summer home, and Beethoven once lived at No 10 Rathausgasse where he composed his *Ninth Symphony*. There are two other museums: the **Rollettmuseum** which houses items related to the history of Baden, and the **Kaiser Franz Josef museum** which has a collection of craft and folk-art works.

On the north side of the elongated Hauptplatz, Pfarrgasse leads to the theatre and to the high-steepled, fifteenth-century **St Stephan's parish church** which has a notable painting of *The Stoning of St*

Baroque trinity column and town hall, Baden

Stephan by Paul Troger (1750). Theresiengasse leads to the Kongresshaus, casino and Roman springs, and to the beautiful **Kurpark**. The park rises up to woodland and has numerous footpaths between lawns and flower beds with a Beethoven temple, summer theatre arena, and a remarkable fountain — the Undinebrunnen. There are several interesting statues — Lanner-Strauss, Kaiser Josef and others.

Baden's second park — **Doblhoffpark** — is on the west side. It is

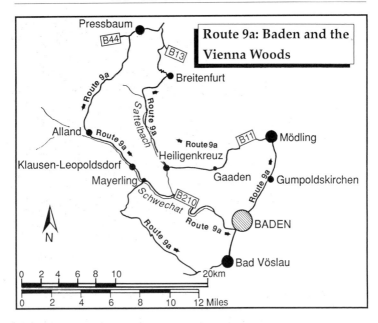

Route 9a: Baden and the Vienna Woods

noted for its lovely rosarium (over 20,000 rose-bushes) and orangery, has a delightful little lake, and large-scale chess. Overlooking the rosarium is the loggia of the former Schloß Doblhoff, now the luxurious Club Hotel. The splendid arcaded courtyard of the castle has been covered over so that it can be used in all weathers for a variety of entertainments.

Further west of the town, past the aqueduct, along Helenen Strasse, is the **church of St Helena**. This late Gothic church has notable reliefs from 1500, and the so-called 'Potter's Altar' (also 1500) from St Stephan's in Vienna. High above the church are the ruins of **Schloß Rauenstein**, and to the south are the ruins of **Schloß Raueneck**, both twelfth century.

Baden is a lively cultural centre with a full programme from May to September of music, drama and other entertainments. For sporting visitors there are indoor and outdoor thermal swimming pools, a fitness course, 40 miles of marked footpaths (from the Kurpark), and many more facilities. Baden also has a trotting racecourse where events are held every Thursday and Sunday during the racing season.

Around Baden

Coach excursions from Baden extend as far as Budapest, cruises on the Danube, the Neusiedler See, Mariazell, and, of course, include a variety of day and half-day trips into Vienna. For the independent

Funicular railway train on the Hochschneeberg

traveller there are several places of interest within easy reach.

It is a short journey to **Puchberg-am-Schneeberg** (35 miles via A2 then Route 26, or by rail via Wiener Neustadt), a pleasant and friendly little holiday resort and winter sports centre and a good base for walking. From the *Bahnhof* a funicular railway climbs slowly up the steep side of the Hochschneeberg Mountain (2,076m, 6,809ft) as far as the hotel-restaurant at 1,795m (5,888ft). The journey takes 80 minutes, including a 10-minute break at the Hengsthütte to water the engine. As well as the views, the alpine flora and the birdlife (there is a good chance of sighting an eagle), at the Hengsthütte there are gigantic hot buns awaiting both up and down passengers. Many visitors come to enjoy the nostalgia of the steam engines which have been running since 1897.

The castle at **Forchtenstein**, 35 miles from Baden, is one of the most impressive castles in Austria. Take the A2 to Wiener Neustadt then Route 53 eastward, then a side road via Wiesen.

The fourteenth-century Burg Forchtenstein, seat of the Princes of Esterházy since 1622, stands on a 500m-high (1,640ft) rock affording views across the Hungarian plain. Entrance is gained over a bridge and through a Renaissance doorway to a courtyard containing a fountain and a 140m-deep (459ft) well which enabled the defenders to withstand the Turkish sieges of the sixteenth and seventeenth centuries. The castle has a museum with a large collection of armoury including Turkish pieces. The castle is also used for dramatic productions.

Eighty miles from Baden via Neunkirchen and Mürzzuschlag, or 75 miles via the slower Route 21 from Wöllersdorf is **Mariazell** (population 2,500) which enjoys a lovely elevated setting surrounded by hills and just 3 miles inside Styria. It is a summer and winter holiday resort with a spacious town square lined with restaurants and shops. There is a cable car to the Bürgeralpe (1,266m, 4,152ft) which has splendid views southward to the Hochschwab Alps. There is also an interesting museum and a beautiful baroque roadside shrine in Wiener Strasse.

Mariazell is famous for its pilgrimage church which was founded in 1157 and has held a very special place in the hearts of the Austrian people — and, indeed, all of the peoples of the old Habsburg Empire — for over 800 years. Such were the numbers of pilgrims that the church had to be enlarged in the late seventeenth century and the present edifice was built by Domenico Sciassia. The Gothic spire flanked by twin baroque, onion-topped domes is a landmark.

The west door has a notable Gothic relief tympanum which depicts pilgrims coming to Mariazell. The original hall was retained by Sciassia and became the west nave, a second nave being added to it. The internal decoration is entirely baroque and the stucco-painted ceilings and dome are very beautiful and best seen from the first-storey gallery.

The chapel of miracles occupies the centre of the church and is surely one of the most wondrous sights in Austria. It houses a silver altar which bears the twelfth-century Romanesque wooden statue of the Virgin of Mariazell holding the Child Jesus and dressed with gold crowns and a magnificent embroidered gown. The chapel, with its twelve silver columns, was designed by J.E. Fischer von Erlach and is enclosed by a silver grille commissioned by Maria Theresa in 1756.

The high altar, by J.B. Fischer von Erlach, dates from 1704 and has a remarkable orb of 2m ($6^1/_2$ft) diameter with serpents, and above it a larger-than-lifesize Crucifixion. There are six side altars including, on the left side, the chapel of St Ladislaus which is the last resting place of Cardinal Josef Mindszenty, Primate of Hungary, who died in exile in 1975. Red-white-and-green ribbons hanging from the wrought-iron screen are evidence of the continued commitment of his followers to the cause of freedom for their country.

The treasury should not be missed. The centrepiece is an old altar with a wonderful fourteenth-century portrait of the *Madonna and Child*. The collection also includes a cedarwood cross from 1531, a gold chalice from 1679, and a gold monstrance from 1736, as well as embroidered articles, and robes for the Virgin of Mariazell.

A visit to Mariazell is highly recommended.

THE VIENNA WOODS

To see the beauty of the Vienna Woods leave Baden via Kaiser Franz Ring/Germer Gasse and drive through the vine-laden countryside to **Gumpoldskirchen**, a celebrated wine village. Its Königswein is one of

West door of the pilgrimage church at Mariazell

the best quality Austrian wines. At the top end of the Wienerstrasse there is an old castle of the Teutonic Order and the Gothic St Michael's church, which has interesting oil paintings and is reached over a small stone bridge. The town hall is sixteenth century and has a tower which houses a local history museum. In front of the town hall there is a pillory column from 1563, and a pretty seventeenth-century town well.

Gumpoldskirchen is known for its wine festivals, held twice a year, when a Festival Queen is crowned, and for the *heurigen* which provide sustenance for visitors all year round. The Bruckberger-beim-Brunnen *heurigen* has a lovely courtyard as well as large dining rooms and is recommended for its memorable meals and excellent wine.

Leave the village along Mödlingerstrasse and after 3 miles turn left opposite the Hochschule. At the main road (Route 11) again turn left. About 4 miles beyond Gaaden turn left into **Heiligenkreuz** abbey.

The beautiful, walled Cistercian abbey of the Holy Cross was founded in 1133 by the Babenberg Leopold III. When construction was completed in 1187 Leopold V gave to the abbey a piece of the True Cross on which Christ died. Amongst the abbey's treasures is also a portion of the Crown of Thorns which was given to Frederick II by

The wine village of Gumpoldskirchen

Ludwig IX, King of France, in 1244.

In the outer courtyard, in front of the abbey tavern, there is a fountain, the Josefsbrunnen, by G. Giuliani. In the inner courtyard there is a notable baroque trinity column, also by Giuliani, in a charming setting beside a group of plane trees, and before the Romanesque west façade of the abbey church. The spacious, simple nave is bare-walled, with large square pillars and a high roof, in contrast to the magnificent choirstalls (1707), surmounted by busts and cherubs, again by Giuliani. The altar dates from 1887 and is by J.M. Rottmayr and M. Altomonte. The thirteenth-century cloister is very peaceful and has a fountain house with notable grisaille windows. The chapterhouse contains the tomb of Frederick the Valiant who died fighting the Hungarians in 1246. He was one of thirteen members of the House of Babenberg buried here. Also buried here is Maria von Vetsera who died at Mayerling.

Leaving the abbey turn left onto Route 11 then immediately right onto a side road which runs up the Sattelbach valley through the village of Grub, and through the leafy woodland to **Breitenfurt** where the parish church dates from 1732. Go north from Breitenfurt over the Little Semmering Pass (463m, 1,519ft) (gradients up to 10 per cent, 1 in 10) through Wolfsgraben, then left to Preßbaum. There turn left onto Route 44, then left again to pass under the A1 motorway (signposted Klausen-Leopoldsdorf). The road winds upward with several small parking places with footpaths into the woods. After the Hengstlhöhe (518m, 6,699ft) it descends, with delightful views, through the valleys to reach the little village of Klausen-Leopoldsdorf. Here bear left onto the side road between the A12 motorway and the Schwechat river. This leads to **Alland**, a pleasant village, convenient for walking, with a well known rock-climbing school on the Pelstein (716m, 2,348ft), and a limestone cave. Take Route 210 to reach Mayerling after just over a mile.

Once the hunting lodge of Crown Prince Rudolf, **Mayerling** is now a Carmelite convent. Its chapel is a memorial to the Crown Prince Rudolf, only son of Franz Josef. Unhappily married, Rudolf fell in love with the beautiful, 17-year-old Countess Maria von Vetsera, daughter of a diplomat. Early on the morning of 30 January, 1889, the trusted valet Loschek found the dead bodies of the young lovers in the royal bedroom at Mayerling, a revolver by their side. Maria Vetsera's body was taken by coach through the snowclad woods to the abbey at Heiligenkreuz and secretly buried there. After some confusion the Emperor revealed that Rudolf had shot himself and buried his son in the Habsburg vault in Vienna. It was only later that her mother reported the death of Maria Vetsera. Speculation about the circumstances of her death have continued to this day. Note that there is a regular post-bus service between Mayerling and Baden.

From Mayerling Route 210 runs down the lovely Helenental to re-enter Baden on the west side. Alternatively, opposite the car park at Mayerling a very enjoyable little road goes south and rises into the hills for about 4 miles. Turn left at the first T-junction and the road then descends gently to meet Route 212 after 7 miles. Turn left to Bad Vöslau.

Bad Vöslau is a very pleasant health resort with a beautiful Kurpark, thermal springs, and a seventeenth-century castle and park which has stone vases by F.A. Zauner (1788), and lovely walks. The Herzberg (496m, 1,627ft), on the west side of the town, affords good views.

From Bad Vöslau it is just 3 miles via Sooß to Baden.

Route 9b   Burgenland, Eisenstadt and the Neusiedler See

The province of Burgenland is a very narrow — at one point just 3 miles wide — strip of land squeezed against the border with Hungary. In the south the terrain is an extension of the Styrian hills and forests as the Alps give way to the eastern plains. In the north the Hungarian plain (*puszta*) has already begun and the Neusiedler See is the dominant feature. This is Europe's only 'steppe lake' and it has unique flora and fauna. The 270,000 people of Burgenland have strong ties with the Croats and Hungarians and these are reflected in their language, architecture and customs. The climate — hot, dry summers and moderate winters — is ideal for the vineyards which cover most of the ground

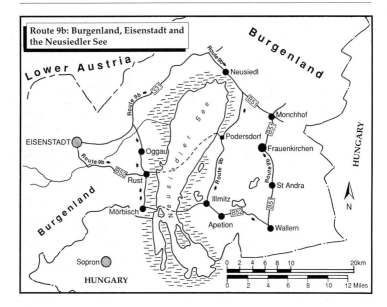

Route 9b: Burgenland, Eisenstadt and the Neusiedler See

around Eisenstadt, and the province produces more than a third of Austria's wine.

Northern Burgenland is very different from the alpine Austria known to most visitors and has a special appeal of its own.

EISENSTADT

On the warm southern slopes of the Leithagebirge hills, enveloped in a sea of vines, Eisenstadt (population 10,000) was once the residence of the Hungarian Esterházy family and home of the great composer Josef Haydn. Today it is the capital of the province of Burgenland and an important wine market town.

   Schloss Esterházy was built in 1673 by Carlo M. Carlone for Prince Paul Esterházy. Behind the garden frontage and impressive façade — decorated by the busts of eighteen generals — there is a simple courtyard. Inside there are elegant furnishings including early nine-teenth-century Chinese wallcoverings and baroque furniture. The high-light of the conducted tour is the Haydn room, now used again as a recital room, which has a magnificent ceiling painted by Carpoforo Tencala. Behind the *Schloß* there is a park with two small lakes, an orangery, and a temple, and footpaths through the trees.

Opposite the *Schloß* is the **town hall** with its colonnaded façade. The Hauptstrasse is the centre of the town and has a fountain — the **Florianibrunnen** — and a trinity column. In Haydngasse is the house

The Esterházy palace at Eisenstadt

in which Josef Haydn lived from 1766 to 1778, now an interesting little **museum** with many original scores — such as *The Creation* — in the composer's precise hand.

Haydn (1732-1809) had the good fortune to enjoy the favour of the Esterházy family, so avoiding the poverty in which his contemporaries lived. In 1761 he became a member of the Prince's court and in 1766 was appointed musical director. He laid the foundations of the modern symphony and achieved fame through his prodigious portfolio of works. He was a close friend and adviser to Mozart. In 1809 he died in Vienna and was buried there, but in 1820 Prince Nikolaus Esterházy had his body brought to Eisenstadt. The head was found to have been stolen by an admirer but it was discovered in 1895 and put on display in a glass case in the museum of the Society of the Friends of Music in Vienna. In 1954 it was reunited with the body in the Haydn mausoleum which had been erected by Prince Paul Esterházy in 1932 in the Bergkirche Maria Heimsuchung at Eisenstadt.

The **Bergkirche** and **Mount Calvary** are located at the west end of the town, on the road to Vienna. The latter is unusual in being wholly artificially constructed. Along the stairs of the Way of the Passion there are caves and chapels, and twenty-four stations leading up to the chapel of the Cross.

In 1960 the **parish church of St Martin**, in Pfarrgasse, was raised to the status of a cathedral. Parts date back to the twelfth century but the fortifications in the massive tower indicate that the present building was designed to repulse the Turks in the fifteenth century. Inside there have been many alterations. The pulpit and organ are baroque, there are two portraits by Dorfmeister (1777), and medieval tombstones.

Until 1938 there was a Jewish community in the lower town and the cemetery has survived as well as three houses which are now part of the **Burgenland museum** (Burgenländische Landesmuseum), in Museumgasse. The comprehensive collection covers every aspect of the history of the province and especially the development of its great vineyards. There is a superb mosaic floor from a Roman villa, and 'moon idols' found in the excavation of a Neolithic settlement at Loretto, about 8 miles north of Eisenstadt on the Leithagebirge.

THE NEUSIEDLER SEE

The Neusiedler See is 35km (22 miles) long, up to 16km (10 miles) wide, and no more than 2m (7ft) deep. Due to the curvature of the earth the middle of the lake is 25m (82ft) higher than the longest axis. It is fed from underground springs and, because it is so low lying, water can only escape by evaporation. In a strong wind the water is driven away from the lee shore and rises onto the other side. On rare occasions (the last time was 1868-72) the lake dries up completely, then there are great disputes about the ownership of the newly revealed land. Around the shoreline, and especially at the southern end, there are thick reed beds which provide homes for a great variety of birdlife so that the lake is popular for birdwatching, as well as angling, shooting and water sports.

Leave Eisenstadt southward on Ruster Strasse (Route 59a), passing the Liszt statue on the right, then bear left onto B52 signposted Rust. Just after St Margarethen there is a Roman quarry which provided stone for *Carnuntum* and which is now used to display modern sculptures and for Passion Plays. From the edge of the low escarpment before Rust the prospect of unbroken flatland stretching to the far horizon is quite astonishing. Rust is 9 miles from Eisenstadt.

The village of **Rust** (population 2,000), said to be the warmest place in middle Europe, is the principal resort on the Neusiedler See. From April to August it is frequented by storks which return every year to their nests on the roof tops of the town. Many of the houses in the town centre have Renaissance or baroque façades and around the small square there are several *heurigen* and wine shops which sell the famous Ruster Ausbruch wine as well as local basketware. Parts of the Fischer- Kirche date from the twelfth century when it was protected by a wall. It has frescoes in the Marienkapelle, and in the choir and transept, and the stone pulpit is decorated with floral paintings.

On the eastern side of the town a causeway runs past the wooden lake huts and the tall rushes to the landing stage where flat-bottomed boats offer cruises on the lake, there is a restaurant and facilities for sailing and bathing.

Three miles south of Rust is the village of **Mörbisch**, known for the musicals and operettas performed on a floating stage during the summer. Here too the storks nest above the houses which have a Magyar style with pretty stairs and porches along the side alleyways. Little more than a mile beyond Mörbisch is the border with Hungary and 6 miles further is the town of Sopron.

Return along the vine-lined road to Rust. Take the road past the new See Hotel through Oggau to the main road, Route 331, via Purbach to **Neusiedl-am-See** (population 4,000). Here there is an interesting lake museum with collections of the flora and fauna of the region. Take Route B51 to Weiden and a mile after the village turn right onto an unnumbered, tree-lined road which runs through flat, open fields to **Podersdorf**. At the entrance to the village note the decorated, single- storeyed house on the right. At the junction turn right to reach a bathing beach. This is one of the most popular beaches on the lake with good facilities for water sports, and for cruising.

Continue southward from Podersdorf through this land of the big sky to **Illmitz** (population 2,500), the lowest village in Austria. A 3-mile-long causeway runs down to the beach and reed huts can sometimes be seen. Here colourful horse-drawn caravans may be hired. Follow Route B52 eastwards through Apetion, passing the Lange Lacke which is a bird sanctuary. The whole of this area is rich in birdlife and flora. Pass, on the right, the Pannonia leisure centre and then the Pamhagen zoo (entrance via Pamhagen, 2$\frac{1}{2}$ miles south of Wallern) where there are typical animals and birds of the Hungarian steppes such as wolves, wild boar and hunting birds. At Wallern turn left onto Route B51 via St Andrä, where some of the roofs are thatched, to **Frauenkirchen**.

A visit to the pilgrimage church at Frauenkirchen is highly recommended. The original church was built in 1335 but suffered at the hands of the Turks in the sixteenth and seventeenth centuries. The present edifice was designed and built in 1702 by the Italian architect Francesco Martielli to the order of Prince Paul Esterházy. The twin towers with their double onion domes are the most striking outside feature. Inside the church is decorated in the most breathtaking baroque style. The magnificent frescoes and stucco decorations are by Luca Antonio Columba and Petro Antonio Conti. On the high altar there is a framed painting of the Madonna and Child, and above it is a lovely thirteenth-century linden wood statue of Maria with the infant Jesus dressed in an embroidered mantle. There are eight superb side altars. The choirstalls with their painted panels are delightful and the pulpit is a masterpiece of baroque artwork. Relatively unknown and unsung, set in the modest flat countryside of the Seewinkel, this is one of the most beautiful churches in Austria.

Return to Eisenstadt through Neusiedl and Route 331. The round tour is just short of 100 miles.

FURTHER INFORMATION

TOURIST OFFICES

Austrian national tourist offices are the best source of advance information. Illustrated material is available on all kinds of accommodation, sports and pastimes, places to visit, travel, shopping, cultural events, and advice is freely available.

Austrian National Tourist Office
30 St George Street
London W1R 0AL
☎ 01 629 0461

Austrian National Tourist Office
500 Fifth Avenue
New York
NY 10110
☎ 212 944 6880

Austrian National Tourist Office
11601 Wilshire Blvd, Suite 2480
Los Angeles
California 90025
☎ 213 477 3332

Austrian National Tourist Office
2 Bloor Street East, Suite 3330
Toronto
Ontario M4W 1A8
☎ 416 967 3380

Austrian National Tourist Office
1010 Sherbrooke Street West
Suite 1410
Montreal PQ H3A 2R7
☎ 514 849 3709

Austrian National Tourist Office
736 Granville Street
Vancouver Block,
Suite 1220
Vancouver, BC V6Z 1J2
☎ 604 683 5808

MUSEUMS, CASTLES, ABBEYS

The following information is relevant to the places mentioned in the text. Opening hours do vary from time to time and should be checked from local sources. All quoted periods are inclusive.

Admont
Abbey
Natural History Museum, Art History Museum, Library
Guided tours: May-September daily 10am-1pm, 2-5pm; April and October, daily, 10am-12noon, 2-4pm; November to March, daily except Monday, 11am-12noon, 2-3pm.

Alberschwende Bregenzerwald
Heimatmuseum Alberschwende
Open: Sundays and holidays, 10-11am.

Altmünster/Traunsee
Neukirchen Local History Museum
Open: June-mid-September Tuesday-Thursday, 2-4 pm; Sunday and holidays, 10am to 12noon.

Aurach-bei-Kitzbühel
The Old Mill
Open: Tuesday-Sunday 1-5pm.

Baden
Beethoven House Museum
Rathausgasse 10
Open: May-mid-October, daily except Thursday, 9-11am, and 3-5pm; mid-October to April, Tuesday and Saturday 3-5pm, Thursday 9-11am.

Rollett Museum
Open: May-October, Saturday and Wednesday, 3-6 pm; Sunday 9-12noon.

Kaiser Franz Josef Museum
Open: Wednesday-Sunday 1-7pm.

Bad Goisern
Anzenau Mill Open-air Museum
Open: daily except Friday 9am-12noon, 2-5pm.

Local History Museum
Open: April-mid-September daily, 9.30-11.30am.

Bad Ischl
Haenel-Pancera Museum
Concordiastrasse 3
Open: May-September, daily 9am to 5pm.

Kaiservilla
Kaiserpark
Open: May-mid-October, daily 9am-12noon, and 1-5pm.

Lehár Villa
Open: Easter-September, daily 9-12noon, 2-5 pm.

Austrian Museum of Photography
Marmorschlößl
Open: April-October, daily 9.30am-5.30pm.

Bad Vöslau
Town Museum
Open: May-September, Thursday 4-7pm; Sunday 9am-12noon.

Bezau/Bregenzerwald
Heimatmuseum Bezau
Verkehrsamt Bezau
Open: Tuesday, Thursday, Saturday 2-4pm; Wednesday 10am-12noon.

Bludenz
Heimatmuseum Bludenz
Obere Tor
Open: Tuesday-Saturday, 10am-12noon, 3-6pm; Sunday 10am-12noon.

Bregenz
Vorarlberg Landesmuseum
Kornmarktplatz
Open: daily except Monday 9am-12noon, 2-5pm.

Döllach im Mölltal
Museum Schloss Großkirchheim
Open: daily 9am-6pm.

Dornbirn
Vorarlberger Naturschau
Marktstrasse 33
Open: Tuesday-Sunday 9am-12noon, 2-5pm.

Ebene Reichenau
Mineralienmuseum Zirbenhof
Turrachehöhe
Open: weekdays 9am-12noon, 2-5.30pm.

Ebensee/Traunsee
Local History Museum
Open: July-mid-September, Monday to Saturday 2-6pm; Sunday 8.30-11.30am.

Eferding
Schloß Starhemberg
Open: May-September 9am-
12noon.

Egg/Bregenzerwald
Heimatmuseum Egg
Verkehrsamt Egg
Open: enquire at the tourist infor-
mation office in Egg.

Eisenstadt
Burgenland Provincial Museum
Open: Tuesday-Sunday 9am-
12noon, 2-5pm.

Haydn House Museum
Open: Easter-October, 9am-
12noon, 1-5pm.

Haydn Room
Schloß Esterházy
Open: summer 9am-5.30pm; winter
9am-4.30pm.

Enns
Enns Museum
Open: daily except Tuesday, 10am-
12noon, 2-5pm.

Feldkirch
Heimatmuseum Feldkirch
Schattenburg
Open: daily 9am-5pm, except Wed-
nesdays when it is open for visiting
groups only.

Friesach
Evangelisches Diözesanmuseum
Open: mid-June-mid-September,
Thursday and Saturday 9am-
12noon, 2-5pm; Sunday 11am-
12noon.

Stadtmuseum Friesach
Fürstenhofgasse 115
Open: June-September, Tuesday,
Thursday, Friday, 3-5pm.

Gmunden
Kammerhof Museum
Open: Tuesday-Sunday 10am-
12noon, 2-5pm; Sunday and
holidays 10am-12noon.

Gmünd
Porsche Automuseum
Helmut Pfeifhofer
Open: mid-May-mid-October, daily
9am-6pm; mid-October-mid-May
10am-4pm.

Goldegg
Pongau Folklore Museum
Schloss Goldegg
Guided tours: May-September:
Thursday and Sunday 3pm and
4pm; July and August also on
Tuesday; October to April, every
Thursday at 2pm.

Golling
Golling Castle
Open: June-September, Wednesday, Saturday, Sunday, 9am-
12noon.

Graz
The Armoury
Open: April-October 9am-12noon
daily and 2-5pm on Monday, Tuesday and Thursday; July and August
also open Wednesday and Friday
afternoons; closed November to
March, 1 May and Corpus Christi
day.

Styrian Folk Museum
Open: 9am-4pm, Monday-Thurs-
day; 9am-1pm, Saturday, Sunday,
and public holidays.

New Gallery
Open: 10am-6pm, Monday-Friday;
9am-12noon Saturday, Sunday and
public holidays; closed 1 May,
Easter, Whitsun, Christmas.

Attems Palace
(Archive department of the
    Joanneum museum)
Open: 8am-4pm, Monday, Tuesday,
Thursday; 8am-1pm, Wednesday,
and Friday.

Joanneum Museum
Open: 9am-4pm, Monday-Friday;
9am-12noon, Saturday, Sunday and
public holidays.

Eggenberg Palace
Pre- and Early History Museum
Open: 9am-5pm daily, February-
November.

Styrian Hunting Museum
Open: 9am-12noon, 2-5pm daily,
February-November.

State Apartments
Open: 9am-1pm, 2-5pm daily, April-
October.

Roman Relic Collection (and the
    Park)
Open: 8am-5pm, daily, January,
February, November, December;
8am-6pm March, April, September,
October; 8am-7pm May-August.

Grein/Danube
Old Town Hall and Theatre
Open: April-October, daily 10.30am-
2.30pm.

Schloß Greinburg Ship Museum
Open: 9am-12noon, 2-5pm daily
except Monday, May-October.

Hallein
Celtic Museum
Open: May-October, 9am-5pm.

Hallstatt
**Prehistoric and Local History
    Museum**
Open: May-September, daily
9.30am-6pm; April-October, daily
10am-4pm.

Hittisau/Bregenzerwald
Alpsennereimuseum Hittisau
Verkehrsamt Hittisau
Open: enquire at the tourist
information centre in Hittisau.

Hüttenberg
Mineralienschau des Bergwerks
Open: April-October, daily 9am-
12noon, 2-5pm.

Innsbruck
Alpenvereinsmuseum
Wilhelm-Greil-Strasse 15
Open: June-September, Monday-
Friday, 9am-12noon, 2-5pm;
October-May, Tuesday-Thursday
9am-12noon, 2-5pm.

**Bergisel Museum and
    Regimentsmuseum
Der Tiroler Kaiserjäger**
Berg Isel
Open: March, Tuesday-Sunday,
10am-3pm; April-October, daily
9am-5pm.

Hofburg
Rennweg 1
Open: guided tours all year, daily
9am-4pm, except mid-October to
mid-May, closed Sundays and
holidays.

Hofkirche
Universitätsstrasse 2
Open: May-September, daily, 9am-
5pm; October-April, daily 9am-
12noon, and 2-5pm.

Olympiamuseum Innsbruck
Open: daily 10am-5.30pm.

Schloß Ambras
Open: May-September, daily except
Tuesday 10am-4pm.

Tiroler Kaiserschützenmuseum
Open: May-September, Monday-
Saturday, 10am-4pm, Sundays and
holidays 9am-12noon.

Tiroler Landeskundliche Museum
Open: May-September, daily 10am-5pm; Thursday evening 7-9pm.

Tiroler Landesmuseum Ferdinandeum
Open: May-September, Monday-Saturday 10am-5pm, Thursday evening 7-9pm; Sunday and holidays, 9am-12noon; October-April, Tuesday-Saturday, 10am-12noon, 2-5pm,Sunday and holidays 9am-12noon, closed on Monday.

Tiroler Volkskunstmuseum
Open: May-September, daily 9am-5pm; October-April, daily 9am-12noon, 2-5pm; Sunday and holidays, 9am-12noon.

Jochberg
Heimatmuseum Jochberg
Open: Tuesday and Thursday, 5-8pm; Sunday 11am-12noon.

Kirchberg in Tirol
The Old Oil Mill
Open: Tuesday 2-4pm; Thursday 10am-12noon.

Kitzbühel
Bauernhausmuseum am Römer-weg
Open: daily 1-6pm.

Heimatmuseum der Stadt
Open: Monday-Friday 9am-12noon.

Klagenfurt
Bergbaumuseum
Radetzkystrasse
Kreutzbergl
Open: May-September, Monday-Saturday, 9am-6pm; October-April, Friday, 9am-12noon, Saturday, 8am-6pm.

Diözesan Museum
Open: Monday-Saturday: May-mid-June, 10am-12noon; mid-June-mid-September, 10am-12noon, 3-5pm; mid-September-mid-October 10am-12noon.

Koschatmuseum
Viktringer Ring 17
Open: Monday-Saturday 10am-12noon.

Landesmuseum fur Kärnten
Open: May-October, 9am-4pm, Sunday 10am-12noon; November-April, Tuesday-Saturday, 10am-2pm.

Knappenberg/Carinthia
Bergbaumuseum und Schaubergwerk Hüttenberg
Open: April-October, daily 9am-12noon, 1-5pm.

Kotschach-Mauthen
Plöckenmuseum
Rathaus
Open: daily 9am-12noon, 1-5pm; closed Friday-Sunday in winter.

Krems/Danube
Dominican Church Museum
Open: Tuesday-Saturday 9am-12noon, 2-5pm. Closed Mondays.

Kremsmünster
Abbey of Kremsmünster
Open: Easter-October, daily 9am-10.30am, 2-3.30pm.

Vintage Car Museum
Schloß Kremsegg
Open: 10am-12noon, 2-4pm Friday and Sunday, 2-4pm Saturday; Tuesday to Thursday by appointment. Closed Mondays.

Launsdorf
Burg Hochosterwitz
Open: Easter-September, daily 9am-6pm.

Lendorf
**Archäologisches und Frühchrist-
liches Museum Teurnia**
Open: July-September, daily 9am-
12noon, 2-5pm.

Lienz
Osttiroler Bezirksheimatmuseum
Schloss Bruck
Open: April-October, 10am-5pm.
Closed Monday; also closed Nov-
ember-March.

Freilichtsmuseum Aguntum
Open: mid-May-mid-September,
daily 9am-5pm.

Linz
Nordico Museum
Open: 9am-6pm, Monday-Friday;
3-5pm Saturday and Sunday.

Schloßmuseum
Open: 9am-5pm, Tuesday-
Saturday; 10am-4pm Sunday;
closed Monday.

**New Gallery/Wolfgang-Gurlitt
Museum**
Open: 10am-6pm Monday, Tuesday,
Wednesday and Friday; 10am-
10pm Thursday; 10am-1pm Satur-
day; closed Sunday.

Maria Saal
Kärntner Freilichtmuseum
Open: May-October, daily 10am-
6pm.

Melk/Danube
Melk Abbey Library etc
Conducted tours: daily, 9am-12noon,
2-5pm.

Micheldorf/Kremsmünster
Wrought-Iron Museum
Open: Tuesday-Sunday, 9am-
12noon, 2-5pm.

Millstatt
Stiftsmuseum Millstatt
Open: May-October, daily 9am-6pm.

Möderndorf-Hermagor
Gailtaler Heimatmuseum
Schloss Möderndorf
Open: May-October, daily 10am-
1pm, 2-5pm.

Mondsee
**Open-air Museum, Rauchhaus,
and Town Museum**
Open: daily 8am-6pm.

Neukirchen — see Altmünster

Neusiedl
Lake Museum
Open: Easter-October, 9am-12noon
and 1-5pm.

Pischeldorf
Magdalensbergmuseum
Open: May-October, 8am-6pm.

Ramingstein
Schloss Finstergrün
Guided tours: June-September,
Monday, Wednesday, Friday,
Saturday, 2pm and 3.30pm.

Riegersberg
Schloß Riegersberg
Guided tours: mid-March-October,
daily 9am-5pm.

St Florian/Linz
Hunting Museum
Schloß Hohenbrunn
Open: 10am-12noon, 2-6pm daily
except Monday.

Traunleiten Railway Museum
Trains run each Sunday and holiday, May-September, 10am-7pm.

Samesleiten Open-air Museum
Open: 10am-5pm, Tuesday-
Sunday; closed Monday.

St Gilgen
Mozart Museum
15 Ischler Strasse
Open: May-September, 9am-6pm.

St Johann in Tirol
Heimatmuseum
Open: daily 9.30-11.30am.

St Paul-in-Lavanttal
Benediktinerstift im Lavanttal
Conducted tours: mid-May-mid-Sep-
tember, daily 10.30am and 3pm.

St Wolfgang
Puppet Museum
Bachler-Rix Villa
Open: all year round, 10am-
12noon, 2-5.30pm.

Salzburg
Mozart Museum
9 Getreidegasse
Open: May, June, September, 9am-
7pm; July, August, 8am-10pm; October-April (1st floor only), 9am-6pm.

Carolinum Augusteum Museum
Open: daily 9am-5pm all year;
library: Monday-Friday, mornings
only.

Cathedral Museum
Open: May-October, Monday-
Saturday, 10am-5pm; Sunday
12noon-5pm.

Cathedral Crypt
Open: April-October, 9am-12noon,
2-6pm.

Hochensalzburg Fortress
Guided tours: every 15 minutes
daily; summer 9am-6pm; winter
9.30am-4.30pm.

Mozarteum
Guided tours: July and August at
11.30am.

Natural History Museum
Open: April-September, 9am-5pm;
October-March, 10am-4pm.

The Residence
Open: June-October, Monday-
Friday, 9am-12noon, 2-5.30pm;
winter, Monday-Friday, 10am-
12noon, 2-4pm; weekends/holidays
10am-12noon.

Salzburger Barockmuseum
Open: Tuesday-Saturday 9am-
12noon, 2-5pm; Sunday 9am-
12noon. Closed Monday.

Schloß Mirabel
Open: May-October, Monday-
Saturday, 9am-12noon, 3-6pm.

Scharnstein/Gmunden
Austrian Museum of Criminology
Open: May-November, daily except
Monday 9am-12noon, 1-5pm.

Schoppernau
Franz Michael Felder Museum
Open: Monday-Friday 8am-12noon,
2-6pm.

Schruns
Montafoner Heimatmuseum
Open: July-mid-September, Tuesday-Saturday, 10am-12noon,
3-6pm, Sunday 10am-12noon; mid-
September-third week of October,
Tuesday and Friday 3-6pm; Jan-
uary-June, Tuesday and Friday
3-6pm.

Schwarzenberg
Heimatmuseum Schwarzenberg
Open: Tuesday, Thursday, Satur-
day 1.30-4.30pm; Sunday 4-6pm.

Seeboden
Kärntner Fischereimuseum
Open: mid-May-mid-September,
daily 9am-12noon, 2-6pm.

Spittal-an-der-Drau
**Bezirksheimatmuseum im
  Schloss Porcia**
Open: May-September, 9am-6pm.

Museum Teurnia
St Peter in Holz
Open: May-October, daily 9am-
12noon, 1-5pm.

Steyr
Innerberger Stadel Museum
Open: April-October, Tuesday-Sun-
day 10am-3pm; November-March,
Wednesday-Sunday, 10am-3pm.

Steyr/Grünberg
Steyrtal Railway Museum
Trains run each Sunday mid-June-
mid-September, 7.30am-7.20pm.

Straßburg/Gurktal
Schloss Straßurg
Open: July and August, daily 9am-
5pm.

Stübing/Graz
Austrian Open-air Museum
Open: 9am-5pm (last admission
4pm), daily except Monday, April-
October.

Tamsweg
Lungauer Folklore Museum
Open: May-October, Christmas and
Easter, daily except Monday 10am-
12noon, 2-5pm.

Vienna
Austrian Film Museum
1 Augustinerstrasse 1
Film shows: October-May, Saturdays 6 and 8pm.

Austrian Gallery
Upper Belvedere
Prinz Eugen Strasse 27
Open: Tuesday-Sunday 10am-4pm.

Beethoven Memorial Rooms
(1) 1 Mölker Bastei 8
(2) 19 Probusgasse 6
(3) 19 Döblinger Hauptstrasse 92
Open: Tuesday-Sunday 10am-
12.15pm, 1-4.30pm.
(4) 6 Laimgrubengasse 22
Open: May-September 10am-
12noon.

Chapel of the Imperial Palace
1 Hofburg
Schweizerhof
Open: guided tours, mid-January-
June, mid-September-mid-Decem-
ber, Tuesday and Thursday 2.30-
3.30pm (mass with Vienna Boys
Choir at 9.15am Sundays and
religious holidays).

Circus and Clown Museum
2 Karmelitergasse 9
Open: Wednesday 5-7pm; Saturday
3-5pm; Sunday 9am-12noon.

Clock Museum
1 Schulhof 2
Open: Tuesday-Sunday, 9am-
12.15pm, 1-4.30pm.

**Federal Collection of Period
  Furniture**
7 Mariahilfer Strasse
Open: Guided tours every hour on
the hour, Tuesday-Friday 8am-4pm;
Saturday 9am-12noon.

Fiaker Museum
17 Veronikagasse 12
Open: first Wednesday in the
month, 9am-1pm.

Firefighting Museum
1 Am Hof 10
Open: Sundays and holidays 9am-
12noon.

Sigmund Freud's House
9 Bergasse 19
Open: Monday-Friday, 9am-1pm;
Saturday, Sunday and public
holidays 9am-3pm.

Haydn's Residence and Brahms Memorial Room
6 Haydngasse 19
Open: Tuesday-Sunday 10am-
12.15pm, 1-4.30pm.

Historical Museum of the City of Vienna
4 Karlsplatz
Open: Tuesday-Sunday 9am-
4.30pm.

Hofburg Imperial Palace
State Rooms and Imperial Apartments
1 Michaelerplatz
Open: Monday-Saturday, 8.30-
4.30pm; Sunday, 8.30-12.30pm.

Imperial Burial Vault
1 Neuer Markt
Open: May-September, daily
9.30am-4pm; October-April, daily
9.30am-1pm.

Imperial Coach Collection
13 Schönbrunn Palace (right wing)
Open: May-September, Tuesday -
Sunday 10am-5pm; October-April,
Tuesday-Sunday 10am-4pm.

Imperial Tableware and Silver Depot
1 Michaelerplatz
Open: Tuesday-Friday and Sunday
9am-1pm.

Mozart Memorial 'Figaro House'
1 Domgasse 5
Open: Tuesday-Sunday 10am-
12.15pm, 1-4.30pm.

Museum of Applied Arts
1 Stubenring 5
Open: Tuesday, Wednesday,
Friday 10am-4pm; Thursday 10am-
6pm; Sunday 10am-1pm.

Museum of Fine Arts
1 Maria-Theresien-Platz
Open: Tuesday-Friday, 10am-6pm;
Saturday and Sunday 9am-6pm.

Museum of Modern Art
Liechtenstein Palace
9 Fürstengasse 1
Open: daily 10am-6pm, except
Tuesday.

Museum of Natural History
1 Maria-Theresien-Platz
Open: daily 9am-6pm, except
Tuesday.

Museum of Technology
14 Mariahilfer Strasse 212
Open: Tuesday-Friday and Sunday
9am-4pm; Saturday 9am-1pm.

Museum of the Cathedral and Diocese
1 Stephansplatz 6 (1st floor)
Open: Wednesday-Saturday,
10am-4pm; Sunday and holidays
10am-1pm.

Museum of Medical History
9 Währinger Strasse 25/1
Open: Monday-Friday 11am-3pm
except holidays.

Schönbrunn Palace
Schönbrunner Schlossstrasse
Open: guided tours: October-April,
daily 9am-12noon, 1-4pm; May-
September, daily 9am-12noon,
1-5pm.

Franz Schubert's Birthplace
9 Nussdorfer Strasse
Open: Tuesday-Sunday, 10am-
12.15pm, 1-4.30pm.

State Opera House
1 Opernring 2
Open: guided tours: July/August,

daily 10am-3pm; May/June and
September/October, daily 1, 2,
3pm; November-April, 2 and 3pm.

Johann Strauss Residence
2 Praterstrasse 54
Open: Tuesday-Sunday 10am-
12.15pm, 1-4.30pm.

Undertaker's Museum
4 Goldeggasse 19
Open: By prior arrangement
(☎ 651631/227)
Monday-Friday 12noon-3pm.

Vienna Streetcar Museum
3 Erdbergstrasse 109
Open: Saturday, Sunday, holidays
9am-4pm; vintage tram tours: May-
October, Saturday 2.30pm, Sunday
and holidays 9am (from the
Karlsplatz).

Villach
Museum der Stadt Villach
Wildmanngasse 38
Open: May to October, Monday to
Saturday 10am-4.30pm.

Wagrain
Heimatmuseum
Open: June-September, Monday
3-6pm; Saturday 4-6pm; Sunday
10am-12noon.

Wels
Burg Museum Wels
Open: all year; Tuesday-Friday
10am-5pm; Saturday and Sunday
10am-12noon. Closed Monday.

Zell-am-See
Heimatsmuseum
Constable's Tower
Open: mid-June-mid-September,
Monday-Friday 10am-12noon,
4-6pm; also if doors are open!

ZOOLOGICAL AND BOTANICAL GARDENS AND WILDLIFE PARKS

Altmünster
Wildpark Hochkreut
Open: April-October, daily 9am-6pm.

Assling/Lienz
Wildpark Assling
Open: daily 10am-5pm.

Aurach bei Kitzbühel
Wildpark Tirol
Bergbauernhof 'Brand'
Open: daily 9am-5pm; feeding time
2.30pm.

Bad Kleinkirchheim
Alpengarten
Weg No 6
Nockalm-Scharte nach St Oswald
Open: mid-June-August, daily
10am-6pm.

Bregenz
Reptile Zoo
Heldendankstrasse 29
Open: daily 9am-6pm.

Fusch-an-der-Glocknerstrasse
Ferleiten Game Park
Ferleiten
Open: May-October, daily from
8am-9pm.

Gänserndorf/Deutsch Wagram
Safari Park
Open: Monday-Friday 10am-
5.30pm; Saturday and Sunday
9am-5.30pm.

Grünau-im-Almtal
Cumberland Game Park
Open: April-October, 9am-6pm;
November-March, Saturday,
Sunday, and holidays 9am-dusk.

Innsbruck
Alpenzoo Innsbruck-Tirol
Weiherburggasse 37
Open: all year, daily 9am-6pm.

Klagenfurt
Reptilian Zoo Happ
Villacherstrasse 237
Open: daily 9am-6pm.

Pamhagen/Seewinkel
Pamhagen Zoo
Open: April-October, daily 9am-dusk; November-March, closed.

Rosegg/Velden
Wildpark Kärnten Rosegg
Open: daily 9am-6pm.

Roßleiten/Windischgarsten
Wildpark Enghagen
Open: All year from 9am-dusk.

Salzburg
Schloß Hellbrunn
Open: April and September 9am-4.30pm; May-August, 8am-5.30pm; October, 9am-12noon, 1-4pm.

Vienna
Alpine Garden in the Belvedere Park
3 Landstrasse Gürtel 1
Open: April-June, daily 9am-6pm; July-September 9am-4.30pm.

Aquarium (Haus des Meers)
6 Esterházypark
Open: daily 9am-6pm.

Botanical Gardens
3 Mechelgasse 2 (near Rennweg) or, Landstrasser Gürtel 1
Open: mid-April-mid-October, daily 9am-dusk.

Schönbrunn Zoo
13 Park of Schönbrunn Palace (entrance Heitzinger Tor)

Open: daily 9am-dusk (latest time 6pm).

Villach
Alpengarten Villacher Alpe
Parkplatz 6
Villacher Alpenstrasse
Open: mid-June-end of August, daily 9am-6pm.

Wels/Linz
Vogelpark Schmiding
Krenglbach
Open: mid-April-November, daily 9am-7pm.

Wels Zoo
Open: all year, 9am-dusk.

OTHER PLACES TO VISIT

Bad Dürrnberg
Bad Dürrnberg Salt Mines
Guided tours: May-October, daily 9am-5pm.

Bischofshofen
Gainfeld Waterfall
Guided tours: May-September, daily.

Dorfgastein
'Entrische Kirche'
Guided tours: mid-March-mid-October, daily except Mondays 10am-6pm, starting on the hour.

Golling
Golling Waterfalls
Open: May-October, daily, all day.

Salzach Gorge
Open: May-October, daily, all day.

Innsbruck
Stadtturm
Herzog-Friedrich-Strasse 21

Open: March-October, daily 10am-5pm, except July and August, daily 10am-6pm.

Riesenrundgemälde
Rennweg 39
Open: April-October, daily 9am-4.45pm.

Klagenfurt
Minimundus
Villacher Strasse 241
Open: May, June, September, daily 8.30am-6.30pm; July and August, daily from 8am-8.30pm.

St Johann-im-Pongau
Liechtenstein Gorge
Open: May-October, daily, all day.

Salzburg
St Peter's Catacombs
Guided tours: May-September, 9am-6pm; winter, 10am-2.30pm.

The Playhouse
Guided tours: summer (except during Festival) 11am and 3pm; winter 3pm Monday-Saturday, 11am Sunday.

Glockenspiel
Guided tours and performances: daily at 6.45am, 10.45am, 5.45pm.

Scheffau
Lammer Gorge
Open: May-October, daily, all day.

Vienna
Austrian Parliament
1 Dr Karl Renner Ring 3
Open: Guided tours: Monday-Friday 11am (except when Parliament is in session); July/August, Monday-Friday 10, 11am, 2, 3pm.

Giant Ferris Wheel
2 Prater

Open: April-September, daily 9am-11pm; March and October daily 10am-10pm.

National Theatre
1 Dr-Karl-Lueger-Ring 2
Open: Guided tours: July/August, daily 11am, 1, 2, 3, 4pm; September/October and May/June, Monday-Saturday 9am and 3pm; November-April, daily 3pm by arrangement.

Planetarium
2 Prater Hauptalle
(near Giant Ferris Wheel)
Performances: Saturday, Sunday, and holidays 3 and 5pm; children's performances on Sunday at 9.30am.

Spanish Riding School
1 Hofburg
Josefplatz
Performances: enquire at tourist office or at the riding school. Training sessions: February, Monday-Saturday 10am-12noon; March-June and September-mid-December, Tuesday-Saturday 10am-12noon (except when on tour).

Villach
Relief von Kärnten
Peraustrasse
Open: May-October, Monday-Saturday 10am-4.30pm.

Weissbach (near Lofer)
Seisenberg Gorge
Open: mid-June-September, Wednesdays and weekends, all day.

Werfen
Eisreisenwelt Ice Caves
Guided tours: May-October, daily from 9.30am.

Werfenweng
Eiskogel Caves
Guided tours: May-October, daily from 10am.

INDEX

MPC

TOUR & EXPLORE WITH MPC VISITOR'S GUIDES

Britain
- Chilterns
- Cornwall
- Cotswolds
- Devon
- East Anglia
- Guernsey
- Hampshire & the Isle of Wight
- Historic Places of Wales
- Jersey
- Kent
- Lake District
- Northern Ireland
- The North York Moors, York & the Yorkshire Coast
- Peak District
- Scottish Borders & Edinburgh
- Severn & Avon
- Somerset & Dorset
- South & West Wales
- Sussex
- Welsh Borders
- Yorkshire Dales

Europe
- Austria
- Bavaria
- Black Forest
- Brittany
- Corsica
- Dordogne
- Finland
- Florence & Tuscany
- French Coast
- Holland
- Iceland
- Italian Lakes
- Loire
- Normandy
- Norway
- South of France
- Sweden
- Turkey
- Tyrol
- Yugoslavia: Adriatic Coast

also:
- Walking in the Alps
- Walking in Austria
- Walking in Northern France
- Walking in Switzerland

Simply the Best

Our policy of regularly revising MPC Visitor's Guides means that some titles may be temporarily unavailable, so send for our up-to-date list of these and our other books.

288